60171-7-$4.95 WASHINGTON SQUARE PRESS

The Pocket Aquinas

Selected from *Summa of Theology* and
more than thirty other
writings of St. Thomas Aquinas

9 780671 601713

50495

0-671-60171-7

THE BOOK

THE POCKET AQUINAS is divided
into eight chapters, each beginning with
a Foreword by the editor. The materials
represent thirty-two of St. Thomas' most
important writings. Each chapter closes
with a short list of recommended works
for further reading.

THE AUTHOR

Born in 13th-century Italy, Thomas
Aquinas entered the Dominican Order
when he was 22. He studied for several
years at Cologne under Albertus Magnus.
He died in 1274 and was canonized by
Pope John XXII in 1323.

THE ACCLAIM

The synthesis of faith and reason, of moral
and political science, and of Hellenism and
Christianity, SUMMA OF THEOLOGY
stands as one of the great achievements of
human thought and the brilliant culmina-
tion of the scholastic philosophy of the
Middle Ages.

The Pocket Aquinas

*Edited and a
General Introduction by*
VERNON J. BOURKE

WSP

WASHINGTON SQUARE PRESS
PUBLISHED BY POCKET BOOKS

New York   London   Toronto   Sydney   Tokyo

Imprimatur: ✠ Joseph E. Ritter, Archbishop of St. Louis
July 11, 1960

A Washington Square Press Publication of
POCKET BOOKS, a division of Simon & Schuster Inc.
1230 Avenue of the Americas, New York, N.Y. 10020

ISBN: 0-671-60171-7

First Pocket Books printing November 1960

24   23   22   21   20   19   18   17   16   15

WASHINGTON SQUARE PRESS and WSP colophon are
registered trademarks of Simon & Schuster Inc.

Printed in the U.S.A.

ACKNOWLEDGMENTS

We hereby acknowledge permission of the following to reprint selections from the works specified; identification by the name of the respective translator will be found at the beginning of each selection:

THE AMERICAN CATHOLIC PHILOSOPHICAL ASSOCIATION for *Physics and Philosophy,* translation of a portion of Aquinas' *Exposition of Aristotle's Physics,* Book I, by J. A. McWilliams, S.J.; copyright, ©, 1946, by The American Catholic Philosophical Association.

DOUBLEDAY & COMPANY, INC., for *On the Truth of the Catholic Faith, Book IV,* translated by Charles J. O'Neil; copyright, ©, 1957, by Doubleday & Company, Inc.

B. HERDER BOOK CO. for *The Soul,* a translation of St. Thomas Aquinas' *De Anima,* by J. P. Rowan; copyright, ©, 1949, by B. Herder Book Co. The two extracts identified as from the *Summa Against the Gentiles,* translated by J. Rickaby, are from *Of God and His Creatures,* translated by Joseph Rickaby, S.J., published by B. Herder Co., St. Louis, and Burns & Oates, London, 1905.

THE PONTIFICAL INSTITUTE OF MEDIAEVAL STUDIES (Toronto) for *On Being and Essence* by St. Thomas Aquinas, translated by A. A. Mauer, C.S.B., and from St. Thomas Aquinas, *On Kingship,* translated by G. B. Phelan, revised by I. Th. Eschmann, O.P.: both copyright, ©, 1959, by The Pontifical Institute of Mediaeval Studies, Toronto.

THE PROVIDENCE COLLEGE PRESS for *On the Virtues in General* by St. Thomas Aquinas, translated by J. P. Reid, O.P.; copyright, ©, 1951, by The Providence College Press.

HENRY REGNERY COMPANY for *Truth* by St. Thomas Aquinas, translated in three volumes by R. W. Mulligan, S.J., J. V. McGlynn, S.J., and R. W. Schmidt, S.J.; copyright, ©, 1952, 1953, 1954, by Henry Regnery Company.

ROUTLEDGE & KEGAN PAUL LTD. (London) for *Aristotle's De Anima and the Commentary of St. Thomas Aquinas,* translated by K. Foster, O.P., and S. Humphries, O.P.; copyright, ©, 1951, by Routledge & Kegan Paul Ltd., London, and published in the United States by Yale University Press.

EDITOR'S NOTE

All selections marked "trans. V.J.B." are newly translated from the standard Latin texts by the editor of this volume.

Contents

vii

II. Nature and Philosophy

V. Moral Life and Ethics

VIII. Revelation and Theology

General Introduction

THOMAS AQUINAS WAS THE SON of Landolfo of Aquino, a minor public official in the service of the Emperor of Sicily. Born at the end of 1224, or early in 1225, at Roccasecca (midway between Rome and Naples), Thomas did his elementary studies with the Benedictines at Monte Cassino. About the year 1239, he began the study of liberal arts at the University of Naples. Some authorities think that he eventually took a master's degree in arts at this university, which was a state institution.

Around 1244, Thomas entered the Order of Preachers, in Naples. After about a year of delay, due to family objections, he entered upon the Dominican course of studies at Paris and Cologne. From 1248 to 1252, Albert the Great was his teacher at Cologne. Selected to do advanced studies in theology at the University of Paris, Thomas prepared for the magistrate (equivalent to our doctorate) in theology, which he received in Paris in 1256. He was admitted to the Paris faculty in 1257. By 1259, he had completed his first course as a professor at Paris. His *Commentary on the Sentences* was probably completed by 1256. In this period he also wrote Scripture commentaries and conducted disputations resulting in some of the *Quodlibetal Questions* and the *Disputed Questions on Truth*. The *Summa contra Gentiles* was begun at Paris.

In his early thirties, Thomas Aquinas was already well known as a brilliant scholar and teacher. His preparatory studies had been more thorough than those of most of his colleagues. He had read widely and profoundly in the available literature of contemporary science, philosophy, and religion. He had studied at four great and dissimilar centers of learning: Monte Cassino, the state University of Naples, the Dominican Institute at Cologne, and the University of Paris. To many of his contemporaries, as to many religious critics in the Reformation period, Aquinas appeared overaddicted to philosophy. As far as we know, he was never a professor of philosophy, but he certainly wrote much on that subject and made full use of his philosophical knowledge in his theological works.

It was customary for the thirteenth-century professor of theology at Paris to teach the complete course once (normally a three-year period) and then be replaced by a new master. Aquinas finished his first Paris professorate in the spring of 1259. With Albert and other Dominican scholars, he then attended an important meeting at Valenciennes, where a general chapter decided to set up more stringent standards for the training of young men in the Order of Preachers. Henceforth, greater emphasis was to be placed on philosophical studies.

Thomas returned to Italy in the summer of 1259 and spent the next decade in residence at various Dominican houses in Rome and neighboring towns. It was a period of study, nonuniversity teaching, and writing. Early in this decade, a Greek-speaking Dominican missionary, William of Moerbeke, was recalled from the East and assigned to the translation and revision of the existing versions of the works of Aristotle. With this aid, for he did not himself know Greek, Aquinas began his expositions of the philosophic works in the Aristotelian corpus. At Naples, in 1260, he was raised to the status of Preacher General, a personal honor from his Order. As a result, he was an active participant in the annual chapter meetings of the Roman province of the Dominicans. The full story of Aquinas' duties in these ten years remains open for further research. He was not idle; this period saw the beginning of many of his large treatises. His advice was coveted by important personages within and without the Order. He perfected his mature position in theology and philosophy.

Roughly the first thousand years of Christianity had been an era in which writers knew but one type of Greek philosophy: Platonism. With the exception of a few logical treatises, Aristotle's philosophic encyclopedia had not been translated into Latin and did not directly affect Western thought. By the time that Aquinas first came to the University of Paris, all this was changed. Aristotelian translations were still incomplete and defective but enough was now known of Aristotle's new-found science and philosophy to make Christian Platonism old hat—and to arouse the concern of ecclesiastical authorities. Repeatedly, in the first fifty years of the century, Church officials at Paris warned against the *teaching* of the Aristotelian treatises on natural philosophy (including the *Metaphysics*) until they had been reviewed by capable Catholic scholars. It is noteworthy that no ecclesiastical regulations in the thirteenth century forbade the personal reading of Aristotle, or of his Jewish and Mohammedan commentators. Eventually, the popes and bishops saw (and it is to their lasting credit in the history of scholarship) that the thing to do was not to outlaw Aristotle or burn his books but to see that he was studied with all due care. It appears that Thomas Aquinas played a central role in this concerted effort of Christian scholarship to assimilate Aristotelianism.

Late in the year 1268, Aquinas returned to Paris, where he taught again as a university professor of theology, from 1269 to 1272. It was a signal honor to be given such a second professorate. The reasons for it are not entirely clear; certainly there were many other competent Dominican masters in theology. It may be that the Dominican superiors felt that the Paris situation demanded the presence of their ablest scholar. This was a time of controversy in intellectual and ecclesiastical circles at Paris. A group of masters in the Arts Faculty, headed by Siger of Brabant, had begun to teach a type of radical Aristotelianism which owed something to the influence of the great Mohammedan commentator Averroes. Though Christians, these Arts teachers in the late 1260's claimed that there is no philosophic evidence of man's personal immortality, that men are not equipped with complete powers of understanding, and that philosophically the world appears to be eternal. There is even some suggestion in this movement (which Renan later called a Latin Averroism) that man is not a free moral agent. It was a challenge from within to some of the basic tenets of Christianity. Aquinas' scholarship was highly respected by these professors in the Arts Faculty (they later wrote an affectionate letter on the occasion of St. Thomas' death, in which they were the first to speak of him as a saint), but he opposed their extreme teachings and worked hard to establish an interpretation of Aristotle that was moderate and acceptable in Christian schools.

At the same time, there were people in Paris who regarded the whole Aristotelian movement in Catholic schools with suspicion. Even Aquinas' teaching was now subjected to criticism. A British Dominican, Robert Kilwardby, and a noted Franciscan scholar, John Peckham, attacked the Thomistic theory that there can be but one substantial form in one substance—say, in a man. In 1270, the Bishop of Paris condemned thirteen propositions which included some views shared by Thomas Aquinas. Later, in 1277, Bishop Tempier issued a much more sweeping list of erroneous teachings. After fifty years had passed, in 1323, these Paris condemnations, insofar as they applied to Thomism, were removed in the diocese of Paris.

Much of Aquinas' literary output came in these years. He continued to work on his expositions of Aristotle and on portions of the Bible, to write shorter treatises on theological and philosophical subjects. He conducted and edited the disputations which completed his series of *Quodlibetal* and *Disputed Questions*. Of course, a large portion of the *Summa of Theology* dates from 1269 to 1272.

By the fall of 1272, Thomas had returned to southern Italy and taken up his duties as a master of theology at the University of Naples. As a professor at this state institution, he was paid a salary of twelve ounces of gold per year. His writing continued and he preached several series of *Sermons*, apparently in the Neapolitan vernacular, though they are now recorded in Latin. Then nearing fifty, Thomas Aquinas was at the peak of his career. An important Church Council was planned for Lyons, France, in 1274. Aquinas was asked to attend. There were rumors that he might be made a cardinal. Shortly after he began his journey, in the month of February, he fell ill and had to stop to rest. He died on March 7, 1274, at the Cistercian monastery at Fossanova, not far from the place of his birth.

Almost fifty years later, careful investigations into the personal life and teachings of Thomas Aquinas were conducted at Naples and Fossanova. One of his early biographers, William of Tocco, was an important instigator of these canonization proceedings. Aquinas was recognized as a saint in 1323.

The theological and philosophical teachings of Thomas Aquinas have been held in high esteem in Catholic scholarship during the ensuing centuries. He has come to be known as the Angelic Doctor. At the end of the nineteenth century, a new impetus was given to Thomism in the *Aeterni Patris* (1879) of Pope Leo XIII. In that letter, as well as in the *Humani Generis* (1950) of Pius XII, St. Thomas is given a special place in Catholic studies. Students in ecclesiastical seminaries are to become familiar with the thought and method (*ratio*) of Aquinas, not to the exclusion of other important writers or of the findings of modern science.

Aquinas is not regarded by modern Thomists as a man who has answered all questions, once and for all. He is considered a model of what the open-minded student may achieve in rethinking the problems of reality, knowledge, and human life, with the aid of what is best in contemporary science and learning.

Thomas Aquinas' thought is the product of a man of genius, coming at a time in which Western intellectualism and education reached a peak in the first flowering of the great universities. Profoundly religious, sensitive to the value of tradition, Aquinas was nonetheless an innovator in both philosophy and theology. Every problem in his *Summa of The-*

ology is presented as an open question; opposed views are
always stated before he offers his own solution. The same
broad vision characterizes the more than thirty other works
represented in the selections that follow. Pagans (Plato,
Aristotle, Plotinus), Mohammedans (Avicenna and Averroes),
and Jewish writers (Avicebron and Maimonides) play almost
as great a role in his scholarly documentation as do Christian
authors and the Bible. Few thinkers have been more open to
the influence of so many diverse traditions.

The following is an alphabetical list of the English titles
of the works from which selections are printed in *The
Pocket Aquinas*. These are Aquinas' most important writings.
For a more complete survey of all the writings, see: I. T.
Eschmann, O.P., "A Catalogue of St. Thomas's Works," in
E. Gilson, *The Christian Philosophy of St. Thomas* (New
York: Random House, 1956, 381-439); or V. J. Bourke,
Introduction to the Works of St. Thomas Aquinas, in Vol. I,
Opera Omnia, Parma Reprint (New York: Musurgia, 1948,
iii-xxx; offprint distributed by Modern Schoolman Office,
St. Louis University).

In each item that follows, the listing includes: English and
Latin titles, standard edition of Latin text, a short descriptive
note with date of writing, and information as to the avail-
ability of English translations. The translations so listed are
not always the source of the excerpts quoted later. For instance, in the case of the *Summa contra Gentiles*, some passages have been reprinted from the Doubleday edition, some
from the older version by J. Rickaby, and some have been
newly translated by the present editor. Much the same diversity of translation source will be found in the extracts from
the *Disputed Questions on Truth* and from the several *Commentaries* on Aristole. Passages from the *Summa of Theology*
are all newly translated, to secure uniformity in the rendition
of this important work. At the beginning of each extract from
Aquinas in the ensuing chapters, the precise source of the
translation that is used will be clearly indicated.

Against the Attackers of the Religious Life (Contra Impugnantes Dei cultum et religionem, in *Opuscula Theologica,* Vol. I. Turin: Marietti, 1954). A short polemical treatise, written in 1256, against William of St-Amour, a critic of the religious Orders. Translation: J. Procter, *An Apology for the Religious Orders.* Westminster, Md.: Newman, 1950.

Compendium of Theology (Compendium theologiae, in *Opuscula Theologica,* Vol. I. Turin: Marietti, 1954). An unfinished treatise arranged under the headings of Faith, Hope, and Charity; date disputed, may have been written in the 1260's or at the end of Aquinas' life. Translation: C. Vollert, *Compendium of Theology.* St. Louis: Herder, 1957. Also by L. Lynch. New York: McMullen, 1947.

Disputed Question on Spiritual Creatures (Quaestio disputata de spiritualibus creaturis, ed. L. Keeler. Rome: Gregorianum, 1946). This question was composed after 1267; an important source of information for the study of the human soul and angelic natures. Translation: J. Wellmuth and M. Fitzpatrick, *On Spiritual Creatures.* Milwaukee: Marquette University Press, 1949.

Disputed Question on the Soul (Quaestio disputata de anima, in *Quaestiones Disputatae,* Vol. II. Turin: Marietti, 1953). This question may date from Paris, about 1270. It should not be confused with the *Exposition of Aristotle on the Soul.* Translation: J. P. Rowan, *The Soul.* St. Louis: Herder, 1949.

Disputed Question on the Virtues in General (Quaestio disputata de virtutibus in communi, in *Quaestiones Disputatae,* Vol. II. Turin: Marietti, 1953). This, with four other questions on the virtues, dates from Paris, 1269-72. Translation: J. P. Reid, *The Virtues (in General).* Providence, R.I.: Providence College Press, 1951.

Disputed Questions on Evil (Quaestiones disputatae de malo, in *Quaestiones Disputatae,* Vol. II. Turin: Marietti, 1953). These disputed questions may be dated about 1268-70. There is no complete English version; q. VI translated by A. C. Pegis, *On Free Choice.* New York: McMullen, n.d.

Disputed Questions on the Power of God (Quaestiones de potentia Dei, in *Quaestiones Disputatae,* Vol. II. Turin: Marietti, 1953). Important for their metaphysical content, these questions may have been disputed in Rome about 1265. Translation: L. Shapcote, *On the Power of God.* Westminster, Md.: Newman, 1952.

Disputed Questions on Truth (Quaestiones disputatae de veritate, in *Quaestiones Disputatae,* Vol. I. Turin: Marietti, 1953). A series of questions important for theory of knowledge; disputed at Paris, 1256-59. A critical edition is being prepared for the Leonine edition. Translation: R. W. Mulligan, J. V. McGlynn, and R. W. Schmidt, *Truth.* 3 vols. Chicago: Regnery, 1952-54.

Exposition of Aristotle on Interpretation (In libros Peri Hermeneias expositio, in Ed. Leonina, Vol. I. Rome: Leonine Commission, 1882. Manual ed., Turin: Marietti, 1955). A commentary on one of the logical works of Aristotle; probably dates from Paris 1269-72. No English translation.

Exposition of Aristotle on the Soul (In libros de anima expositio, ed. R. M. Spiazzi. Turin: Marietti, 1955). This commentary was composed in 1268-71; a key source for psychology and theory of knowledge. Translation: K. Foster and S. Humphries, *Aristotle's de Anima with the Commentary of St. Thomas Aquinas.* London: Routledge and Kegan Paul, 1951; New Haven: Yale University Press, 1951.

Exposition of Aristotle's Ethics (In decem libros Ethicorum expositio. Turin: Marietti, 1949). A famous commentary on the *Nicomachean Ethics,* composed about 1271-72. No English translation.

Exposition of Aristotle's Metaphysics (In duodecim libros Metaphysicorum expositio. Turin: Marietti, 1950). Composed at Paris, 1270-72. No translation published, but J. P. Rowan has one forthcoming from Regnery.

Exposition of Aristotle's Physics (In octo libros Physicorum expositio, ed. A. Pirotta. Naples: D'Auria, 1953. Also in Ed. Leonina, Vol. II. Rome: Leonine Commission, 1884). This commentary may have been composed in 1265-68. No complete English version has been printed, but the work has been translated under the direction of R. J. Blackwell, John Carroll University. Book I, translated by R. Kocourek. St. Paul: North Central Publishing Company, 1947. A portion of Book III is translated in J. A. McWilliams, *Physics and Philosophy.* Washington: American Catholic Philosophical Association, 1945, 28-49.

Exposition of Aristotle's Politics (In libros Politicorum expositio. Ed. Parma, 1866. Reprinted New York: Musurgia, 1949, Vol. XXI, 364-716). Authentic only to Book III, lectio 6; this commentary may have been composed in 1270-72. No English translation.

Exposition of Aristotle's Posterior Analytics (In libros posteriorum Analyticorum expositio, ed. R. M. Spiazzi. Turin: Marietti, 1955. Also in Ed. Leonina, Vol. I. Rome: Leonine Commission, 1882). Possibly composed in 1268-70, this commentary on part of Aristotle's logic is of epistemological importance. Translation: P. Conway and W. H. Kane, *Exposition of the Posterior Analytics.* Quebec: M. Doyon, 1956, mimeographed.

Exposition of Boethius on the Trinity (Expositio super librum Boethii de Trinitate, ed. B. Decker. Leiden: Brill, 1955). Written about 1258-59, at Paris; valuable for discussions of scientific methods. The translation by Sister Rose E. Brennan (St. Louis: Herder, 1946) was not made from the critical edition; questions V and VI are well translated in: A. Maurer, *Division and Methods of the Sciences.* Toronto: Pontifical Institute of Mediaeval Studies, 1953.

Exposition of Dionysius on the Divine Names (Expositio in Dionysii de divinis nominibus, ed. C. Pera. Turin: Marietti, 1956). Possibly written in Italy, 1262-68; discusses a type of Neoplatonic metaphysics. No English translation.

Exposition of Job (Expositio in Job ad litteram. Ed. Parma, 1863, Vol. XIV, 1-147. In preparation for the Leonine edition). Done about 1260, this Scripture commentary contains many philosophic reflections. No English translation.

Exposition of St. John's Gospel (Expositio in evangelium Joannis. Turin: Marietti, 1952). Composed at Paris, 1269-72, this is the most highly regarded of Aquinas' works on Scripture. No English translation.

Exposition of the Book of Causes (Super librum de Causis expositio, ed. H. D. Saffrey. Fribourg: Société Philosophique, 1954). A commentary of metaphysical interest on a compilation from Proclus; written about 1270-71. No English translation.

Exposition of the Lord's Prayer (Expositio devotissima Orationis Dominicae, in *Opuscula Theologica,* Vol. II. Turin: Marietti, 1954). Part of a series of Sermons preached in the vernacular at Naples, 1272-73. Translation: J. B. Collins, *The Catechetical Instructions of St. Thomas.* New York: Wagner, 1953.

Letter to the Duchess of Brabant (De regimine Judaeorum, ad Ducissam Brabantiae, in *Opuscula Philosophica.* Turin: Marietti, 1954). A letter answering eight political questions, possibly to Marguerite, daughter of Louis IX of France; possibly written after 1270. No English translation.

On Being and Essence (De ente et essentia, ed. Perrier. Paris: Lethielleux, 1949). One of Aquinas' most influential short works, on metaphysics; written in Paris, 1252-56. Translation: A. Maurer, *On Being and Essence.* Toronto: PIMS, 1949.

On Buying and Selling (De emptione et venditione ad tempus, in *Opuscula Theologica,* Vol. I. Turin: Marietti, 1954). A short letter giving Aquinas' views on usury. Translation: A. O'Rahilly, "Notes on St. Thomas on Credit," *Irish Ecclesiastical Record,* XXXI (1928), 164-165.

On Kingship (De Regno ad regem Cypri, in *Opuscula Philosophica,* Vol. I, ed. Perrier. Paris: Lethielleux, 1949. A more accurate edition is a desideratum). Addressed to the King of Cyprus, this political work was written about 1267; the text is in a corrupted condition. Translation: G. B. Phelan and I. T. Eschmann, *On Kingship.* Toronto: PIMS, 1949. This translation is based on a careful study of the MSS and the text tradition.

On the Articles of the Faith and the Sacraments of the Church (De articulis fidei et sacramentis ecclesiae, in *Opuscula Theologica,* Vol. I. Turin: Marietti, 1954). A letter of theological significance, possibly written in Italy, about 1262. Translation: J. B. Collins, *The Catechetical Instructions of St. Thomas.* New York: Wagner, 1953.

On the Perfection of the Spiritual Life (De perfectione vitae spiritualis, in *Opuscula Theologica,* Vol. II. Turin: Marietti, 1954). A work of controversy, written in 1270, against Gerald of Abbeville, a critic of the religious Orders. No published English translation. There is a translation by G. J. Guenther, C. G. Kloster, and J. X. Schmitt, in three master's theses done at St. Louis University, 1942-44.

On the Principles of Nature (De principiis naturae, ed. J. Pauson. Fribourg: Société Philosophique, 1950). A companion treatise to *On Being and Essence;* written in Paris, 1252-56. Translation: R. Kocourek, *The Principles of Nature.* St. Paul: North Central Publishing Company, 1948.

On the Sentences (Scripta super IV libros Sententiarum Petri Lombardi. Ed. Parma, 1856, Vols. VI-VIII. Ed. Mandonnet-Moos, Paris: Lethielleux, 1929, 1933, 1949, 4 vols., still incomplete.) This is Aquinas' original course in theology, Paris, 1252-56. No English translation.

Quodlibetal Questions (Quaestiones Quodlibetales. Turin: Marietti, 1949). A series of questions on miscellaneous topics, dating from Paris, 1256-59 *(Quodlibets VI-XI),* and again from Paris, 1270-72 *(Quodlibets I-VI,* possibly XII). No English translation.

Sermon on the Creed (Expositio devotissima super symbolum apostolorum, in *Opuscula Theologica,* Vol. II. Turin: Marietti, 1954). Preached at Naples, 1272-73. Translation: L. Shapcote, *The Three Greatest Prayers.* London: Burns, Oates, 1937, 39-89. Also J. B. Collins, *The Catechetical Instructions of St. Thomas.* New York: Wagner, 1939, 3-66.

Summa Against the Gentiles (Summa de veritate fidei Catholicae contra Gentiles, in Ed. Leonina. Tomes XIII-XV. Rome: Leonine Commission, 1918, 1926, 1930. Reprinted, Turin: Marietti, 1934). One of the most widely read works of Aquinas; written 1259-1264; important in theology and philosophy. Translations: J. Rickaby, *On God and His Creatures.* St. Louis: Herder, 1905. L. Shapcote, *The Summa contra Gentiles.* 5 vols. London: Burns, Oates; New York: Benziger, 1928-29. A. C. Pegis, J. F. Anderson, V. J. Bourke, C. J. O'Neil, *On the Truth of the Catholic Faith.* New York: Doubleday, 1955-57.

Summa of Theology (Summa Theologiae, in Ed. Leonina. Tomes IV-XII. Rome: Leonine Commission, 1888-1906. Also in 5 vols., Ottawa: Studium Generale Ordinis Praedicatorum, 1941-45). This great work was written 1265-1273; it was left incomplete by Aquinas. Translation: English Dominican Fathers (L. Shapcote), *The Summa Theologica.* 22 vols. London: Burns, Oates, 1912-36. A revision of part of this translation appears in *Basic Writings of Saint Thomas Aquinas,* ed. A. C. Pegis. 2 vols. New York: Random House, 1945.

RECOMMENDED READINGS

CHESTERTON, G. K. *St. Thomas Aquinas*. London: Hodder and Stoughton, 1947.

COPLESTON, F. C. *Aquinas*. London: Penguin Books, 1955.

FOSTER, K. *The Life of Saint Thomas Aquinas*. London: Longmans, Green; Baltimore: Helicon Press, 1959.

GILSON, E. *History of Christian Philosophy in the Middle Ages*. New York: Random House, 1955.

GRABMANN, M. *Thomas Aquinas, his Personality and Thought*. Translated by V. Michel. London and New York: Sheed and Ward, 1928.

MARITAIN, J. *St. Thomas Aquinas, Angel of the Schools*. Translated by J. F. Scanlan. London: Sheed and Ward, 1931.

VAN STEENBERGHEN, F. *Aristotle in the West*. Translated by L. Johnston. Louvain: Nauwelaerts, 1955.

WALZ, A. *Saint Thomas Aquinas: a Biographical Study*. Translated by S. Bullough. Westminster, Md.: Newman Press, 1951.

The Pocket Aquinas

I. Knowledge and Method

Foreword

IN HIS THEORY OF KNOWLEDGE, Thomas Aquinas was a cautious realist: he thought that human beings acquire knowledge of real things as they exist in man's environment—bodily things—through sense perception. On this level of knowing, man begins to know in much the same way that any of the higher vertebrates do. His external sense organs are stimulated or impressed by colored, audible, odorous, gustatory, and tactile qualities of individual bodies. If a vital response, rational or irrational, on the part of the animal occurs, then the result is a cognitive awareness of green trees, barking dogs running about, flowers with a distinctive odor, the warmth of sunlight, and so on. Such sense perception is a primary experience, not of disembodied qualities but of things that are at once colored, noisy, smelly, hot, and qualified in many other ways. To explain how men perceive such a thing as a dog, with its many characteristics, Aquinas adopted an already traditional theory (in both Aristotle and Augustine) that men are equipped not only with vision and hearing and the other capacities of external sensation but also with certain powers of internal sensation. These senses are "internal" because they are stimulated or actuated by means of images that are already within man's cognitive experience as a result of external sensation. Moreover, the internal senses, though organic powers, are not so obviously equipped with specialized organs. Aquinas seems to have agreed with the Arabian physiologists that certain brain centers are the organs of internal sensation. He distinguished

four such internal sense powers. A central or general sense
grasps what is seen, heard, and smelled as one thing—this
individual dog. A second internal sense, imagination, retains
the impressions made on the external senses long after their
stimulation has ceased and their objects have departed. A
third internal sense, memory, associates the objects of sense
perception with past time and is probably the psychological
basis of our awareness of the temporal continuum. Finally,
a fourth power, the cogitative sense (called estimative in
nonhuman animals), collates sense impressions and achieves
judgments that are quite concrete and individualized. Using
this fourth sense, a man (or a sheep) may decide: this dog
is dangerous, or this carrot is good to eat.

Thus analyzed, sensory cognition is doubtless rather complicated, involving the use of any number of the five or
more external senses, plus the additional responses of the
central sense and any of the other three internal senses.
Such complexity is the result of reflective analysis; Aquinas
would admit that the ordinary person perceives a dog in one
natural, easily performed, global act of sensory awareness.

Sense experience has another dimension: the perceiver
often responds to what he knows, with affective attitudes or
inclinations. Man likes some of the things that he sees; he
inclines toward them and may endeavor to get them or use
them in some way. He dislikes other objects that are sensed,
feels a repugnance to them, endeavors to avoid them. This
is the area of sensory appetition; the movements of sense
appetition are called passions or emotions. Aquinas distinguishes two powers here: the concupiscible appetite undergoes feelings in regard to sense objects that are easy to attain
or avoid; the irascible appetite undergoes feelings of an
emergency character in regard to sense objects perceived
as difficult to attain or avoid. My desire for an apple is a
feeling of concupiscence; my feeling of anger which may
prompt me to fight a fierce dog is an irascible passion. It
should be noted that such feelings appear to be the sources,
or conscious stimuli, of spontaneous motor activity in men.

Now, all the foregoing cognitive and appetitive sensory

functions have reference to objects that have one item in common: these objects are individual bodies or their individual parts. There is not much difference between such human experience and the parallel responses of the higher brute animals to things in their environment. Sense perception is valuable to man but Aquinas does not think that it is peculiarly characteristic of the human being.

On a separate and higher level are those truly human activities of cognition and appetition that are associated with intellectual understanding of the natures, or general meanings, of the things already perceived through sensation. In Aquinas' view, all of man's natural knowledge starts in sensation. What he considers peculiar to man as a knower is the ability to understand the universal characteristics (*rationes*) of things. The power to know things in this generalized manner is called intellect or understanding. Following Aristotle's lead, he distinguishes three acts of the intellect. The first is the simple apprehension of some meaning or intelligibility arising out of sensory experience. Simple intellection expresses its intelligible content in the form of one concept or idea. Thus, I think "dog," or "brown," or "big." This simple apprehension results in a knowledge which commits one to no judgment; it is a mere cognitive awareness of something that has meaning for the intelligence.

The second act of the intellect is judgment, or as Aquinas often names it, intellectual composition or division, combination or separation. Logically, judgment may be described as the identification (or nonidentification) of two concepts, or the attribution of one concept to another. However, what is thought in the usual judgment is not two concepts but two realities, or aspects of reality, that are either combined or separated. Psychologically then, judgment is a simple cognitive action in which something is known to be in a certain manner, or not to be so. Obviously such an act of judging can be either true or false, depending on whether the thing that is judged is so, or not. If I judge that Lassie is a dog, my judgment is true, provided the thing (*res*) "Lassie" exists in the way that my understanding (*intellec-*

tus) thinks of it. This is the basis of the famous Thomistic
definition of truth as the conformity of the thing and the
understanding (*adaequatio rei et intellectus*). Aquinas does
not claim that it is always possible to verify our human judgments. He is a realist but not a naïve one. Man's judgment
is fallible but often verifiable by further observation, study,
and experimentation. Even verified judgment is not taken as
exhaustive: Aquinas often remarks that definitive knowledge
of the nature of sensible things is rarely achieved.

The third act of understanding is the process of discursive
reasoning—ratiocination. One can move in thought from one
or more known judgments to a new judgment which involves
either the discovery of new knowledge or the verification of
something suspected but not clearly known before. The pat-
terns of valid reasoning are studied in logic. Aquinas regards the syllogism as the typical pattern of demonstration.
He often refers to geometry as a field in which it is well
used. However, he is fully aware of the possibilities of other
types of reasoning, in particular the "if A then B" sequence.
Successful reasoning terminates in a judgment which is the
optimum act of understanding. We reason in order to be
able to judge. Aquinas considers reasoning a laborious and
imperfect way of knowing but characteristic of man's intellectual processes. He speculates that more perfect intellects
(those of angels) may be able to judge all things within the
competence of their natures, without recourse to discursive
reasoning. When man is defined as a rational animal, then,
this is no compliment. It would be better if he could be
called an intellectual animal, but man rarely rises to an act
of pure intellection; his intellect is forced by its own imperfection to think in the step-by-step process which is a poor
substitute for first-rate, intuitive intelligence.

Will is rational appetite, the power of inclining affectively
toward or away from universally apprehended objects of
understanding. It is impossible to will what is not known
through the intellect. One wills health; one desires a steak,
by a movement of the concupiscible appetite. The objects
of volition are universal goods; those of sensory appetition

are individual. The will is not in any way a knowing power.

The foregoing sketches Aquinas' attempt to explain how man perceives and understands bodily things. The natures and characteristics of such things are what man is best equipped to know here on earth. In a way, then, Aquinas is a naturalist, and even a materialist, in his theory of knowledge. He never admits that men on earth have a natural "vision" of immaterial beings. Of course, he is convinced that some real beings exist without matter in them. The three examples of such immaterial beings that he talks about are human souls, angels, and God. There is no sensory experience of such beings, because they are not bodies and have not the qualities of corporeal things. This means that such spirits cannot be seen, or heard, or sensed in any way. Nor can there be any direct, natural apprehension of them by man's intellect.

How, then, can a person know anything about his own soul, or another soul, or an angelic spirit, or God? The only explanation open to Aquinas is that our knowledge of immaterial beings must be achieved by indirect and laborious reasoning to judgments about them. One method that is available is by negation, that is, a judgment of division or separation from matter. If an angel is nominally defined as an incorporeal being, then it follows that it does not occupy space and will not be subject to the sort of time that applies to bodies in motion. This is not the way to show that angels do exist, however. Another way to proceed in reasoning toward a judgment about spirits is from their effects. If it can be shown that certain events occur within our experience which cannot be explained by reference to bodily causes, then it may be possible to argue that these events point to the existence of nonbodily causes. Such reasoning is used by Aquinas to show that men have souls. Briefly, he thinks that man's intellectual and volitional activities cannot be caused by bodily forces; he patiently reasons (as we shall see later, in Chapter III) to the judgment that there must exist in each man an intellectual soul capable of performing such actions.

It is doubtful whether Aquinas ever attempts a formal

demonstration of the existence of angels, that is, of immaterial real beings that are finite but not substantially united
with any bodies. At most, he thinks that the existence of such
beings is a fitting complement to the perfection and diversity
of things in the universe. Of course, he accepts the existence
of angels on religious faith.

The epistemological situation is different in regard to God.
Aquinas does think that man can know, by careful discursive
reasoning, that God exists. This reasoning moves from man's
understanding of certain caused characteristics of bodies to
the conclusion that there must be a first and uncaused cause
of these effects. We shall see more of this in Chapters IV and
VIII, but it is to be noted here that Aquinas does not claim
that it is easy to achieve demonstrative knowledge of God.
Moreover, he thinks that we can only demonstrate *that* God
exists. We cannot know *what* He is, during this life, in any
adequately positive way. We may define God, nominally, as
a supreme or perfect being. We may make certain negative
judgments about Him: He is not a body. We may make
certain analogous judgments about Him: He is a being, good,
powerful, free. But we cannot know positively and directly
what He is, apart from these limping comparisons.

From what has been said, it will have been gathered that
Aquinas has special views on the distinctions and methods of
the various kinds of demonstrative knowledge that man can
achieve. Let us say once and for all that the Latin word
scientia originally means knowledge. Today, "science" suggests a highly specialized kind of knowledge possessed by
certain experts who are called scientists. In Aquinas' writings,
scientia (science) usually means a special kind of knowledge,
too. For him, it names any kind of demonstrative intellectual
knowledge. We shall see him, in the selections at the end of
this chapter, describing three kinds of speculative science:
physics, mathematics, and metaphysics. Physics is also called
natural philosophy; and metaphysics is another name for first
philosophy or divine science. The last name is a literal translation by Boethius of the Greek term *theologia*, which should
not be confused with the theology that is sacred, or based on

revelation. What Aquinas has to say about this supernatural theology will be seen in Chapter VIII.

Physics or philosophy of nature deals with bodies, their motions and principles, and their qualitative aspects. Mathematics treats the quantitative aspects of things. Metaphysics studies being as being, in its noncategorical aspects, wherever it is found. The foregoing distinctions depend on differences of subject matter but there are also differences of method. The philosophy of nature gives most play to discursive reasoning; in it there is a place for probability and judgments that admit of further revision. Its method is *ratiocinative*. Mathematics is taken as a very clear kind of knowledge, capable of being taught even to youngsters without much difficulty. Its method is called that of *learning*. Finally, metaphysics is viewed as a kind of knowledge characterized by the simplicity and unity of its thought; not that it is easy knowledge but rather that it represents those rare instances in which the human intellect is used at peak capacity, where the thinking is *intellectual*.

A Description of Cognitive Agents

Knowing agents differ from those that do not know in the fact that the nonknowers possess their own form only, while the knower is adapted from its origin to possess also the form of another thing, in the sense that the species of the known thing may be present in the knower.

It is clear, then, that the nature of a noncognitive thing is more restricted and limited, while the nature of knowing things has greater fullness and extension. This is why the Philosopher [Aristotle] says in the third book, *On the Soul* (8, 431b21), that "the soul is in a way all things."

Now, the limitation of the form is due to matter. Hence we said above that the more immaterial forms are, the more do they approach some sort of infinity. It is plain, then, that the immateriality of a thing is the reason why it is able to know; and the level of cognition depends on the level of immateriality. So, it is stated in the second book, *On the Soul* (12, 424a32), that plants do not know, because of their materiality. But the sense power is cognitive because it takes in species without matter; and the intellect is still more cognitive because it is more "separated from matter and unmixed," as is said in the third book, *On the Soul* (4, 429a18).

Summa of Theology, I, 14, 1, c. Trans. V.J.B.

How Men Know Corporeal Things

The answer should be that (as we said, q. 84, a. 7) the knowable object is proportioned to the knowing power. Now, there are three levels of knowing powers. One kind of knowing power is the act of a corporeal organ, namely sensation. Therefore, the object of any sensitive potency is the form as it exists in corporeal matter. Since this kind of matter is the principle of individuation, every power of the sensitive part of the soul is able to know particular things only.

Another kind of knowing power is that which is neither the act of a corporeal organ nor in any way associated with corporeal matter: the angelic intellect, for instance. So, the object of this knowing power is a form subsisting apart from matter; although they may know material things, they see them only in immaterial beings—either in themselves, or in God.

Now, the human intellect occupies a middle position: it is not the act of any organ, yet it is a power of the soul which is the form of the body, as we explained previously (q. 76, a. 1). So, it is appropriate to it to know a form that is existing individually in corporeal matter, yet not in the way that it is in such matter. Now, to know that which exists in individual matter, but not as it is in such matter, is to abstract the form which the phantasms represent from the individual matter. So, it must be said that our intellect understands material things by abstracting from phantasms, and that we reach some knowledge of immaterial things by proceeding from material things that are known in this way, just as angels, on the contrary, know material things through immaterial ones.

On the other hand, Plato, concentrating solely on the immateriality of the human intellect and not on the fact of its being united to a body in some manner, claimed that separate ideas are the object of the intellect, and that we understand

Summa of Theology, I, 85, 1, c, reply to Obj. 1, 2. Trans. V.J.B.

not indeed by abstracting but rather by participating in things already abstracted, as we said above (q. 84, a. 1).

[*Answer to first objection*]

It should be said that there are two ways of abstracting. One way is by composition and division; thus do we understand that something is not present in another, that it is separated from it. Another way is through simple and absolute consideration; thus do we understand one item while giving no thought to the other.

To abstract by means of the intellect those things which in reality are not abstracted, using the first way of abstracting, is not done without falsity. However, to abstract intellectually in the second way those things that are not abstracted in reality is not to falsify, as is clear on the level of sensation. If we say that color is not present in a colored body, or that it is separated from it, it will be a case of falsity either in opinion or in speaking. But if we consider color as its property, giving no thought to the colored apple, or if we speak about what has been so considered, there will be no falsity of opinion or speech. Indeed, an apple is no part of the intelligible meaning of color; so nothing prevents color from being understood without any understanding of apple.

In the same way, I say that the items that belong to the intelligibility [*ratio*] of the species of any material thing (an apple, a man, or a house) can be considered apart from the individual principles which do not belong in the intelligible meaning of the species. Now, this is to abstract the universal from the particular, the intelligible species from the phantasms, namely, to consider the specific nature without thinking of the individual principles that are represented by the phantasms.

So, when it is said that understanding is false when it understands a thing other than it is, this is true if the word "other" refers to the thing that is understood. Then, indeed, the understanding is false when it understands the thing to be other than it is. Thus, understanding would be false if it abstracted the species of a stone from matter, in such a way that it understood it not to exist in matter (as Plato asserted).

However, the proposition is not true if the word "other" is taken as applying to the knower. Indeed, there is no falsity in the statement that the mode of the knower in performing the act of understanding is different from the mode of the thing in real existence, for the thing understood is in the one who is understanding according to the manner of the intellect, and not materially, according to the manner of the material thing.

[*Answer to second objection*]

It should be said that some people have thought that the species of a natural thing is simply the form, and that matter is not a part of the species. According to this theory, matter would not be included in the definitions of natural things. So, a different explanation must be given, that there are two kinds of matter, namely, *common* and signate or *individual*. The common is, for instance, flesh and bone; while the individual is, for example, these fleshy parts and these bones.

The intellect, then, abstracts the species of a natural thing from individual sensible matter but not from common sensible matter. Thus, it abstracts the species of man from these fleshy parts and these bones, which do not belong to the intelligible content of the species but are individual items (as is said in the *Metaphysics*, VI, 10, 1035b28), and therefore it can be considered apart from them. However, the species of man cannot be intellectually abstracted from flesh and bones.

Of course, mathematical species can be abstracted intellectually not only from individual sensible matter but also from the common matter—not from common intelligible matter but only from the individual. Sensible matter is called corporeal matter, inasmuch as it is the subject of the sensible qualities such as hot and cold, hard and soft, and the like.

Intelligible matter is called substance, inasmuch as it is the subject of quantity. Now, it is evident that quantity is present in substance prior to the sensible qualities. Hence, quantities, such as numbers, dimensions, and shapes (which are quantitative factors), can be considered apart from the sensible qualities—and this is to abstract from sensible matter. Yet, they cannot be considered apart from an understanding of the substance that is the subject of quantity, for this would be to abstract them from the common intelligible matter. However, they can be considered without this or that substance—and this is to abstract them from individual intelligible matter.

Of course, there are some things that can be abstracted even from common intelligible matter, items such as being, one, potency, and act, and others such, which can be without any matter, as is clear in the immaterial substances.

Because Plato did not consider what has been said about the two ways of abstracting, he claimed that all the items that we have called abstract, through understanding, are abstract in reality.

Sense Knowledge and Truth

Our knowledge, taking its start from things, proceeds in this order. First, it begins in sense; second, it is completed in the intellect. As a consequence, sense is found to be in some way an intermediary between the intellect and things; for, with reference to things, it is, as it were, an intellect; and with reference to intellect, it is, as it were, a thing. Hence, truth or falsity is said to be in sense in two respects. The first is in

Disputed Questions on Truth, I, 11, c. Trans. Mulligan, McGlynn, and Schmidt, *Truth*, vol. I, pp. 48–49.

the relation of sense to intellect. In this respect, the sense is said to be true or false as a thing is, namely, insofar as it causes a true or false judgment in the intellect. The second respect is in the relation of sense to things. In this, truth and falsity are said to be in sense as they are said to be in the intellect, namely, insofar as the sense judges that what is, is or is not.

Hence, if we speak of a sense in the first meaning, in a way there is falsity in sense, and in a way there is not. For sense, in itself, is a thing; and it also passes judgment on other things. If, in its relation to the intellect, it is considered as a thing, then there is no falsity in sense, for a sense reveals its state to the intellect exactly as it is affected. Hence, Augustine says, in the passage referred to: "The senses can report to the mind only how they are affected." On the other hand, if sense is considered in its relation to the intellect as representing some other thing, it may be called false in view of the fact that it sometimes represents a thing to the intellect other than it actually is. For, in that case, as we said about things, it is such as to cause a false judgment in the intellect—but not necessarily, since the intellect judges on what is presented by sense just as it judges about things. Thus, in its relation to the intellect, sense always produces a true judgment in the intellect with respect to its own condition, but not always with respect to the condition of things.

If sense is considered in its relation to things, however, then there are truth and falsity in sense in the manner in which these are in the intellect. For truth and falsity are found primarily and principally in the judgment of the intellect as it associates and dissociates, and in the formation of quiddities, only in their relation to the judgment following upon this formation. Hence, truth and falsity are properly said to be in sense inasmuch as it judges about sensible objects, but inasmuch as it apprehends a sensible object, there is not properly truth or falsity, except in the relation of this apprehension to the judgment, insofar as a judgment of this or that sort naturally follows upon a particular apprehension.

The judgment of sense about certain things—for example, proper sensibles—takes place spontaneously. About other things, however, it takes place by means of a certain comparison, made in man by the cogitative power, a sense power, whose place in animals is taken by a spontaneous estimation. This sensitive power judges about common sensibles and accidental sensibles. However, the spontaneous action of a thing always takes place in one way, unless by accident it is impeded intrinsically by some defect or extrinsically by some impediment. Consequently, the judgment of sense about proper sensibles is always true unless there is an impediment in the organ or in the medium; but its judgment about common or accidental sensibles is sometimes wrong. Thus, it is clear how there can be falsity in the judgment of sense.

As regards the apprehension of the senses, it must be noted that there is one type of apprehensive power, for example, a proper sense, which apprehends a sensible species in the presence of a sensible thing; but there is also a second type, the imagination, for example, which apprehends a sensible species when the thing is absent. So, even though the sense always apprehends a thing as it is, unless there is an impediment in the organ or in the medium, the imagination usually apprehends a thing as it is not, since it apprehends it as present though it is absent. Consequently, the Philosopher says: "Imagination, not sense, is the master of falsity."

Three Intellectual Operations

As the Philosopher states in the third book, *On the Soul* (6, 430a26), the operation of the intellect is twofold: one operation is called the understanding of indivisibles, that is, it apprehends by this function the essence of each thing in itself; the other operation pertains to the intellect as combining and

Exposition of Aristotle on Interpretation, I, Lect. 1. Trans. V.J.B.

distinguishing. Now, there is also a third operation, reasoning; by it the reason proceeds, from items that are known, to search for things that are unknown.

The first of these operations is directed to the second, for there cannot be combination and distinction, except of apprehended simple items. And the second is ordered to the third, because the intellect must proceed from some truly known thing to which the intellect assents, in order to acquire certitude concerning any unknown things. Since logic is called rational science, its consideration must be directed to those factors that characterize the three rational operations that have been mentioned.

Aristotle explains what is pertinent to the first operation of the intellect in his *Categories*. Then the Philosopher explains the second operation, affirmative and negative judgment, in his book *On Interpretation*. And he explains the third operation in the *Prior Analytics* and the subsequent treatises, in which there is a treatment of the syllogism without qualification, and then of the various kinds of syllogism and arguments by which reason moves from one thing to another.

Truth in Understanding and in Being

When a predicate is used primarily and secondarily of many things, it is not necessary that that which is the cause of the others receive the primary predication of the common term, but rather that in which the meaning of the common term is first fully verified. For example, *healthy* is primarily predicated of an animal, for it is in an animal that the nature of health is first found in its fullest sense. But inasmuch as medicine causes health, it is also said to be healthy. Therefore, since truth is predicated of many things in a primary and a second-

Disputed Questions on Truth, I, 2, c, reply to Obj. 1. Trans. Mulligan, McGlynn, and Schmidt, *Truth*, vol. I, pp. 10-12.

ary sense, it ought to be primarily predicated of that in which
its full meaning is primarily found.

Now, the fulfillment of any motion is found in the term of
the motion; and, since the term of the motion of a cognitive
power is the soul, the known must be in the knower after the
manner of the knower. But the motion of an appetitive power
terminates in things. For this reason the Philosopher speaks
of a sort of circle formed by the acts of the soul: for a thing
outside the soul moves the intellect, and the thing known
moves the appetite, which tends to reach the things from
which the motion originally started. Since good, as mentioned
previously, expresses a relation to appetite, and true, a relation
to the intellect, the Philosopher says that good and evil are
in things, but true and false are in the mind. A thing is not
called true, however, unless it conforms to an intellect. The
true, therefore, is found secondarily in things and primarily
in intellect.

Note, however, that a thing is referred differently to the
practical intellect than it is to the speculative intellect. Since
the practical intellect causes things, it is a measure of what
it causes. But, since the speculative intellect is receptive in
regard to things, it is, in a certain sense, moved by things
and consequently measured by them. It is clear, therefore, as
is said in the *Metaphysics*, that natural things from which
our intellect gets its scientific knowledge measure our intellect. Yet these things are themselves measured by the divine
intellect, in which are all created things—just as all works of
art find their origin in the intellect of an artist. The divine
intellect, therefore, measures and is not measured; a natural
thing both measures and is measured; but our intellect is
measured and measures only artifacts, not natural things.

A natural thing, therefore, being placed between two intellects is called *true* insofar as it conforms to either. It is said
to be true with respect to its conformity with the divine intellect insofar as it fulfills the end to which it was ordained by
the divine intellect. This is clear from the writings of Anselm
and Augustine, as well as from the definition of Avicenna,
previously cited: "The truth of anything is a property of the

act of being which has been established for it." With respect to its conformity with a human intellect, a thing is said to be true insofar as it is such as to cause a true estimate about itself; and a thing is said to be false if, as Aristotle says, "by nature it is such that it seems to be what it is not, or seems to possess qualities which it does not possess."

In a natural thing, truth is found especially in the first, rather than in the second, sense; for its reference to the divine intellect comes before its reference to a human intellect. Even if there were no human intellects, things could be said to be true because of their relation to the divine intellect. But if, by an impossible supposition, intellect did not exist and things did continue to exist, then the essentials of truth would in no way remain.

[*Answers to difficulties*]

1. As is clear from the discussion, *true* is predicated primarily of a true intellect and secondarily of a thing conformed with intellect. *True* taken in either sense, however, is interchangeable with being, but in different ways. Used of things, it can be interchanged with being through a judgment asserting merely material identity, for every being is conformed with the divine intellect and can be conformed with a human intellect. The converse of this is also true.

But if *true* is understood as used of the intellect, then it can be converted with being outside the soul—not as denominating the same subject, but as expressing conformity. For every true act of understanding is referred to a being, and every being corresponds to a true act of understanding.

True Understanding and Judgment

Just as the true is found primarily in the intellect rather than
in things, so also is it found primarily in an act of the intellect joining and separating, rather than in an act by which
it forms the quiddities of things. For the nature of the true
consists in a conformity of thing and intellect. Nothing becomes conformed with itself, but conformity requires distinct terms. Consequently, the nature of truth is first found
in the intellect when the intellect begins to possess something
proper to itself, not possessed by the thing outside the soul,
yet corresponding to it, so that between the two—intellect
and thing—a conformity may be found. In forming the quiddities of things, the intellect merely has a likeness of a thing
existing outside the soul, as a sense has a likeness when it
receives the species of a sensible thing. But when the intellect begins to judge about the thing it has apprehended, then
its judgment is something proper to itself—not something
found outside in the thing. And the judgment is said to be
true when it conforms to the external reality. Moreover, the
intellect judges about the thing it has apprehended at the
moment when it says that something is or is not. This is the
role of "the intellect composing and dividing."

For these reasons, the Philosopher says that composition
and division are in the intellect, and not in things. Moreover,
this is why truth is found primarily in the joining and separating by the intellect, and only secondarily in its formation of
the quiddities of things or definitions, for a definition is called
true or false because of a true or false combination. For it
may happen that a definition will be applied to something
to which it does not belong, as when the definition of a circle
is assigned to a triangle. Sometimes, too, the parts of a definition cannot be reconciled, as happens when one defines a
thing as "an animal entirely without the power of sensing."

Disputed Questions on Truth, I, 3, c. Trans. Mulligan, McGlynn, and
Schmidt, *Truth*, vol. I, pp. 13-14.

The judgment implied in such a definition—"some animal is incapable of sensing"—is false. Consequently, a definition is said to be true or false only because of its relation to a judgment, as a thing is said to be true because of its relation to intellect.

From our discussion, then, it is clear that the true is predicated, first of all, of joining and separating by the intellect; second, of the definitions of things insofar as they imply a true or a false judgment. Third, the true may be predicated of things insofar as they are conformed with the divine intellect or insofar as, by their very nature, they can be conformed with human intellects. Fourth, true or false may be predicated of man insofar as he chooses to express truth, or insofar as he gives a true or false impression of himself or of others by his words and actions; for truth can be predicated of words in the same way as it can be predicated of the ideas which they convey.

Judgment as Combining and Distinguishing

Since intellectual conceptions are the likenesses of things, the factors involved in the understanding may be treated and designated in two ways: either in themselves or according to the rational characteristics of the things of which they are likenesses. Thus, a statue of Hercules in itself is called and is a piece of copper; but insofar as it is the likeness of Hercules, it is called a man. So, too, if we direct our attention to those factors that relate to understanding in itself, then wherever there is truth or falsity there is always combination; for these are never found in understanding, unless because of the fact that the intellect compares one simple concept with another. However, if it be a comparison with the thing, sometimes it is called combination, sometimes distinction.

It is combination when the intellect compares one concept

Exposition of Aristotle on Interpretation, I, Lect. 3. Trans. V.J.B.

with another, apprehending as it were the conjunction or identity of the things to which the conceptions pertain; and it is distinction when it compares one concept with the other in such a way that it apprehends that the things are different. In this way, also, in the sphere of vocal expressions, combination is called affirmation (in that it signifies a joining together on the side of reality), and distinction is called negation (in that it signifies a separating of real things).

Relational Character of Human Truth

From our previous discussion it is clear that truth is properly found in the human or divine intellect, as health is found in an animal. In things, however, truth is found because of some relation to intellect—just as health is said to be in things other than animals insofar as they bring about or preserve animal health. Truth, therefore, is properly and primarily in the divine intellect. In the human intellect, it exists properly but secondarily, for it exists there only because of a relation to either one of the two truths just mentioned.

In his gloss on these words of Psalm II (5:2), *Truths are decayed from among the children of men*, Augustine writes that the truth of the divine intellect is one, and from it are drawn the many truths that are in the human intellect—"just as from one man's face many likenesses are reflected in a mirror." Now, there are many truths in things, just as there are many entities of things. But truth predicated of things because of their relation to the human intellect is, as it were, accidental to those things; for, supposing that the human intellect did not or could not exist, things would still remain essentially the same. But truth predicated of things because of their relation to the divine intellect is inseparably attendant on them, for they cannot exist except by reason of the divine in-

Disputed Questions on Truth, I, 4, c. Trans. Mulligan, McGlynn, and Schmidt, *Truth*, vol. I, pp. 17-18.

tellect which keeps bringing them into being. Again, truth is primarily in a thing because of its relation to the divine intellect, not to the human intellect, because it is related to the divine intellect as to its cause, but to the human intellect as to its effect, in the sense that the latter receives its knowledge from things. For this reason, a thing is said to be true principally because of its order to the truth of the divine intellect rather than because of its relation to the truth of a human intellect.

So, if truth in its proper sense be taken as that by which all things are primarily true, then all things are true by means of one truth, the truth of the divine intellect. This is the truth which Anselm writes about. But if truth in its proper sense be taken as that by which things are said to be true secondarily, then there are many truths about many true things, and even many truths in different minds about one true thing. Finally, if truth in its improper sense be taken as that by which all things are said to be true, then there are many truths for many true things, but only one truth for one true thing.

Things are called true from the truth in the divine or human intellect, just as food is called healthy, not because of any inherent form, but because of the health which is in an animal. If, however, a thing is called true because of the truth in the thing, which is simply its entity conformed with intellect, then it is so called because of something inhering in it after the manner of a form, as food is said to be healthy because of a quality of its own—which is the reason for its being said to be healthy.

Falsity and Understanding

The name "intellect" arises from the intellect's ability to know the most profound elements of a thing; for to understand

Disputed Questions on Truth, I, 12, c. Trans. Mulligan, McGlynn, and Schmidt, *Truth*, vol. I, pp. 50-51.

[*intelligere*] means to read what is inside a thing [*intus legere*]. Sense and imagination know only external accidents, but the intellect alone penetrates to the interior and to the essence of a thing. But even beyond this, the intellect, having perceived essences, operates in different ways by reasoning and inquiring. Hence, "intellect" can be taken in two senses.

First, it can be taken merely according to its relation to that from which it first received its name. We are said to understand, properly speaking, when we apprehend the quiddity of things or when we understand those truths that are immediately known by the intellect, once it knows the quiddities of things. For example, first principles are immediately known when we know their terms, and for this reason intellect or understanding is called "a habit of principles." The proper object of the intellect, however, is the quiddity of a thing. Hence, just as the sensing of proper sensibles is always true, so the intellect is always true in knowing *what a thing is*, as is said in *On the Soul*. By accident, however, falsity can occur in this knowing of quiddities, if the intellect falsely joins and separates. This happens in two ways: when it attributes the definition of one thing to another, as would happen were it to conceive that "mortal rational animal" were the definition of an ass; or when it joins together parts of definitions that cannot be joined, as would happen were it to conceive that "irrational immortal animal" were the definition of an ass. For it is false to say that some irrational animal is immortal. So it is clear that a definition cannot be false except to the extent that it implies a false affirmation. (This twofold mode of falsity is touched upon in the *Metaphysics*.) Similarly, the intellect is not deceived in any way with respect to first principles. It is plain, then, that if intellect is taken in the first sense—according to that action from which it receives the name "intellect"—falsity is not in the intellect.

Intellect can also be taken in a second sense—in general, that is, as extending to all its operations, including opinion and reasoning. In that case, there is falsity in the intellect. But it never occurs if a reduction to first principles is made correctly.

Intellectual Meaning and Vocal Signs

For the understanding of this term "Word" [*Verbum*], we should note that, according to the Philosopher (*On Interpretation*, 16a3), spoken terms are signs of mental experience. Now, it is customary in Scripture to designate the basic meanings by using the names of their symbols. Thus, there is the text in I Cor. 10:5: *But the rock was Christ*. Now, it was necessary for that meaning within our soul, signified by our external word, to be called a word. Whether the term "word" primarily belongs to the vocalization externally expressed or to the mental conception is not important at the moment. However, it is clear that what is signified in speaking, as internally existing in the mind, is prior to the external word expressed in speech, for it is the cause of the latter's existence. Therefore, if we wish to know what the internal word of the mind is, we may examine the meaning that is expressed by the external vocable.

Now, there are three items within our understanding: the potency of the intellect, the species of the thing that is understood (its form, related to the intellect itself as the species of color is to the pupil of the eye), and thirdly, the very working of the intellect, the act of understanding. But none of these is signified by the word that is vocally expressed, for the name "stone" does not signify the substance of the intellect, since this is not what the speaker intends to say; nor does it signify the species, which is that whereby the intellect understands, for even this is not intended by the speaker; nor again does it signify the act of understanding, since understanding is not an external action proceeding from the knower but something remaining within him. So, that which the knower forms in the act of understanding is what is properly called the internal word.

Of course, the intellect forms two things, on the basis of its two operations. By its operation that is called the

Exposition of St. John's Gospel, c. 1, Lect. 1. Trans. V.J.B.

understanding of indivisibles, it forms the definition; and
by its operation whereby it combines and separates, it forms
the enunciation, or something of that type. Therefore, what
is so formed and expressed by the working of the intellect,
either as defining or enunciating, is what is signified by the
external vocalization.

Consequently, the Philosopher says that the intelligibility
[*ratio*] that the name signifies is the definition. So, that
which is so expressed, that is to say, formed in the mind, is
called the internal word. Hence, it is related to the intellect,
not as that whereby the intellect understands but as that
in which it understands, because it sees the nature of the
thing that is understood as expressed and formed in it.
Thus, then, do we get the meaning of this term "Word."

Secondly, from what has been said we can conceive that
the word is always something proceeding from the intellect
as actuated. Again, the word is always the intelligibility and
likeness of the thing understood. And if the same thing be
both the agent and the object of the act of understanding,
then the word is the intelligibility and the likeness of the
intellect from which it proceeds. But if the knower and the
thing understood be different, then the word is not the likeness and intelligibility of the knower but of the thing understood; thus the conception that a person has of a stone is
the likeness of the stone only. But when the intellect understands itself, then this kind of word is the likeness and intelligibility of the intellect.

Man's Knowledge of His Own Soul

Because it is natural for our intellect, in the condition of this
present life, to be concerned with material and sensible
things (as we have explained before), it follows that our
intellect understands itself by virtue of the fact that it is
actuated by species that are abstracted from sensible things

Summa of Theology, I, 87, 1, c. Trans. V.J.B.

by the light of the agent intellect (which is the act of these objects of understanding). It is by means of these species that the possible intellect understands. So, our intellect knows itself not through its own essence but through its act.

Now, this works in two ways. One is particular, as when a Socrates or a Plato perceives that he has an intellectual soul, due to his perception that he is performing the act of understanding. The other way is universal, as when we consider the nature of the human mind from the action of the intellect. . . .

Moreover, there is a difference between these two cognitions. To have the first kind of knowledge of the mind, the very presence of the mind is enough, for it is the principle of the act from which the mind perceives itself. So it is said to know itself through its own presence. But to have the second kind of knowledge of the mind, its presence is not enough; instead, a careful and subtle investigation is required. As a result, many people do not know the nature of the soul and many have erred, too, concerning the nature of the soul.

How the Human Intellect Is Known

To exist as a reality in nature is not proper to prime matter, unless it be made actual by form, for it is in potency. Now, our possible intellect has a status in the order of the objects of understanding similar to that of prime matter in the order of things in physical nature, in the sense that it stands in potency toward intelligibles just as prime matter does toward things in physical nature.

Consequently, our possible intellect cannot have an intellectual operation, unless it be perfected by an intelligible species from some real thing. So, it understands itself through an intelligible species, just as it does other things. Now, it is plain that it understands its own act of understand-

Summa of Theology, I, 14, 2, reply to Obj. 3. Trans. V.J.B.

ing when it knows any object of the intellect, and it knows its intellectual power through its act. God, of course, exists as a pure act both in the order of existing beings and in that of objects of understanding; so He understands Himself through Himself.

On Knowing God

Knowledge occurs by virtue of the fact that the thing known is present in the knower. Now, the thing known is in the knower according to the mode of the knower. Hence, for each type of knower its knowledge is present according to the mode proper to its nature. So, if the mode of existing of any known thing surpasses the mode proper to the nature of the knower, then the knowledge of that thing must be above the nature of this knower.

There are many modes of existing for things. There are some things whose nature cannot exist except in individual matter; things like this are all corporeal. There are others whose natures are subsistent in themselves and not in any matter. However, these are not identical with their own act of existing, but they have an act of existing; they are incorporeal substances and we call them angels. Now, for God alone is that mode of being proper in which He is His own subsisting act of existing [*esse*].

It is connatural for us to know those things that exist only in individual matter, because our soul by which we know is a form in matter. It has two powers of knowing. One is the act of a corporeal organ. It is connatural to this power to know things as they exist in individual matter; as a consequence, this sense power knows singulars only. Its other knowing power is the intellect, which is not the act of any corporeal organ. Hence, it is connatural for us through the intellect to know natures that in fact exist only in individual matter, yet not to know them as they are in individual matter

Summa of Theology, I, 12, 4, c. Trans. V.J.B.

but as they are abstracted from it by means of intellectual consideration. Consequently, we are able to know intellectually things of this kind in a universal way that is above the capacity of sense power.

Of course, it is connatural to the angelic intellect to know natures that are not existing in matter, and this is above the natural capacity of the intellect proper to the human soul in its present state of life when it is united to a body.

The conclusion remains, then, that to know the subsistent act of existing itself is connatural only to the divine intellect, for this is above the natural capacity of any created intellect since no creature is its own act of existing but a creature has participated existence. Therefore, the created intellect cannot see God in His essence—unless God through His grace joins Himself to the created intellect as a thing to be understood by it.

Demonstrative Science as an Intellectual Habit

An intellectual virtue is speculative when the speculative intellect is perfected by it in order to think about what is true; for this is its good work. Now, the true may be considered in two ways: first, as known directly in itself; second, as known through something else. What is known directly in itself stands as a principle and is perceived at once by the intellect. So, the habit perfecting the intellect for the consideration of a true object of this kind is called the understanding as the *habit of principles*.

The true that is known through something else is, of course, not perceived at once by the intellect but as a result of rational searching; so, it has the character of a terminus. Now, this is possible in two ways. One way is for it to be ultimate in any genus; the other way is for it to be ultimate

Summa of Theology, I-II, 57, 2. Trans. V.J.B.

in regard to the whole of human cognition. Since "things that are known later by us are prior and more knowable in their own nature" (as is said in the *Physics,* I, 2, 184a18–20), therefore, that which is ultimate in regard to the whole of human cognition is what is first and most knowable in its own nature. Now, dealing with this kind of object is *"wisdom,"* for it considers the highest causes," as is said in the *Metaphysics* (I, 1, 981b28). Hence, it evidently judges and orders all matters, because it is impossible to have perfect and universal judgment except by resolution to the first causes.

Now, for what is ultimate in this or that genus of knowable objects, *science* perfects the intellect. So, according to the generically different kinds of knowable things, there are different habits of the sciences, while of course there is but one wisdom.

Answers to objections

1. We would have to say that wisdom is somewhat a science, to the extent that it has what is common to all sciences, namely, the function of demonstrating conclusions from principles. But, since it has something peculiar to itself above the other sciences, that is, its function of judging all things not only as to conclusions but even as to the first principles, it therefore has a more perfect character as a virtue than does science.

2. When the objective intelligibility [*ratio objecti*] comprised under one act is related to a potency or habit, then the habit or potency is not distinguished on the basis of the intelligibility of the object and the material object. For instance, it pertains to the same visual potency to see color and also light; for the latter is the principle of the seeing of color and yet it is seen at once along with it. Now, principles of demonstration can be considered separately, without the conclusions being considered. They can also be considered along with their conclusions, in the sense that the principles are brought forward to their conclusions. So, to consider

principles in this second way is proper to science, for it also considers conclusions; but to consider principles in themselves is the function of understanding.

Hence, if a person thinks about this correctly, he will not distinguish these three virtues as items on the same level, but on the basis of a certain ranking, as happens in the case of potential wholes where one part is more perfect than another; for example, the rational soul is more perfect than the sensitive, and the sensitive than the vegetative. In fact, science in this way depends on understanding as on something more primary. And both depend on wisdom as on something most primary, which includes both understanding and science, for it passes judgment on the conclusions of the sciences and even on their principles.

How We Know First Principles

As a thing has its act of being [*esse*] through its proper form, so does the knowing power possess its act of knowing [*cognoscere*] through a likeness of the known thing. Hence, just as a natural thing is not deficient in the act of being that is appropriate to it because of its form, though it can be deficient in regard to certain accidental or associated items (for instance, from the fact that he is, it is not necessary that he have two feet, but from the fact that he is, he must be a man), so also the knowing power is not deficient in its act of knowing with regard to the thing whose likeness informs the power. However, it can be defective in regard to anything that is merely associated with, or accidental to, its object. As was said, the power of sight is not deceived in regard to its proper object but it may be in regard to common sensibles which are related to the object as consequences, and also in regard to accidental sensibles.

Now, just as the sense power is informed directly by the likeness of its proper sensibles, so is the intellect informed

Summa of Theology, I, 17, 3, c. Trans. V.J.B.

by the likeness of the essence of the thing. Hence, the intellect is not deceived about what is, any more than the sense is about proper sensibles.

However, it can be deceived in the act of judging by composition or division, when it attributes to a thing whose quiddity it understands something that does not go along with it, or is opposed to it. In fact, the intellect stands in regard to the judging of items like this in the same way that the sense power does in regard to the judging of common or accidental sensibles. Of course, this difference is maintained (as was mentioned previously in connection with truth): falsity can be present in the intellect, not only because the intellect's knowledge is false but also because the intellect knows the falsity, as also the truth. In the sense, however, falsity is not present as something known, as was said.

Though intellectual falsity is essentially connected with the compositive [judging] function of the intellect, there also may be falsity in the operation of the intellect whereby it knows quiddity, by virtue of the fact that some intellectual composition is mixed with this operation. This may occur in two ways. First, the intellect may attribute the definition of one thing to another, as when the definition of a circle is attributed to a man. Thus, the definition of one thing is false in regard to another thing. Second, it may put together the parts of a definition when these parts are incompatible; in this case the definition is not only false in relation to a certain thing, it is false in itself. Suppose it forms this definition: a rational four-footed animal; the intellect is false in making this act of definition, because it is already false in forming this compositive judgment: *Some rational animal is a quadruped.* For this reason, the intellect cannot be false in knowing simple quiddities; instead, it is either true or it understands nothing at all. The intellect is always right when engaged in the understanding of principles; it is not deceived about these, for the same reason that it is not deceived about that which is. For the self-evident principles are those which, when their terms are understood, are at once known from the fact that the predicate is included in the definition of the subject.

On Indemonstrable Propositions

Aristotle first states that the immediate principle of a syllogism is of two kinds. One is called a postulate [*positio*]; it is not susceptible of demonstration and that is why it is called immediate. Yet, it is not necessary for the pupil, the person whose role is to be taught in a demonstrative science, to have it, that is, to intuit it mentally or to assent to it. The other kind, however, is what is called an axiom [*dignitas*], or a maximal proposition. Now, everyone whose function is to be taught must have this sort of proposition in his mind and give assent to it.

It is clear that some principles are of this latter kind, as is shown in the fourth book of the *Metaphysics* (3, 1005b20), concerning the principle that affirmation and denial are not simultaneously true. No one can believe the contrary of this in his mind, although in speaking he may pretend that he does. For such principles, we use the term axioms or maximal propositions, because of the certitude of this type of principle in the process of making other propositions evident.

To make this division clear, note that every proposition whose predicate is within the rational meaning of its subject is immediate, and is known by itself, in the sense that it stands by itself. But the terms of some propositions are such that they are present in the knowledge of all things: for example, being and one, and others such that pertain to being as being. Indeed, being is the primary intellectual conception. Consequently, such propositions, not only in themselves but also as far as we are concerned, must be as it were self-known: for example, that the same thing cannot both be and not be, that the whole is greater than its part, and the like.

Exposition of Aristotle's Posterior Analytics, I, Lect. 5. Trans. V.J.B.

Hence, all the sciences take principles of this kind from metaphysics, for its function is to consider being without restriction, and also the items that pertain to being. Of course, there are some immediate propositions whose terms are not known to all people. Hence, though their predicate does belong to the rational meaning of their subject, it is not necessary that such propositions be conceded by all. For instance, this proposition: *all right angles are equal,* is in itself self-evident or immediate, because such equality falls within the definition of the right angle. In fact, a right angle is what a straight line produces when it falls upon another straight line in such a way that the angles are made equal on both sides. So, this type of principle is accepted with a certain element of postulation.

There is also another way in which some propositions are called suppositions. There are some propositions that cannot be proved except through the principle of another science; so, they have to be posited within one science even though they may be proved by the principles of another science. Thus, the geometer takes it that a straight line extends from one point to another, while a natural scientist proves this by showing that between any two points there is a mediating straight line.

Sensory Induction to First Principles

He [Aristotle] shows in the foregoing how the knowledge of first principles comes about within us. He concludes from what has been said that memory arises out of sensation; that is so in the case of those animals in whom the sensible impression endures, as was said above. Then, out of memory that has been produced many times concerning the same thing (under a variety of different individual conditions, however), there comes experience; for experience is obvi-

Exposition of Aristotle's Posterior Analytics, II, Lect. 20. Trans. V.J.B.

ously nothing but the taking of something from many instances retained in memory.

Nevertheless, experience requires some reasoning about particulars, by which it relates one item to another, and that is characteristic of reason. For instance, when it is remembered that a certain herb has many times cured many people of fever, we say that it is our experience that there is such a remedy for fever.

Of course, reason does not stop with the experience of particular instances; rather, from the many particulars of which it has experience it takes one common item that is established in the mind and thinks of it without considering any of the singulars; and this it takes as a principle of art and science. Say a physician has thought for a long time that a given herb has cured Socrates of a fever, and also Plato, and many other individual men; then, when his consideration has risen to this point, that such a species of herb cures fevered people without qualification, this is taken as a rule in the art of medicine. So, this is what Aristotle says: just as experience arises out of memory, so also out of experience or, even further, out of the universal lying at rest in the mind it is taken as so in regard to all, just as it has been experienced in regard to some.

Indeed, the universal is said to be lying at rest in the mind, in the sense that it is considered apart from the singulars in which motion occurs. Furthermore, the fact that he speaks of it as one apart from the many does not mean in real existence but in the consideration of the intellect which thinks of any nature, say that of man, without relating it to Socrates and Plato. Though, on the basis of intellectual consideration, it is one apart from many, nevertheless it is one and the same in all the singulars—not numerically so, as if there were the same numerical humanity for all men, but according to the specific rational character. For, just as this white thing is the same as that white thing, in whiteness, but not in the sense that one numerical whiteness is existing in both, so also is Socrates like Plato, in humanity, but not in the sense that one numerical humanity is existing in both.

And so, from this experience and from such a universal taken from experience, there is present in the mind that which is the principle of art and science. He distinguishes between art and science, as in the sixth book of the *Ethics* (3, 1039b20), where it is stated that art is right reason concerning things that are to be made. Therefore, he says here that if from experience one takes a universal concerned with production, that is, with any things whatever that can be made, for instance, things concerned with healing or with agriculture, then this pertains to art. On the other hand, science deals with necessary things, as he says in the same place. So, if the universal under consideration applies to items that are always the same, it belongs to science, for example, if it concern numbers or figures.

Now, this method that has been explained applies to the principles of all the sciences and arts. Consequently, he concludes that the habits of principles do not pre-exist in us as something determined and perfected; nor are they produced anew from some better-known pre-existing habits, as a habit of science is generated within us from previously known principles; instead, the habits of the principles are present in us from prior sensation. . . .

He clarifies what has been said in the foregoing, in regard to the point that the universal is taken from the experience of the singulars. He says that because it was not clearly explained above how the universal is produced in the mind from experience of the singulars, he must again state it so that it will be more clearly presented.

If many singulars are taken and they are not different in regard to some one item existing in them, this one item according to which they do not differ, when received in the mind, is the first universal, whatever it may be, whether it pertains to the essence of the singulars or not. Because we find Socrates and Plato, and many others, to be not different in regard to whiteness, we take this one item, namely *white*, as the universal; and in this case it is an accident. Similarly, because we find that Socrates and Plato and others are not different in regard to rationality, we take this one item in which they do not differ, namely *the rational,* as a universal; and this is a specific character.

Now, how this one item can be taken he explains in the following section. Indeed, it is obvious that the singular is sensed properly and directly in itself; yet sensation is also in some way of the universal itself. For it knows Callias, not only as Callias but also as he is this man—and similarly, Socrates as he is this man. As a result of such reception in prior sensation, the intellectual soul can consider "man" in both. If the case were such that sensation could only apprehend what belongs to particularity and could in no way apprehend the universal along with this particular object, it would not be possible for universal knowledge to be caused in us from sensory apprehension.

He shows this same point, next, in the process that goes from species to genus. He adds that, again, in the case of these, say "man" and "horse," the mind stays with its consideration until it reaches something that is indistinguishable in them, and this is the universal. For example, we consider this animal and that one, a man and a horse, until we reach the common "animal" that is the higher genus. So, since we receive the knowledge of universals from singulars, he concludes that we must know the first universal principles by induction. For thus, that is by way of induction, does sense make the universal within the mind, according as all the singulars are considered.

Different Kinds of Science

Theoretical or speculative understanding is properly distinguished from operative or practical understanding by the fact that the speculative has for its end the truth that it contemplates, while the practical directs the truth under consideration toward activity as an end. So, the Philosopher says in the third book, *On the Soul* (10, 333a15) that they differ

Exposition of Boethius on the Trinity, V, 1, c. Trans. V.J.B.

from each other according to their end; and in the second
book of the *Metaphysics* (1, 993b20) is the statement that
the end of speculative knowledge is truth but the end of
operative knowledge is action.

Therefore, since matter must be in proportion to its end,
the matter of the practical sciences must be those things that
can be done by our working; for, in this event, the knowledge
of these things can be directed toward activity as an end.
On the other hand, the matter of the speculative sciences
must be things that are not produced by our working; thus,
the consideration of these things cannot be directed toward
activity as an end.

It is according to this distinction of things that the
speculative sciences must be distinguished. However, we
should note that when habits or potencies are differentiated
by virtue of their objects, their distinction is not effected by
merely any differences in these objects; it must be by those
differences that are essential to the objects as objects. For
instance, it is incidental to a sense object as sensible whether
it be an animal or a plant. The distinction of the sense
powers is not based on such a difference but rather on a
difference such as that between color and sound. Therefore,
the speculative sciences must be distinguished by means of
speculative differences, insofar as they are objects of speculation. Now, such an object, one that is an object of a
speculative power, has one aspect that pertains to the intellectual potency and another that pertains to the scientific
habit by which the intellect is perfected. From the side of
the intellect comes the fact that it is immaterial, because
the intellect itself is immaterial; while from the viewpoint
of the science arises the fact that it is necessary, since
science deals with necessary matters, as is proved in the
Posterior Analytics (I, 6, 75b5). Now, everything that is
necessary is, as such, immobile; because everything that is
subject to change is, as such, able to be and not to be,
either absolutely or in some restricted way, as is said in the
Metaphysics (IX, 8, 1050b11-15). And so, to that which
can be viewed speculatively, to that which is an object of

speculative science, there belongs essentially either separation from matter and motion, or some sort of relation to them. Thus, the speculative sciences are distinguished according to their degree of removal from matter and motion.

Thus, there are some objects of speculative knowledge that depend on matter according to their actual being, because they cannot exist except in matter. And these are further subdivided. For some depend on matter according to actual being and also understanding, as do those things in whose definition sensible matter is included and which as a result cannot be understood apart from sensible matter. For instance, in the definition of man it is necessary to include flesh and bones. Now, *physics* or *natural science* deals with these objects.

On the other hand, there are some things which, though they depend on matter according to their act of being, do not do so when they are understood, because sensible matter is not included within their definitions: for instance, lines and numbers. Now, *mathematics* deals with these objects.

Then, there are some objects of speculative knowledge that do not depend on matter in their act of being, because they can exist without matter; either they never exist in matter, as is so of God and an angel; or in some cases they are in matter while in others they are not, as is so for substance, quality, being, potency, act, one and many, and the like. Dealing with all such is *theology,* the divine science, because chief among its knowable objects is God. Under another name it is called *metaphysics,* that is to say, "beyond physics," because it comes after physics in the things that we learn; for we must proceed from sensible objects to the nonsensible ones. It is also called *first philosophy,* in the sense that all the other sciences follow after it in receiving their principles from it. Now, there could not be another kind of things such that they would be dependent on matter for their being understood but not for their existence, because understanding of itself is immaterial. So, there is no fourth kind of philosophy beside the foregoing ones.

Methods Characteristic of
Different Sciences

One method of procedure in the sciences is called "ratiocinative" [*rationabilis*], in three ways. One way depends on
the principles from which the thinking process starts; for
example, when a person proceeds to prove something from
constructs of reason, from such items as genus, species, the
contrary, and thoughts like that, of which logicians treat.
According to this way, a procedure will be called ratiocinative
when a person uses in any science propositions that are
taught in logic: that is to say, as we use logic as a teaching
device in other sciences. But this method of proceeding cannot belong to any special science as its own special method;
error develops in these sciences unless they follow their
own proper procedure. However, this method may be followed, appropriately and suitably, in logic and metaphysics,
because both are general sciences and have the same subject
matter, in a way.

In a second sense, a procedure is called ratiocinative because of the terminus at which the process stops. Of course,
the ultimate terminus to which a rational investigation can
lead is an understanding of principles, in which we achieve
a judgment by way of resolution. Now, when this goes on,
the procedure is not called a ratiocinative one but rather a
demonstrative one. However, sometimes rational investigation cannot be conducted to such a terminus; it stops within
the process of investigation itself, that is, while the way of
the investigator is still open to diverse outcomes. This occurs
when the method of procedure uses probable arguments
that are by their nature productive of opinion or belief but
not science. In this sense, the ratiocinative procedure is in
contrast to the demonstrative. It is possible to proceed in this
ratiocinative way in any science, in order that the way to

Exposition of Boethius on the Trinity, VI, 1, c. Trans. V.J.B.

necessary proofs may become evident from probable arguments. And this is the other way in which we use logic in the demonstrative sciences, not as a teaching device but as a tool. . . .

In a third sense, a method is called rational from the rational power, that is, inasmuch as we follow in our procedure the method of a rational soul in its knowing. So understood, the ratiocinative procedure is appropriate to natural science. Indeed, natural science in its own procedures observes the proper method of the rational soul, in regard to two points. First, there is the fact that just as the rational soul takes its information about intelligible things (that are more knowable in their own nature) from sensible objects (that are better known to us), so does natural science proceed from things that are better known to us but less knowable in their own nature, as is evident in the first book of the *Physics* (1, 184a20). Besides, demonstration accomplished through a sign or an effect is most commonly used in natural science.

Secondly, since it is proper to reason to move discursively from one point to another, this is especially the case in natural science, where from a knowledge of one thing one comes to a knowledge of another: for instance, from the knowing of an effect to the knowing of a cause. And the process is not only a movement from one item to another one within reason, where there is no real difference, as when the process moves from [the genus] animal to [the species] man. In the mathematical sciences, the process works through those items that pertain merely to the essence of a thing, since these sciences demonstrate only by means of the formal cause. So, in them something is not demonstrated about one thing by means of another thing, but by the proper definition of that thing. For, although some demonstrations are given concerning the circle from the triangle, or conversely, this is done only because the triangle is potentially in the circle, or the converse. But, in natural science, where demonstration is accomplished through extrinsic causes, something is proved about one thing by means of another thing that is completely extrinsic. And so, the method of reason is chiefly followed in natural science and, because of this, natural science is of all the most suited to the understanding of man. Therefore, to proceed by ratiocination is the attribute of natural science, not as merely suitable to it but as a principal characteristic of it. . . .

In the second place, to proceed according to a *learning* method [*disciplinaliter*] is characteristic of mathematical science; not that it alone progresses by learning but because this is especially appropriate to it. Indeed, since to learn simply means to get scientific knowledge from another, we are said to use the method of learning when our procedure leads to sure knowledge which is called science. Now, this happens chiefly in the mathematical sciences.

Since mathematics is intermediate between natural and divine science, it is more certain than either of them; more so than the natural because its thinking is cut off from motion and matter, while the thinking of the natural scientist is directed to matter and motion. Now, due to the dependence of the thinking of natural science on matter, its knowledge depends on many factors: on a consideration of matter itself, of form, of material structures and properties that are associated with form in matter. Whenever one has to consider plural items in order to know something, knowledge is more difficult. Thus, it is said in the *Posterior Analytics* (I, 27, 87a34) that a science that results from adding on something, as geometry does to arithmetic, is less certain. In the event that its thinking deals with mobile things that do not remain uniform, a science is less stable because its demonstrations often proceed by probability, due to the fact that what is contingent sometimes occurs in a different way. So, too, the more a science approaches singulars (as is the case with operative sciences like medicine, applied chemistry, and moral science), there is less possibility of certainty because of the multitude of items that must be considered in such sciences; for, if any one of them is omitted, error may follow, and also there is the variability of these items.

Moreover, the procedure of mathematics is more certain than that of divine science because the things that divine science studies are more removed from the objects of sensation from which our knowledge takes its start; in the case both of immaterial substances (for the knowledge of which these objects that we know through sensation are an inadequate guide) and also of those items that are common to all beings (for they are most universal, and thus most removed from the particulars falling within sense experience). Now, the objects of mathematics do fall within sense experience and are subjects for the imagination: for instance, figures, lines, numbers, and the like. Thus, human understanding grasps the knowledge of these items from the phantasms more easily and more certainly than the knowledge about an intelligence, or even than about a substantial essence, act, potency, and other similar items. So, it is clear that mathematical thinking is easier and more certain than physical or theological, and much more so than that of the other operative sciences. Hence, it is said to proceed in a most distinctive manner, according to the method of learning. . . .

In answer to the third difficulty, the reply is that in learning we begin with the easier thing, unless necessity dictates otherwise. Of course, it is sometimes necessary in the process of learning to make a start, not with what is easier but with that on which the knowledge of the consequents depends. For this reason, we must begin with logic in the learning process, not because it is easier than other sciences (indeed, it presents very great difficulties since it deals with second intentions) but because the other sciences depend on it, for it teaches the method of proceeding in all the sciences. . . .

In the third place, just as proceeding in a ratiocinative manner is characteristic of natural philosophy, due to the fact that the method of reasoning is chiefly used in it, so to proceed by the method of *intellection* is characteristic of divine science, because the method appropriate to understanding is principally followed in it. Now, reasoning differs from understanding as multiplicity does from unity. Hence, Boethius says in the *Consolation of Philosophy* (IV, prose 6) that reasoning stands in relation to understanding as time does to eternity, and as a circle to its center. Indeed, it is

appropriate to reason to be spread out over many items
and to gather in one simple point of knowledge from them.
. . . On the other hand, intellection first of all considers a
unified and simple truth and then grasps in it some knowledge of a whole multiplicity: thus does God know all things
in understanding His own essence. . . .

So, it is evident that ratiocinative thinking terminates in
intellective thinking, by following the process of resolution
whereby reason gathers in one simple truth from many items.
Again, intellective thinking is the starting point for ratiocinative thinking, by following the process of composition or discovery whereby the intellect understands a multiplicity in one
item.

Therefore, the kind of thinking that is the terminus of
the whole process of human ratiocination is in a special way
intellective thinking. Now, in the case of all the sciences, the
whole process of ratiocinative thinking, following the way of
resolution, terminates in the thinking proper to the divine
science. Reasoning, as we said before, sometimes proceeds
from one thing to another in the order of reality: for instance,
in the case of demonstration by means of causes or effects
that are extrinsic—by composition, when the process moves
from causes to effects—by resolution, when it moves from
effects to causes, by virtue of the fact that causes are more
simple, immobile, and uniformly constant than their effects.
So, the ultimate termination of resolution in this process
occurs when one reaches the most simple supreme causes,
and these are the substances separated [from matter].

At other times, the process moves from one item to another
in the order of reason: for instance, when there is a process
based on intrinsic causes—by way of composition, in the case
where the process is from the most universal forms to the
most particular items; by resolution, however, when the
process is reversed, because of the fact that the more universal is the more simple. Now, the most universal items
are those that are common to all beings. Therefore, the
ultimate termination of the way of resolution, during this
life, is the consideration of being and of those items that

belong to being in this manner. Of course, these are the objects that divine science considers, as we said above, the separated substances and the items common to all beings. Hence, it is evident that its thinking is especially intellectual. As a further consequence, there is the fact that it bestows principles on all the other sciences, because intellective thinking is the starting point of rational thinking. This is why it is called first philosophy, even though it is learned after physics and the rest of the sciences. And because intellective consideration is the terminus of the ratiocinative thinking, this is why it is called metaphysics, as if to say *beyond physics,* since it comes after physics in the way of resolution.

A Sequence of Philosophic Studies

As the Philosopher says in the tenth book of the *Ethics,* (1177a12) the ultimate happiness of man consists in the best activity of man, and that is of his highest potency, the intellect, in regard to the best intelligible object. Now, since an effect is known through its cause, it is obvious that a cause is more intelligible in its nature than an effect; although sometimes, from our point of view, effects are better known than causes, because of the fact that we receive knowledge of universal and intelligible causes from particulars that fall under sensation.

Speaking without qualification, then, the first causes of things must be in themselves the greatest and best objects of understanding, because they are the greatest beings and the truest things, since they are the essences of other things and the causes of truth, as is apparent from the Philosopher in the second book of the *Metaphysics* (993b28). However, these first causes are less and later known as far as we are concerned. Our intellect is related to them as the bat's eye is to sunlight, which latter it cannot perceive perfectly because of its excessive brightness. So, the ultimate happiness that man

Exposition of the Book of Causes, Lect. 1. Trans. V.J.B.

can possess in this life must consist in the consideration of the first causes, for what little can be known of them is more lovable and worthy than all the things that can be known about inferior realities, as is shown by the Philosopher in the first book *On the Parts of Animals*. And since this knowledge is perfected within us after this life, man is established as perfectly happy in accord with the Gospel text: *Now this is eternal life: that they may know thee, the only true God* (John 17:3).

Hence it is that the interest of the philosophers was chiefly directed to this aim: to achieve knowledge of the first causes by means of all the things that they considered in reality. Consequently, they put the science of the first causes last in the order of learning and assigned its consideration to the last period in a person's life. They began first with logic, for it teaches the method of the sciences. Then they went to mathematics, which even boys can grasp. Thirdly, they advanced to natural philosophy, which requires time because of its need of experience. Fourthly, they proceeded to moral philosophy, of which a young person cannot be a suitable student. They gave the final place to divine science, for it considers the first causes of beings.

So, they found something about first principles written down in various separate propositions, somewhat in the style of discrete thoughts about certain truths. And indeed, we do find in Greek such a book that has come down from Proclus, the Platonist, containing one hundred and nine propositions, which is entitled the *Elements of Theology* [*Elevatio theologica*]. But this book, called *On Causes* among Latin scholars, is found in Arabic and it is agreed that it has been translated from the Arabic and there is practically no evidence that it exists in Greek. Hence, it seems that it was excerpted by some Arabian philosopher from the aforementioned book by Proclus, particularly because everything contained in it is contained in the other [i.e., the Greek] book in much fuller and more extended form.

RECOMMENDED READINGS

HOENEN, P. *Reality and Judgment according to St. Thomas.* Translated by H. F. Tiblier. Chicago: Regnery, 1952.

MARITAIN, J. *The Degrees of Knowledge.* New York: Scribner's, 1959.

MAURER, A. "Introduction," to St. Thomas Aquinas, *Division and Methods of the Sciences.* (Toronto) Pontifical Institute of Mediaeval Studies (1953), vii-xxxvi.

MAZIARZ, E. A. *The Philosophy of Mathematics.* New York: Philosophical Library, 1950.

RÉGIS, L. M. *Epistemology.* New York: Macmillan, 1959.

——. *St. Thomas and Epistemology.* Milwaukee: Marquette University Press, 1946.

SMITH, G. *The Truth That Frees.* Milwaukee: Marquette University Press, 1956.

SMITH, V. E. *St. Thomas on the Object of Geometry.* Milwaukee: Marquette University Press, 1953.

VEATCH, H. *Realism and Nominalism Revisited.* Milwaukee: Marquette University Press, 1954.

WILHELMSEN, F. D. *Man's Knowledge of Reality.* New York: Prentice-Hall, 1956.

II. Nature and Philosophy

Foreword

FOR THOMAS AQUINAS, the philosophy of nature is the study of a certain kind of beings: those that exist with matter as one of their components and which are in consequence subject to change or motion. These things are observed in sense experience. They are the familiar items in man's environment: rocks, trees, donkeys, human beings, oceans, the heavens, and the stars and planets moving about in them. He did not think that our knowledge of these mobile beings is restricted to sense perception but he insisted that it must always start with information received through the senses. What is distinctive of human knowledge of such things is, however, the intellectual understanding resulting from the effort to interpret sense experience and the reports of contemporary science.

There is no doubt that in this area of natural philosophy Aquinas is very dependent on the *Physics* of Aristotle and its associated treatises. He does not clearly distinguish physics and descriptive natural science from this philosophy of nature. Moreover, he is indebted to Aristotle for much of the terminology and even some of the facts in his discussion of the nature of things. Of course, Aquinas' view of the physical universe is not identical with that of Aristotle. For one thing, Aristotle thought that the world of material things had neither beginning nor end. Aquinas acknowledges the validity of this conclusion of Aristotle, on the basis of the information that the Stagirite had; but, because of his Christian belief, Thomas pointed out (*see* Chapter VIII) that this world has been created by God at the beginning of time and that it will come to an end.

The explanation that Aquinas offers for change in the material world is very faithful to the text of the third book of Aristotle's *Physics*. Three sorts of accidental change are recognized in bodies: local motion, change in size, and change in quality. A fourth kind of change is more basic: the corruption of one substance and the concomitant generation of another kind of substance. When a pig eats an apple, the apple is corrupted but at least some of its matter becomes part of the pig. The general explanation of such substantial change is very thoroughly presented in the treatise *On the Principles of Nature*, printed here in its entirety. We are introduced in it to the four causes, the theory of elements and principles, and other terminological precisions.

Matter and form are regarded as intrinsic components of every body. Prime matter is not itself a body but that *part* of any body which makes it subject to change and which endures through change. Nor is form a body; it is another *part* of a body, that which makes it exist as a member of some definite species of material things. Dogs and trees are not specifically distinguished by their matters but they have specifically distinct forms. Thus, the differences between various "matters" are due only to their association with forms. Two exceptions should be made to the foregoing statement. First of all, Aquinas thought that matter in conjunction with form becomes quantified. The matter that is in Socrates' body is a different piece or amount of matter from that which is in Plato's body. Thus matter, "as quantified," is used to explain the numerical distinction of individuals within the same species. In this sense, there is numerical diversity between different instances of matter—but matter does not exist without form. Secondly, Aquinas was led into a factual error by Aristotle's notion that the celestial bodies (stars and planets) are subject to but one kind of change: locomotion. Due to this mistake, Aquinas speaks vaguely of celestial matter, as if it were a special type, subject only to change in place. In the age of Sputnik, it is clear that this part of his astronomical physics requires correction.

His attempts to define place and time are also limited by their Aristotelian ancestry. Doubtless, the "box" theory of space is still exerting its influence on Aquinas, as it will continue to influence thinking down to the period of Newton and later. Sometimes, it appears that there is an absolute up and down, fore and aft, right and left. Yet, it will be seen that Aquinas is not so much concerned with space as with place. His explanation of the location of a given body in a moving medium and in relation to larger place limits is not without interest. Here again, ancient astronomy was misleading, with its well-known view that the earth is situated at the center of a number of larger concentric spheres in which the celestial bodies move. The outermost sphere would be the place limit of this physical universe. It was considered the outermost, or first, mobile thing. This was what contemporary science taught in the thirteenth century and Aquinas felt the limitations of this astronomy, as did Dante and others.

The last extract in this chapter shows in striking fashion that Aquinas knew he was in an area of opinion when he took a position on the motions of the planets. Much that is offered as the last word in science is but the most recent opinion of the experts. This final selection also shows how far Thomas Aquinas is from dogmatism on such points. Few philosophers have so stressed the need for an open mind on problems of this sort.

What the Philosophy of Nature Is

Since the *Physics,* which we intend to explain, is the first book of natural science, it is necessary at its beginning to indicate what the matter and subject of natural science are. Since every science is present in the intellect, it should be noted, then, that a thing becomes actually intelligible by the

Exposition of Aristotle's Physics, I, Lect. 1. Trans. V.J.B.

fact that it is in some manner abstracted from matter. According as different things are variously related to matter, they belong to different sciences. Again, since every science is achieved by demonstration, and since the means of demonstration is definition, the methods of the sciences must be distinguished by a difference of definition.

We should note, then, that there are some things whose actual being [*esse*] depends on matter—and they cannot be defined without matter. And there are other things such that, though incapable of actual being apart from sensible matter, nevertheless, their definition does not include sensible matter. These two types differ as the curved does from the snub-nosed; for the snub-nosed is found in sensible matter and it is necessary that sensible matter fall within its definition. In fact, snub means a curved nose and this is the characteristic of all natural things, such as man and stone.

Now a curve, though it cannot exist except in sensible matter, does not, however, include sensible matter in its definition. This is the way that all mathematicals are, for instance, number, size, and figure.

Furthermore, there are still other things that depend on matter neither for their actual being nor for their rational meaning [*ratio*]—either because they never exist in matter, as in the case of God and the other separate substances, or because they are not in all cases found in matter, for example, substance, potency, and act, and being itself.

Mathematics is concerned with these things which depend on sensible matter for their actual being but not for their rational meaning [*ratio*]. The natural science that is called physics is concerned with those things which depend on matter not only for actual being but also for their rational meaning.

Since everything that possesses matter is mobile, as a consequence, mobile being is the subject of natural philosophy. Now, natural philosophy is concerned with natural things. Natural things are those whose principle is a nature. Nature is the principle of motion and rest in that in which it is present. So, natural science deals with those things that have a principle of motion within them.

However, since those items that are associated with something common must be determined first of all and especially, lest it be necessary to repeat this many times in treating all the divisions, one book on natural science had to be first set forth in which a treatment would be offered of the characteristics of mobile being in general. In the same way, first philosophy, in which a determination is given of the items that are common to being as being, is set before all the sciences.

Now, this is the book of *Physical Things,* which is also called *Physics,* or the course on nature, because it was handed down in the fashion of a teaching addressed to students. Its subject is mobile being without qualification. I do not say mobile body; for, that every mobile thing is a body is proved in this book and no science proves its own subject. So, immediately at the start of the treatise *On the Heavens,* which comes next after this treatise, a beginning is made from the knowledge of body. Other books of natural science follow, in which there is a treatment of the species of mobile beings: for instance, in the book *On the Heavens,* of the mobile according to local motion which is the first kind of motion; in the book *On Generation,* of motion toward form and the primary subjects of motion, namely the elements, in regard to their general transmutations; while in the book *On Meteorology,* it is of their special changes; on mobiles which are mixtures [of the elements] and inanimate is the book *On Minerals;* on animated ones, the book *On the Soul* and those which go along with it.

The Empirical Character of Natural Science

When the properties and accidents of a thing that are evidenced by sensation adequately express the nature of the

Exposition of Boethius on the Trinity, VI, 2, c. Trans. V.J.B.

thing, then the judgment that understanding makes concerning the nature of that thing must conform to the items that sense perception shows concerning the thing. Now, all physical things are of this kind; they are restricted to sensible matter. Thus, in natural science, our knowledge ought to terminate in the sense order, so that we may make judgments about natural things in the way that sense perception presents them (as is clear from the treatise *On Heaven and Earth*, III, 7, 306a16). He who neglects sensation, in the natural sciences, will fall into error. Natural things, in this sense, are those that are inseparable from sensible matter and motion, both in their actual being and in the way that they are studied.

An Explanation of Motion and Change

Lectio 1. Motion and Its Implications

1-2. Nature is the source of motion and mutation, as is clear from the definition given in the Second Book. (The difference between motion and mutation will be explained in Book Five.) And since motion enters the definition of nature, then not to know motion is not to know nature. So, our purpose being to expound the science of nature, we must explain motion.

3. Aristotle first takes up certain concomitants of motion; because, first of all, when one discusses any subject he must discuss the questions it gives rise to. The subject and its concomitants form one science.

Intrinsic to motion is the "infinite." That is because motion involves the study of continuities. And the "infinite" enters the definition of the continuum. The additive infinite of number derives from the infinite division of the continuum. Thus, authors defining the continuum say, for example, that it is divisible *in infinitum*. There is also another definition

Exposition of Aristotle's Physics, III, Lect. 1-3. Trans. McWilliams, *Physics and Philosophy*, pp. 28-37.

given in the *Predicamenta:* a continuum is that whose parts
are inclosed within a single common boundary. Since a
continuum is a total, it can be defined by its parts. But the
parts are regarded in two ways with respect to the total:
as the continuum is composed of these parts; or is resolved
into these parts. The definition here is by way of resolution;
in the *Predicamenta* by way of composition. It follows that
the "infinite" is intrinsic to motion.

Other things are extrinsically consequent on motion; these
are its extrinsic measures, as place, vacuum and time. Time
is the measure of motion itself. Of the mobile *body* the
measure really is place; though in the opinion of some vacuum
is the measure. That is why he says there cannot be motion
without place, vacuum and time. The fact that not every
motion is local is no obstacle, because only what exists in a
place is subject to motion. Every sensible body is in a
place, and only of such can there be motion. Besides, the
first motion [that of the outer sphere] is local motion; if
it be stopped, all others will stop. Hence, for the reason given,
these four concomitants of motion are subjects for the
philosopher of nature.

4-5. Another reason he gives is that these four are common
to all things physical. Since therefore the *Physics* is about
all of corporeal nature, these subjects must be taken up
first; because, as was said at the beginning, the study of the
general attributes precedes that of the specific. And among
the general, motion must be treated first, because the others
are consequent on it.

6. He sets down three headings. The first is that "being"
is divided into potency and act. This is not a division into
categories, because potency and act are found in every
category. Secondly, "being" is divided into the ten categories.
Of these the first is *hoc aliquid,* that is a substance; another
is "how much" or "what kind" or some of the other predicamenta. The third heading is about a single category, relation;
because motion in some way belongs to this category, in that
the mover is related to the mobile.

About this last it is to be remarked that, since relation has a most tenuous existence, consisting as it does only in a reference to something else, it has to be founded on some other accident. The more perfect accidents are nearer to the substance, and it is through their mediation that the other accidents inhere in the substance. Now relation is especially founded on the two that have respect to something else, namely quantity and action. For quantity can be the measure of something *external* to it; and an agent activates something *else*. Some relations therefore are founded on quantity; and in particular on number, which is basic to measuring, as is clear from "twice," "half," "the square" and other powers, and the like. So also "same," "like," "equal" are founded on "unity," which is the elemental constituent of number. Other relations are founded on "*actio*" and "*passio*," either by past act, as father is related to son, or by the power to act, as master to a slave over whom he has control. This heading the Philosopher explains fully in the Fifth Book of the *Metaphysics*. In the present passage he touches on it briefly, saying that one kind of relation is by way of excess and defect, and this is founded on quantity, as "twice" and "half"; another relation is that of agent and patient, mover and moved, which clearly have relation to one another.

7. Then he shows how motion is reduced to these headings. There are two steps. He first shows that there is not any motion outside the categories of those things *in* which motion may occur. Secondly, motion is divided as the categories are divided. About the first, it is to be noted that, since motion, as will appear later, is an imperfect actuation, and since the imperfect comes under the same category as the perfect, not indeed as a species of it, but by reduction (as prime matter is in the category "substance"), it follows that motion is not outside the categories of the things in which motion can occur. . . . And this is clear from the fact that everything which is being moved is being moved either with respect to substance, or quantity, or quality, or place, as will be shown in the Fifth Book. But we are not to understand that to these categories there is something univocally common, as their genus, something not restricted to a single category,

but the genus of them all. "Being" of course is *analogously* common to them, as will be shown in the Fourth Book of *Metaphysics*. It is plain then that neither motion nor mutation is outside the said categories; because nothing is outside them, seeing that they are a complete division of being. How motion is connected with the category of action or passion, will be shown later.

8. He then shows that motion is divided as the categories are divided. A thing may belong to any of the categories in one of two ways, either as perfect or as imperfect. The reason for this is that privation and possession is the prime contrariety, and is found in all contraries. Hence, since all the categories are open to contraries, there must be in all the categories the perfect and the imperfect. Thus in "substance" one thing is like form, another like privation; in "quality" one is like white, which is perfect, the other like black, which is as it were imperfect; in "quantity" the one is the perfect size, the other imperfect; in "place" one is high, which is like the perfect, one low as imperfect; or the light and heavy which are put under "place" because of their tendency. Hence there are as many classes of motion as there are classes of being. For the species of motion vary according to the different categories of beings; thus augmentation, a motion in "quantity," is different from generation, which is motion in "substance." The species of motion also differ as perfect and imperfect in the same category; for generation is a motion in "substance" toward form, corruption toward privation; and in "quantity" growth is toward the perfect size, diminution toward the imperfect size. Why two species are not indicated in "quality" and "place" will be explained in Book Five.

Lectio 2. The Definition of Motion

1. The Philosopher has discussed the necessary preliminaries to the definition of motion. Here he defines motion. First in general, then in particular.

2. About motion in general, it is to be noted that some authors define motion as any transit that is not sudden, from potency to act. Their mistake is to insert in the definition of motion things that are posterior to motion. For transit is a species of motion. Also the "sudden" in their definition brings in time; because that is sudden which happens in an indivisible instant of time. But time is defined by means of motion.

3. Hence it is altogether impossible to define motion by the prior and the better known, in any way except as Aristotle here defines it. As was said, each category is divided into potency and act. Now, since potency and act are prime divisions of being, they naturally are prior to motion; and that is why Aristotle uses them to define motion.

It is to be noted, then, that one thing may be in act only, a second in potency only, and a third midway between potency and act. Now what is in potency only is not yet being moved; what is already in completed act has already *been* moved; therefore that thing is *being* moved which is midway between pure potency and act, partly in potency and partly in act. This is clear in the case of alteration. For when water is only in potency hot, it is not yet being heated; but when it is already boiling, the process of heating is terminated. On the other hand, when it is acquiring something of heat, though imperfectly, then it is being moved toward heat; for what is being heated acquires gradually more and more heat. This imperfect actuation of heat existing in the heatable subject is motion; not indeed by reason of what it already actually is, but because, already existing in act, it is still tending toward further actuation. This is so because, if the tending to further actuation were stopped, its very actuation, however imperfect, would be, not motion, but the terminus of motion. This is the case when something is halfway heated. On the other hand the tending toward further actuation belongs to an "existent in potency to such actuation." Likewise if the imperfect act be considered *only* as potency to additional actuation, it has not the nature of motion, but is the starting-point of motion. As the process of boiling can begin from the freezing-point, so too can it begin from the lukewarm.

Therefore the imperfect actuation has the nature of motion, at once as a potency with respect to further actuation, and as an act with respect to the less perfect. Consequently motion is neither the potency of the existent in potency, nor the act of the existent in act; instead, it is the actuation of the existent in potency. It is called "act" in reference to a preceding potency; whereas it is said to be "of a thing in potency" in reference to further actuation. Therefore, most properly does the Philosopher define motion as the "entelechy," i.e., *the actuation, of an existent in potency, precisely as being actuated.*

4. He then exemplifies the definition in all the species of motion. Thus alteration is the actuation of the alterable as being altered. But motion in "quantity" and "substance" have not a single name, as motion in quality is called alteration; so he gives two names for motion in quantity. He says that the actuation of the augmentable and its opposite, the diminishable, is augmentation and diminution. That of the generable and corruptible is generation and corruption. That of the locally mutable is local motion. He here takes motion broadly for mutation, not strictly, as contrasted with strict generation and corruption, as will be explained in the Fifth Book.

5. He next explains the different parts of the definition. First with regard to motion as "act," then "of the existent in potency," and thirdly "as being actuated."

About the first he makes two observations. An act is that by which a subject previously in potency to something, actually becomes that something. But a subject previously in potency is actually *becoming* while it is being moved. He says it is clear, then, that motion is just that, namely an actuation. For instance, "buildable" implies a potency to something. But when in keeping with that implied potency, the buildable is being reduced to act, we then say that it is being built. The fashioning it is receiving is its actuation. The same holds for all other motions, as teaching, healing, tumbling, dancing, adolescence [growth] and aging [diminution]. It is to be noticed that *before* anything is moved it is in potency to *two* actuations; namely to the perfect actuation, which is the terminus of the motion; and to the imperfect actuation, which is the motion. Thus water before it begins to be heated is in potency both to being heated, and to boiling. But while it is being heated it is being reduced to imperfect actuation, namely motion; but not yet to the perfect actuation which is the terminus of the motion; with respect to that it continues in potency.

6. Secondly, he explains how motion is "the actuation of an existent in potency." Here is his reasoning. Every actuation is properly the actuation of that in which it is always found. Daylight is always found in the atmosphere, and for that reason it is the actuation of the atmosphere. But motion is always found in some "existent in potency." Therefore motion is the actuation of an existent in potency. To explain the minor premise, he says that in some cases the identical thing is both in potency and in act, though not simultaneously nor in the same respect. Thus a thing is hot in potency and cold in act. So, too, many things act and are acted upon by one another, in the sense that each in its own way is in potency and in act with respect to the other. And since all the sublunary natural bodies have the same sort of matter, therefore in each there is a potency to that which is actual in another. Thus in all such there is something which acts and is acted upon, moves and is moved. For that reason it has seemed to some that absolutely every mover is also being moved. More will be said about that later on. As will be shown in the Eighth Book of this work and in the Twelfth of the *Metaphysics,* there is a mover which is immobile, because it is not in potency but in act only. When, however, any actual existent, possessed of a potency, is moving either itself or something else, in whatever way it is "mobile" (that is, capable of being reduced to the act of motion); then, whether it be moved by itself or by another, its motion is its actuation. Whence it is that things in potency, whether they are acting or being acted upon, are being moved; because in acting they are subject to reaction, in moving they are being moved. Thus fire when it acts on kindling is reacted upon to the degree of the smokiness of the flame.

7. Lastly he explains that clause in the definition of motion which reads "as being actuated." First by an example. He says it was necessary to add "as being actuated," because the thing which is in potency is also something in act. And although the existent in potency and in act is the same subject, it is not the same with respect to its being in potency and its being in act. Thus the brass is actually brass and in potency to being a statue, but the reason why it is brass as such is not the same as its potency for the statue. Now the motion [molding] is not the actuation of the brass as brass, but its actuation as in potency to the statue; otherwise as long as it remained brass it would have to continue being molded, which is clearly false. So it was correct to add "as being actuated."

8. He then gives an argument from the "contraries." It is evident that the same given subject is in potency to contrary things. Thus lymph or blood is a single subject in potency to health or disease. But being in potency to health is one thing, being in potency to disease is another. (I mean of course with respect to the different objectives.) Otherwise, if *"can* be sick" and *"can* be well" were the same, it would follow that to *be* sick and to *be* well were the same. It is evident then that the reason why the subject is a certain kind of being is not identical with its potency to something else. Otherwise, the potency to one thing would essentially be the same as the potency to its opposite. So also color does not mean the same as being seen. Hence it was necessary to say that motion is the actuation of an actuable subject [*possibilis*] precisely as being actuated [*possibile*]; lest it be thought that motion is the act of the thing itself which is in potency, considered as that precise kind of subject.

Lectio 3. Defense of the Definition

1. After giving the definition of motion and explaining its several phrases, he here turns to defining the correctness of the definition; first directly, then indirectly.

2. His direct defense is the following. A thing in potency is one that *can* be in act. Now, a buildable is in potency. Therefore there can be some actuation of the buildable precisely as being built. This is either the house or the building process. But the house is not the actuation of the buildable as being built, because the "being built" as such is being reduced to act while the building process is going on. But when it is already a house, it is no longer being built. We are left with the conclusion that the building process is the actuation of the "being built" as such. But the building process is a motion. Therefore motion is the actuation of an existent in potency precisely as being actualized. The same holds for all motions. It is evident then that motion is the kind of actuation it was declared to be. Only while anything is being moved, is it in such actuation; neither before nor after that. Before that, when it is in potency only, the motion has not begun. After that, when it has altogether ceased to be in potency, there is no motion because it is in completed actuation.

3. His indirect defense of his definition is that motion is not correctly defined any other way. There are three steps to his argument. He first states his own position; secondly he sets down and refutes the definitions given by other authors; thirdly he gives the reason why they have so defined motion. Under the first heading he declares that it is clear that motion is correctly defined, from two considerations: from the fact that the definitions which others have given are inapplicable; and from the fact that motion cannot be defined any other way. The reason is, because motion cannot be put in any other classification than that of the actuation of an existent in potency.

4. Under the second heading he rejects other definitions of motion. Others have defined motion in three ways. They have said that motion is *otherness*, because that which is being moved is always other and other. Likewise they have said that motion is *inequality*, because what is being moved is always nearer and nearer to its term. They also said that motion is that which *is not*, or *non-being*, because that which

is being moved, while it is being moved, does not yet have
that to which it is being moved. Thus what is being moved
toward whiteness is not yet white.

These definitions the Philosopher disposes of by three considerations. First, with regard to the subject of motion. For
if motion were otherness or inequality or non-being, then
whatever subject these inhere in, must necessarily be being
moved; because whatever is the subject of motion is being
moved. But things which are other need not, simply because
they are other, be in motion; neither must the unequal, nor
the non-beings. It follows that otherness, inequality, non-
being are not motion. Secondly, with regard to the terminus
ad quem, motion and mutation are no more toward otherness
than toward likeness, no more toward inequality than equality,
no more toward non-being than toward being. Generation is a
mutation toward being, corruption toward non-being. Hence
motion is not otherness rather than likeness, or inequality
rather than equality, or non-being rather than being. Thirdly,
with regard to the terminus *a quo*, just as there is a motion
away from otherness, and from inequality, and from non-
being, so there is also a motion away from their opposites.
Therefore motion should not be put in these classes any more
than in their opposites.

5. Lastly he gives the reason why his predecessors have
so defined motion; first the immediate reason, then the under-
lying cause. First, then, the reason why the Ancients put
motion in the said classifications (namely otherness, inequality
and non-being) is that motion seems to be an indeterminate
thing, that is, incomplete and imperfect, as though it had no
determinate nature. And because it is indeterminate, it ought,
so it seems, to be put in the class of privations. For Pythagoras
set down two orders of things, and in each of these he set
down ten principles. The principles in the second order were
called by him "indeterminates," because they are privatives.
They are not determined by a form in the category of substance, nor by a form of quality, nor by any special form
existent in one of these, nor by the form of any of the other
categories. In the one order the Pythagoreans were wont to

put these ten: finite, odd, one, right, masculine, rest, straight, light, good, equilateral triangle. In the other: infinite, even, plurality, left, feminine, motion, curved, darkness, evil, not equilateral.

6. He then gives the reason why motion is put among the indeterminates. It is because motion can neither be put under potency nor under act. If it be put under potency, then anything in potency, say, to a certain size, would be changing in size. If it be included under act, then anything that had actually attained its size, would still be changing in size. Now it is indeed true that motion is an act, but it is an imperfect act, intermediate between potency and act. That it is an imperfect act is clear from the fact that the thing whose act it is, is an existent in potency, as was said above. And that is why it is difficult to grasp what motion is. At first thought it seems that it is either simply act, or simply potency, or is contained under privation, just as the Ancients said it was contained under non-being and inequality. But none of these is possible, as has been shown. There is left, then, only the aforesaid way of defining motion: that it be such an act as we have declared; an act, namely, of an existent in potency. Though such an act is difficult to comprehend, because of the mixture of act and potency; nevertheless it is not impossible that such an act occur, for it does occur.

Principles, Causes, and Natural Generation

Observe that some things can exist though they do not exist, while other things do exist. That which can be is said to exist in potency; that which already exists is said to be in act. But there are two sorts of existence: the essential or substantial existence of a thing, for example, a man is, and this is to be in the unqualified sense; and the other is accidental existence,

On the Principles of Nature, complete treatise. Trans. V.J.B.

for example, a man is white, and this is to be in some qualified way.

Now, something may be in potency to either sort of existence. For it may be in potency to be a man, as is the case with male seed or the menstrual blood; or it may be in potency to be white, as is the case with a man. Both that which is in potency to substantial existence and that which is in potency to accidental existence may be called matter; as the seed in regard to man, and the man in regard to whiteness. But there is this difference: the matter that is in potency to substantial existence is called the matter *out-of-which;* while that which is in potency to be accidentally is called the matter *in-which.*

Again, properly speaking, that which is in potency to be substantially is called prime matter; but what is in potency to be accidentally is called the subject. So, we say that accidents are in a subject but not that the substantial form is in a subject. This is the difference between matter and a subject: the subject does not get its existence from that which comes to it; of itself it has complete existence. For example, a man does not get his existence from his whiteness. But matter does get existence from that which comes to it, for by itself it possesses incomplete existence. So, to speak without qualification, form gives existence to matter but an accident does not give existence to a subject, rather a subject gives existence to an accident. However, at times one is used for the other, that is, matter for subject, and the reverse.

Just as everything that is in potency can be called matter, so everything from which a thing gets existence, either substantial or accidental, may be called form. Thus a man, when potentially white, becomes actually white through whiteness; and the seed [*sperma*], when potentially man, becomes an actual man through the soul. Because the form makes something to be actually, the form is said to be an act. Now, that which makes substantial existence actual is called substantial form, and that which produces actual accidental existence is called accidental form.

Moreover, since generation is a movement toward a form, there are two kinds of generation corresponding to the two sorts of form. Generation terminating in accidental form is the qualified sense. In fact, when a substantial form is introduced, something is said to come into being without any qualification; thus, we say that a man comes to exist or is generated. However, when an accidental form is introduced, we do not say that a thing simply comes into existence but that it becomes this sort of thing; thus, when a man becomes white, we do not say that he comes into being or is generated in the unqualified sense, but that he becomes or is generated as a white man.

Again, two kinds of corruption stand in opposition to these two meanings of generation. Of course, generation and corruption in the unqualified sense occur only in the genus of substance. Yet, in the qualified sense generation and corruption occur in all the other genera, and since generation is a change from nonbeing to being, while conversely corruption moves from being to nonbeing, generation does not come about from merely any instance of nonbeing but from that nonbeing which is being in potency. Thus, a statue comes from the copper which is potentially, but not actually, a statue.

So, three items are needed in order that generation may occur: potential being, that is, matter; the fact that the product does not actually exist, and this is privation; and that through which it comes to be actually, namely the form. For example, when a statue is made from copper, the copper which is in potency to the form of the statue is the matter; the fact that it is shapeless or not structured is the privation; and the shape by which it is called a statue is the form—not the substantial form, of course, for the copper actually existed before the advent of this form, and its existence does not depend on this shape which is an accidental form. Indeed, all artificial forms are accidental. As a matter of fact, art operates only on that which is already established in existence by virtue of nature.

There are, then, three principles of nature, namely matter, form, and privation. One of these, form, is that toward which generation is directed; the other two are on the side of that from which generation begins. Consequently, matter and privation are identical in their subject but differ in meaning. Thus, the same thing which is bronze is also an unshaped thing prior to the incoming of the form; but it is called bronze for one reason, and shapeless for a different reason. Hence, privation is called a principle not essentially but accidentally, for it coincides with matter. In the same way, we say that a physician builds a house accidentally. For the fact that a physician builds is not because he is a doctor but rather because he is a builder and this coincides in one subject with the physician.

However, there are two sorts of accident: the necessary, which is inseparable from the thing, as the risible in man, and that which is not necessary but is separable, as whiteness is from man. Consequently, though privation is an accidental principle, it does not follow that it is unnecessary for generation, since matter is never stripped from privation. In fact, inasmuch as it exists under one form, it has privation for another, and conversely. For example, in fire there is a privation of air and in air a privation of fire.

We should note, further, that though generation starts from nonexistence, we do not say that negation is a principle, but rather privation, for negation does not determine its subject. The inability to see may be predicated even of nonbeings, as in the phrase "a chimera does not see"; and it can be predicated of beings not equipped by their origin to have sight, as in the case of a stone. But privation is predicated only of a subject that is determined, that is, one born to become so endowed, as blindness is attributed only to those that are born to see. Moreover, since generation does not come about from nonbeing in the unqualified sense but from the nonbeing which is in some subject—not just any subject but one of a determinate kind (for fire does not come about from just anything but from that kind of nonfire that is by origin disposed to the form of fire)—therefore, we say that privation is a principle.

Yet, it differs from the other principles by the fact that the others are principles both in the act of being and in that of becoming. In order that a statue may come into being, there must be bronze and that which finally is the shape of the statue; and then, when the statue is already existing, these two principles must be present. Privation, on the other hand, is a principle in the act of becoming but not in that of being; because, while a statue is being made, it cannot as yet be a statue. If it were, then it could not come into being, since that which is becoming has no existence, except for items whose existence is successive, as are time and motion. But as soon as the statue is in existence there is no longer a privation of statue there, for affirmation and negation are not capable of coexistence, and likewise privation and possession. Privation is also an accidental principle, as explained above, while the other two are essential principles.

From what has been said, it is obvious that matter differs in meaning from form and privation. For matter is that in which form and privation are understood; thus, it is in regard to copper that shape and the shapeless are understood. Indeed, sometimes matter is denominated along with privation, and sometimes without privation. In the case of bronze, when it is the matter of a statue, then it does not imply a privation, for, from the fact that I say, "bronze," there is no suggestion that it is without structure or shape. On the other hand, flour, taken as matter in relation to bread, implies essentially a privation of the form of bread, for, from the fact that I say, "flour," there is signified a lack of disposition or an inordination opposed to the form of bread. And since matter or the subject endures throughout the process of generation, while privation does not, nor does the combination of matter and privation, therefore the matter that does not imply privation is enduring, but that which does imply it is transient.

Yet, we should note that in some cases, matter includes form in its composition; for instance, though bronze is matter in relation to a statue, nevertheless this very bronze is composed of matter and form. Thus, bronze is not called first matter, for it possesses a matter already. On the other hand, that matter which is understood without any form and privation but which is the subject of form and privation is called prime matter because there is no other matter prior to it. This is also called "hyle."

Now, since every definition and act of knowing depends on form, prime matter cannot be known or defined in itself but only in terms of the composite, as it may be said that prime matter is that which is related to all forms and privations as bronze is to the statue and to the shapeless. In this sense, it is called prime without qualification. Of course, it is possible for something to be called prime with respect to some definite genus, as water is prime matter in the genus of wet things. Yet, it is not prime in the simple sense, for it is composed of matter and form and consequently has a prior matter.

It should be noted, also, that prime matter, and form, too, are not generated or corrupted, because every generation is from something to something. Now, that from which generation takes place is matter, and that to which it is directed is form. So, if matter or form were generated, there would be matter for matter, and form for form, on to infinity. Hence, to speak strictly, there is generation of the composite only.

Observe, also, that prime matter is said to be numerically one in all things. Numerically one, of course, has two meanings: it may mean that which possesses one form which is numerically determined, as in the case of Socrates. Now, this is not the way in which prime matter is said to be numerically one, since it does not have in itself any form. Another meaning of numerically one is that which exists without dispositions making it numerically different. It is in this way that matter is said to be numerically one, for it is understood without any dispositions by which it is numerically differentiated.

Again, we should note that although prime matter includes no form or privation in its rational character, yet it is never stripped away from form and privation. Sometimes it exists under one form, sometimes under another. But it can never exist by itself because, since it has no form within its own rational character, it possesses no actual existence, for to be in act is impossible without a form; it is in potency only. So, whatever is in act cannot be called prime matter.

It is clear from the foregoing that there are three principles of nature, namely, matter, form, and privation. Yet, these are not enough for generation. In fact, that which is in potency cannot reduce itself to act. Thus, the copper which is potentially a statue does not make itself into a statue; it needs an operating agent to draw the form of the statue from potency into act. Now, the form cannot draw itself from potency into act—I am talking about the form of the product of generation, what we call the terminus of the process of generation. As a matter of fact, the form is not present except in that which actually exists: that which is being worked on is in the process of becoming, that is, while the thing is being made. So, beside the matter and form there must be some principle that acts and this is called a producer, a mover, or an agent, or that from which change takes its beginning.

Again, because everything that acts does so only by tending toward something, as Aristotle explains in the second book of the *Metaphysics* (II, text 8-9), there must be a fourth principle, namely, that which is intended by the agent. This is called the end. It should also be noted that although every agent both natural and voluntary intends an end, it does not follow that every agent knows its end or deliberates about its end. To know their end is necessary in the case of those agents whose actions are not determined but are open to opposite possibilities, as is true of voluntary agents. So, they must know their end, whereby they may determine their own actions. On the other hand, in the case of physical agents, their actions are determined; consequently, they do not have to choose the means to their end. Avicenna gives the example of a harpist (*Physics*, II, 10) who does not have to deliberate over each plucking of the strings, because the pluckings have become determinate in his case; otherwise, there would be a delay between the pluckings and that would not sound right.

Now, it is more obvious that the voluntary agent deliberates than that the physical agent does. So, there is greater force to the conclusion that if even the voluntary agent (in whose case deliberation is more evident) sometimes does not deliberate, therefore the physical agent does not. It is possible for the physical agent to tend toward its end without deliberation; and this intending is nothing but having a natural inclination toward something.

From the previous explanations, then, it is clear that there are four causes: material, efficient, formal, and final. Now, although "principle" and "cause" may be employed interchangeably (as is stated in the *Metaphysics*, V, 1, 1013a17), still, Aristotle in the *Physics* (I, 7, 191a20; II, 3, 195a15) gives four causes and three principles. He takes causes as extrinsic as well as intrinsic. Matter and form are said to be intrinsic to a thing, in the sense that they are constitutive parts of the thing. The efficient and final causes are called extrinsic because they are outside the thing. But he is taking principles as intrinsic causes only. Now, privation is not named among the causes because it is an incidental principle, as they say. So, when we speak of four causes, we mean essential [*per se*] causes, to which the incidental causes may be reduced; for everything that is incidental may be reduced to what is essential.

However, although in the first book of the *Physics* Aristotle speaks of principles as intrinsic causes, still (as is stated in the *Metaphysics*, XII, 4, 1070b22), "principle" is properly used of extrinsic causes and "element" of causes that are parts of the thing, that is, of intrinsic causes. However, "cause" is used for both; sometimes one of these terms is used for the other, since every cause may be called a principle and every principle a cause. Nevertheless, "cause" seems to add something to the usual way of speaking about a principle; for, whatever is first, whether the being of the consequent follows from it or not, can be called a principle. Thus, a metalworker is called the principle of a knife, because the existence of the knife is due to his work; but when something is changed from black to white, we also say that black is the principle of this change (and generally, everything from which a change takes its start is called a principle), yet black is not that from which the existence of the white flows as a consequent. Rather, we only use "cause" for that sort of first item from which the existence of the consequent follows. Hence, the statement is made that a cause is that from whose being another being follows. So, that first item from which motion takes its start cannot be called an essential cause, though it may be called a principle. For this reason, privation is placed among the principles and not among the causes; for privation is that from which generation takes its start. Of course, it can also be called an incidental cause, in the sense that it is coincident with matter, as has been explained above.

In the proper sense, "element" is used only in reference to the causes out of which the thing is composed, and these are properly the material ones. Again, this will not apply to every material cause but to that from which the primary composition takes place. Thus, we do not say that bodily members are elements of a man, because his members are also composed of other items. But we do say that earth and water are elements, for they are not composed of other bodies. Rather, the primary composition of natural bodies is made out of them.

As a result, Aristotle in the *Metaphysics* (V, 3, 1014a26) says that "element" means the primary component of a thing, immanent in it, and indivisible into other kinds of stuff. The meaning of the first phrase, "the primary component of a thing," is clear from what we have just said. The second phrase, "immanent in it," is included to differentiate "element" from matter that is wholly corrupted by generation. For example, food is the matter for blood, but blood is not produced unless the food is used up; hence, the food does not remain in the blood, and so, food cannot be called an element of blood. Of course, elements must remain in some way, for they are not completely corrupted, as is explained in the book *On Generation* (I, 10, 327b30). The third phrase, "and indivisible into other kinds of stuff," is included to differentiate "element" from things that have parts that are formally or specifically different; for instance, the hand, whose parts are flesh and bones which do differ in kind. But an element is not divisible into parts that differ in kind; water, for example, each part of which is water. It is not required that an element be indivisible quantitatively; it is enough if it be indivisible into different kinds of stuff. Of course, if it is also indivisible in all ways, it is called an element; thus, letters are called the elements of words. It is obvious, then, from what has been said that principle is as it were a more extensive term than cause, and cause more extensive than element. This is what the Commentator says in explaining Book V of the *Metaphysics* [Averroes, *Metaphysica*, Venice, 1552, fol. 50].

Having seen that there are four kinds of causes, we should next observe that it is not impossible for the same thing to have several causes. Thus, the cause of a statue is the copper and the sculptor, but the sculptor as efficient, the copper as matter. Nor is it impossible for the same thing to be the cause of contrary effects. For instance, a pilot may be the cause of saving or sinking a ship: of the former by his presence, of the latter by his absence.

It is even possible for one thing to be both cause and effect with regard to another item, but in a different fashion. Thus, walking, taken as efficient, is the cause of health; but health, as an end, is the cause of walking, for walking is sometimes done for the sake of health. So, too, the body is as matter to the soul; while the soul is as form to the body. In fact, the efficient is called a cause in relation to the end, since the end does not actually function without the activity of the agent. On the other hand, the end is called the cause of the agent, since the latter will not work unless it tend toward the end. Hence, the efficient is the cause of the fact that a certain item stands as an end, for instance, walking in order that there may be health; however, it does not cause the end to be an end, so it is not the cause of the causality of the end; it does not make the end a final cause. For example, a physician may make health to be present actually but he does not cause health to be an end. On the other hand, the end is not the cause of the fact that a given being is efficient but it is the cause of the fact that the agent is acting. Health does not make a physician exist as a physician (I am talking about the health that is produced by the physician's activity) but it does result in the fact that the physician is acting. Hence, the end is the cause of the causality of the agent, because it makes the agent to be an agent; likewise, it makes matter function as matter, and form as form. For matter will not take on form except for the sake of an end; and form will not perfect matter except for the sake of an end. That is the reason for the statement: the end is the cause of causes, for it is the cause of the causality in all the causes.

Matter is also called the cause of the form, in the sense that the form does not exist except in the matter. Likewise, the form is the cause of the matter, because the matter has no actual being except by virtue of the form. In fact, matter and form are correlatives, as is stated in the *Physics* (II, 2, 194b10). They are predicated of the composite as parts of the whole, and as the simple in relation to the complex.

Moreover, since every cause as cause is naturally prior to its effect, we should note that "prior" has two meanings, as Aristotle says in the treatise *On Animals* (XVI, 743a19-22). As a result of these different meanings, a thing can be called both prior and posterior in the same relationship, and the cause can be called the effect. Indeed, something is said to be prior to another, (1) in generation and time, and (2) in substance and perfection. So, since a natural activity proceeds from the imperfect to the perfect, and from the incomplete to the complete, the imperfect is prior to the perfect according to generation and time; however, the perfect is prior to the imperfect in substance. Thus, one can say that the man is before the boy in substance and perfection, but the boy is before the man in generation and time. However, although the imperfect is prior to the perfect, and potency is prior to act, in the order of generable things (considering the fact that in any one thing the imperfect is prior to the perfect and it is in potency before it is in act), yet, absolutely speaking, act and the perfect must be prior. For that which reduces potency to act exists actually; and that which perfects the imperfect is something perfect. Matter, then, is prior to form in generation and time, for that to which something happens is prior to the fact that it happens. But form is prior to matter in substance and complete being, for matter has no complete being without form. Likewise, the agent is prior to the end in generation and time, since motion toward the end comes from the agent. However, the end is prior to the agent, as agent in substance and perfection, since the action of the agent is only completed by virtue of the end. And so, these two causes, material and efficient, are prior in the way of generation; but the form and the end are prior in the way of perfection.

Note, next, that necessity is twofold: namely, absolute and conditional. Absolute necessity is that which proceeds from causes that are prior in the way of generation, and these are the matter and the end. Such is the necessity of death; it results from matter, that is, from the disposition of its constituent contraries. This is called absolute because nothing impedes it. It is also called the necessity of matter. On the other hand, conditional necessity proceeds from causes that are posterior in the process of generation, that is, from the form and the end. Thus, we say that if a man is to be generated, there must be an act of conception. This kind is called conditional because in the absolute sense there is no necessity that this certain woman conceive, but only under this condition, namely, if a human being is to be generated. This is also called the necessity of the end.

It is to be noted, too, that three of the causes can coincide: namely, form, end, and agent. This is illustrated in the production of fire. Indeed, fire generates fire, and thus fire is an efficient cause, inasmuch as it generates. Then, fire is a form, since it makes something that was previously in potency to be actually. Again, it is an end, in that the agent's activity terminates in it. Of course, the end is twofold: namely, the end of the process of generation and the end of the thing that is generated. This is evident in the production of a knife: the form of the knife is the end of the process of production, but cutting (which is the work of a knife) is the end of the thing itself that is produced, of the knife. Now, the end of the process of generation sometimes coincides with the two causes under discussion—that is to say, when generation takes place from a specifically similar being. For instance, when a man generates a man, or an olive produces an olive. But this does not apply to the end of the thing that

is generated. Still, we should note that the end coincides
with the form numerically; for numerically the same item
that is the form of the thing generated is the end of the
process of generation. However, this end does not coincide
with the agent numerically but only specifically. It is impossible for the maker and his product to be numerically
identical but they can be of the same species. For instance,
when a man generates a man, the man generating and the
one that is generated are numerically different but specifically the same. Matter, however, does not coincide with the
other causes, for matter has the character of something imperfect because it is being in potency; while the other causes,
since they are in act, have the character of something perfect.
Now, the perfect and the imperfect do not coincide in the
same subject.

Now that we have seen that there are four causes, the
efficient, material, formal, and final, we should observe that
each of these causes can be analyzed in many ways. We
speak of something as a prior cause and of something else as
a posterior cause. For instance, we say that art and the
physician are the cause of health: art being the prior cause
and the physician the posterior one. The same distinction
applies to the formal and the other causes. Observe that we
should always reduce a question to the primary cause. For
example, if the question is: *Why is this man healthy?*, the
answer should be: *Because a physician has cured him;* and
again: *Why did the physician cure him? Because of the art
of healing which he possesses.*

Note also that the so-called proximate cause is the same
as the posterior cause; and the remote cause is the same as
the prior cause. Hence, these two analyses of the causes—
sometimes as prior and posterior, sometimes as remote and
proximate causes—mean the same thing. Moreover, it is to
be observed that, in all cases, that which is more general
is called the remote cause, while that which is more special
is the proximate cause. Thus, we say that man's proximate
form is his definition, rational mortal animal, but "animal"
is a more remote form, and "substance" is still more remote.

Indeed, all higher things are as forms to lower things. Likewise, the proximate matter of a statue is bronze, the remote is metal, and still more remote is body.

Next, one kind of cause is essential [*per se*] and another incidental [*per accidens*]. A cause is called essential when it is the cause of a certain thing as such. Thus, a builder is the cause of a house and wood is the material cause of a bench. An incidental cause means that which happens incidentally to an essential cause; for instance, when we speak of a grammarian who is building. In fact, the grammarian is called the cause of the building incidentally, not because he is a grammarian but because it is incidental to the builder that he is a grammarian. The same thing holds in the case of the other causes.

Again, some causes are simple and some are composite. A cause is called simple when it alone is assigned as cause to that of which it is the essential cause, or also when it alone is the incidental cause. Thus, we say that the builder is the cause of the house, and we may also say that the physician is the cause of the house. It is called composite when both are assigned as cause; thus we might say the physician-builder is the cause of the house. It is also possible to talk about simple cause in the way that Avicenna explains it (*Physics*, II, 8), as that which is a cause without the addition of anything else; thus is bronze for the statue (for the statue is made from bronze without the addition of any other matter). Similarly, we may say that the physician causes health, or that fire causes heating. Then, the composite cause means that several items must combine in order that there be a cause. For example, one man is not the cause of the motion of a ship but many are; and one stone is not the material cause of a house but many are.

Furthermore, some causes are in act and some in potency. A cause in act is one that is actually causing something; for example, the builder when he is building. Note that in speaking of causes in act, it is necessary for cause and effect to be simultaneous, in the sense that if one is, then the other is, too. In fact, if there is a builder in act, then he must be building; if the building process is in act, then there must be a builder in act. However, this is not required in the case of causes that are only in potency. Observe, too, that the universal cause is correlative with the universal effect, while a singular cause corresponds to a singular effect. Thus, we say that a builder is the cause of a house, and this builder of this house.

We should also note that in speaking about intrinsic principles, that is, matter and form, the points of resemblance or difference in the principles depend on the resemblance and difference of the consequents. Some are numerically the same, as Socrates and this man is, when we are pointing at Socrates. Others are numerically different but the same in species: for instance, Socrates and Plato, though alike in their human species, are nevertheless different in number. Still others differ specifically but are the same in their genus: thus, man and donkey agree in their animal genus. Of course, others are different generically and are the same only according to analogy: thus are substance and quantity, which do not agree in any genus but agree only according to analogy. Indeed, they agree only in the fact that each is a being; but being is not a genus, because it is not predicated univocally but analogically.

To understand this, we should observe that an item is predicable of several things in three ways: univocally, equivocally, and analogically. It is predicated univocally when the predication uses the same name and the same meaning or definition; thus is animal predicated of man and donkey. Both mean animal, and both mean an animate substance capable of sensing, since this is the definition of an animal. Predication is equivocal when the predication applies the same name to several things but with different meanings; thus we use "dog" to speak of a thing that barks and of a constellation in the heavens. They agree in name only and not in definition or signification. In fact, that which is signified by a name is the definition, as is stated in the *Metaphysics* (IV, 7, 1012a24). It is said to be predicated analogically when the predication applies to several items whose meanings are different but are attributed to some one meaning that is the same. For example, "healthy" is predicated of the animal body, of urine, and of a drink, but the meaning is not entirely the same in all the cases. It is predicated of urine as a sign of health, of a body as of its subject, of a drink as of its cause; nevertheless, all these meanings are attributed to one end, namely, health. Sometimes, items that agree analogically (that is, proportionally, comparatively, or by way of adaptation) are attributed to one end, as appears in the preceding example; and sometimes to one agent, as when "physician" is predicated of a person who practices by means of the art of medicine, and of one who practices without the art, like a midwife. And it may even be predicated of instruments, but by way of attribution to one basic item, as being is predicated of substance and of quantity, quality, and the other categories. For, the meaning whereby substance is being is not entirely the same as that for quantity and the others; but all are called being from the fact that they are attributed to substance, which is, indeed, the subject of the others. So, being is predicated primarily of substance and secondarily of the others. Thus, being is not the genus of substance and quantity, because no genus is predicated primarily and secondarily of its species, but being is predicated analogically. This is why we say that substance and quantity differ generically but are similar by way of analogy.

Of those items that are numerically the same, both form and matter are the same in a numerical unit, as in the example of Tully and Cicero [two names for the same man]. On the other hand, in things that are the same specifically but different numerically, the matter and form are also not the same in number but only in species: as in the case of Socrates and Plato. Similarly, for those things that are generically the same, the principles are also the same in their genus: thus the soul and body of a donkey and of a horse are different in species but the same in genus. Likewise, in those things that are in agreement by analogy only, the principles are the same by analogy only, or by proportion. For matter, form, and privation, or potency and act, are principles of substance and also of the other genera. Yet, the matter of substance and of quantity, and similarly their form and privation, differ generically but agree only by way of pro-portion—in the sense that just as the matter of substance is related to the substance according to the characteristic mean-ing of matter, so, too, is the matter of quantity related to quantity. However, as substance is the cause of the rest of the genera, so are the principles of substance principles for all the others.

Efficient Causes and Infinite Series

We must say that, in efficient causes, it is impossible to pro-ceed to infinity *per se;* for example, that the causes that are required *per se* for a certain effect be multiplied to infinity, as if a stone were moved by a stick, a stick by a hand, and so on to infinity. However, it is not deemed impossible to proceed to infinity *per accidens* in agent causes; for instance, if all the causes that are multiplied to infinity have the rank of but one cause and their multiplication be but accidental (suppose an artisan works with many hammers accidentally, because one after another is broken). It is quite accidental, then, to a given hammer that it acts after the action of an-other hammer. Similarly, it is accidental to a given man as an agent of generation that he has been generated by another man, for he generates as a man and not as the son of another man. Indeed, all men who generate have one level among efficient causes, that is, the level of a particular agent of generation. Hence, it is not impossible for man to be generated from man to infinity. Now, it would be impossible if the generation of this man depended on that man, and on an elemental body, and on the sun, and so on to infinity.

Summa of Theology, I, 46, 2, reply to Obj. 7. Trans. V.J.B.

An Argument for the Immobility of Place

He shows how the immobility of place is to be understood, in order to refute the preceding opinion. So, he says that a vessel and place are seen to differ in this way: the vessel may be moved but not the place. Hence, as the vessel may be called a movable place, so may place be called an immovable vessel.

So, when something is moved in another body that is also moving (for example, a boat in a river), it uses that in which it is moving more like a vessel than like a containing place, because place "wishes to be immovable," that is to say, it pertains to the aptitude and nature of place to be immobile. For this reason, one can better say that the whole river is the place of the boat, because the whole river is immobile. In this sense, the whole river, taken as immovable, is the common place. However, since proper place is a part of common place, one has to take the proper place of the boat in the river water, in the sense that it has a relation to the whole river considered as immobile. So, one is to understand the place of the boat in the flowing water, not according to this water that is flowing, but according to the relation or position that this flowing water has in regard to the whole river; and this relation of the position remains the same in the flowing water. Therefore, although in a material way the water is flowing by, yet in the sense that it has the intelligible character of place, insofar as it is considered in a certain relation and position to the whole river, it is not changed.

In this same way, we ought to understand how place stands within the outer boundaries of the mobile bodies in nature, in relation to the whole body of the spherical heavens, which has stability and immobility due to the immobility of the center and the poles. And so, although this portion of the air that is containing something, or this part of the water,

Exposition of Aristotle's Physics, IV, Lect. 6. Trans. V.J.B.

flows and is moved inasmuch as it is this water—yet, insofar
as this water has the character of place, that is, position and
a relation to the whole sphere of the heavens, it always stands
still. Similarly, one could also say that the same fire remains
as far as the form is concerned, even though in the material
sense it may vary with the burning and addition of various
pieces of wood.

Thus, against our statement that place is the terminus of
the container, the objection gives way (that since the container is movable the boundary of the container will be
movable, and so, a thing that is at rest will occupy different
places). This does not follow, because the boundary of the
container is not place, in the sense that it is this surface of
a certain mobile body, but rather according to the relation
or position that it has in the immobile whole. From which
it is evident that the whole meaning of place in all containers
comes from the first container and principle of place, namely, the heavens. . . .

He concludes from the foregoing to this definition of place:
"Place is the first immobile boundary of the container." And
he says "first" in order to designate proper place and to
exclude common place.

Time: Philosophically and Theologically

Time is spoken about in two ways. In one way, it is the
number of before and after as these are found in the motion
of the heavens. This kind of time derives continuity from
motion, and the motion depends on size. Thus, we measure
by this time all things that are ordered in relation to the
motion of the heavens, either directly in themselves, as are
bodily motions, or accidentally, as are some activities of the
soul on the basis of their connection with the body. It is
understood in this way only, by the philosophers.

In another way, time is more generally spoken of as the

On the Sentences, I, 8, 3, reply to Obj. 4. Trans. V.J.B.

number of that which has a before and after in any manner at all. Thus, we speak of time measuring the simple conceptions of our understanding in their succession. This sort of time need not have continuity because the motion with which it is associated is not continuous. This is the way in which time is taken in this text, and frequently by the theologians.

How Time Is Related to Motion

First, then, he studies the statement that time is something pertaining to motion. So, he says that since we are asking what time is, we should start at this point in order to grasp what time is in connection with motion.

That time is something related to motion is clear from this: we perceive motion and time together. It sometimes happens that we perceive the flow of time though we may not sense any particular sensible motion. For instance, if we are in darkness and do not perceive any motion of an external body through sight—and if we do not undergo any alteration in our bodies caused by an external agent—we do not sense any bodily motion. Yet, if any movement occurs in our soul, say a succession of thoughts and images, immediately it is apparent to us that some time is going on. Thus, in perceiving any kind of movement, we perceive time. Likewise, on the other hand, when we perceive time, we perceive motion along with it. Hence, since time is not motion itself, as has been shown, the conclusion remains that it is something connected with motion.

There is a difficulty expressed here concerning the perception of time and motion. Indeed, if time is associated with a sensible motion occurring outside the mind, it follows that a person who does not sense such a motion will not sense time. The contrary of this is expressed here, for if it accompanies a movement of the soul, it follows that a thing is not related to time except by means of the soul. Thus, time would

Exposition of Aristotle's Physics, IV, Lect. 17. Trans. V.J.B.

not be a thing in nature but an intention in the soul, after the fashion of genus and species. And if it were associated with every motion in general, it would follow that there are as many times as there are motions. This is impossible because two times are not identical, as was stated previously.

To clear up this difficulty, we should note that there is one primary motion which is the cause of every other motion; hence, any things whatever that are subject to movement owe this condition to this first motion, which is that of the first subject of motion [*primi mobilis*]. So, whoever perceives any sort of motion, whether occurring in sensible things or in the soul, perceives a being subject to motion, and consequently he perceives the first motion with which time is associated. Hence, whoever perceives motion of any kind perceives time, even though time is only connected with the one first motion by which all others are caused and measured. Thus, there remains but one time.

Secondly, at the phrase "However, since," he studies the second clause in the definition of time. Granted that time is something pertaining to motion, something that goes along with it, we still have to investigate the basis for this association of time with motion—that it is on the basis of before and after. . . .

He shows what time is in connection with motion: it is the number of motion. This he also shows by the same means, that is, by the knowing of time from motion. For, it is plain that we determine when time is going on, whenever we grasp one item and then another within motion, and then grasp something in the middle between them. For, when we understand the different extremes of something in the middle, and the mind says, "These are two 'nows,' one before and the other after," numbering as it were the before and after in a motion, that is when we say that this is time. Time seems to be determined from the "now"; this is taken for granted at this point because it will be more clear later.

So, when we perceive one "now" and do not distinguish a before and after in motion, we do not take the same "now" as the end of the before and the beginning of the after—

and time does not seem to be going on; in fact, motion is not, either. However, if we take before and after, and number them, then we say that time is occurring. This is so because *time is nothing other than the number of motion according to before and after.* Indeed, we perceive time, as we said, when we number the before and after in motion. So, it is clear that time is not motion but it is associated with the numbering of motion. Hence, it is the number of motion.

If one were to object to the definition as just given, that before and after depend on time and so the definition is circular, we would have to say that before and after are used in the definition of time in the sense that they are produced by the size of the motion, not in the sense of being measured by time. So, in order to refute this objection, Aristotle shows above that before and after apply to size prior to their occurrence in motion, and to motion prior to their occurrence in time.

Eternity and Time

Just as we have to come to the knowledge of simple beings by way of composites, so we must come to the knowledge of eternity by way of time. Now, the latter is nothing but "the number of motion according to before and after."

Since there is succession in any kind of motion, and one part after another, we apprehend time due to the fact that we number the before and after in motion. It is nothing other than the number of the before and after in motion.

However, in that which lacks motion and is always in the same condition, one cannot grasp the before and after. Therefore, just as the intelligibility of time consists in the numbering of before and after in motion, so, too, the intelligibility of eternity consists in the apprehension of the uniformity of that which is altogether apart from motion.

Furthermore, "those things are said to be measured by

Summa of Theology, I, 10, 1, c. Trans. V.J.B.

time which have a beginning and end in time," as is stated in the *Physics* (IV, ii, 220a25). This is so because in the case of everything that is moved, some beginning and some end must be accepted. However, what is altogether immutable can have neither beginning nor end, just as it can have no successiveness. And so, eternity becomes known from two characteristics: first, from the fact that whatever is in eternity is interminable, that is, lacking beginning and end, taking terminus as applicable to both; second, from the fact that eternity itself lacks successiveness, existing entirely at once [*tota simul*].

A Discussion of Light

There have been several different views on the nature of light. Some people have thought that light is a body—as is said in Aristotle's text. They have been motivated, in saying this, by certain ways of speaking which we use in talking about light. Indeed, we have become accustomed to saying that a ray passes through the air, that it is reflected, that rays intersect—and all these are suggestive of the behavior of a body.

Yet, this view cannot stand up, for the reasons which Aristotle mentions in his text; in fact, several other criticisms could easily be offered. It would be difficult to explain, for instance, how a body of this kind could be suddenly expanded throughout a whole hemisphere—or how it could be generated or corrupted—or, in fact, how the mere intervention of an opaque body could bring about the corruption of this light body in a certain area of the medium of light [*diaphani*]. As a matter of fact, statements about the motion of light, or its reflection, are metaphorical—just as we can also say that heat moves forward, when more objects are heated, or that heat is reflected when it meets an obstacle.

A second group of thinkers have claimed that light is some

sort of spiritual nature. Their argument is based on the fact that we use the term "light" in speaking about intellectual functions. Indeed, we do say that there is a certain intelligible light in intellectual substances. Yet, this view is also impossible.

Indeed, it is not possible for a spiritual and intelligible nature to fall under the perception of the senses, because this is a corporeal power and can know only bodily things. Of course, if a person says that spiritual light is different from the kind which the senses perceive, there is no point in arguing with him, provided he grants that in this event the light which the visual power perceives is not a spiritual nature. In fact, nothing prevents one name being applied to several things, however different they may be.

The fact that we use the word "light," and other visual terms, in reference to intellectual functions is due to the nobility of the sense of sight, which is more spiritual and subtle than the other sense powers. This is apparent for two reasons, one of which is from a consideration of the object. In fact, some beings are objects of vision because of properties which earthly bodies share in common with bodies in the heavens. On the other hand, the sense of touch perceives properties which belong to the elements, namely, warmth, cold, and the like; while taste and smell perceive properties of bodies that are mixtures, composed according to various combinations of the elemental qualities of warmth, cold, humidity, and dryness. And sound is caused by local motion which is also common to the heavenly and earthly bodies, though the kind of motion which produces sound does not belong to the heavenly bodies, according to Aristotle's opinion. Hence, it is evident, from the nature of its object, that sight occupies a higher position among the sense powers, hearing being next to it, while the other senses are farther removed.

Secondly, it is evident that the sense of sight is more spiritual from the way in which it is stimulated. Indeed, in none of the other senses is there a spiritual change of condition unaccompanied by a physical change. Now, I mean by a physical change the reception of a quality in a subject undergoing this change in its natural being, as when a thing is cooled or heated, or is moved in regard to place. However, a spiritual change occurs when a species is received in a sense organ or in a medium intentionally and not in the fashion of a natural form. In fact, a sensible species is not received in a sense power in the same way that the specific form exists in the sensible thing. It is clear, however, that in the case of touch, and of taste, which is a sort of tactual sense, that a physical change does take place. In fact, a thing becomes hot or cold through contact with something that is hot or cold, and this is not merely a case of spiritual change. In the same way, the stimulating change in the sense of smell involves some movement of vapors, and the change in the case of sound is accompanied by local motion. However, in the motion which stimulates sight, the change is simply spiritual. From this it is evident that of all the sense functions, sight is the most spiritual, and after it comes hearing. For this reason, these two senses are the most spiritual and they are the only ones capable of learning. Thus, also, we use terms that belong to them in reference to the functions of understanding, and especially those which belong to sight.

Still another group of thinkers say that light is nothing more than the appearance of color. But this is obviously false in the case of things which shine at night, when of course their color cannot be seen.

A fourth group say that light is the substantial form of the sun and that the illumination flowing from a source of light has only intentional being, like the species of colors in the air.

Now, both of these views are false. The first is, because a substantial form is not a direct object of sensation but is capable of being apprehended by the understanding only. And if it be said that what is seen in the sun is not light but splendor, there will be no argument about the name, provided this item that we call "light" is not a substantial form. The second view is false, too, because things which possess intentional being only do not produce physical change. Now, the rays from heavenly bodies do change the whole of nature below them. Hence, we say that just as the elemental bodies have active qualities through which they act, so also is light an active quality of a heavenly body through which it acts, and it [light] belongs in the third species of quality, just as heat does.

However, light is different from heat, for light is a quality of the first mobile body, and this has no contrary; hence, light has no contrary but there is a contrary for heat. Since nothing is the contrary of light, then light is incapable of possessing a contrary disposition. For this reason, its passive receptor, namely, the diaphanous medium, is always in ultimate disposition to form. This is why it can be illuminated instantaneously, while the receptor of heat is not heated instantaneously. Now, this participation or effect of a source of light [lux] on the diaphanous medium is called illumination [lumen]. And if it be accomplished by rectilinear motion toward the illuminated body, it is called a ray. However, if it be caused by the reflection of a ray toward the illuminated body, it is called splendor. Now, illumination [lumen] is what is common to every effect of a light source [lux] on the diaphanous medium.

Now that we have seen these points about the nature of light, the reason is easily seen why some bodies are actually luminous, some diaphanous, and others opaque. For, since light is a quality of the first subject of change, and this is most perfect and formal among bodies, therefore those bodies which are most formal and subject to motion are actually luminous. And those which are nearest to them are receptive to illumination, as is the case with the diaphanous medium. But those bodies which are grossly material have neither illumination in their nature nor any receptivity to light, and they are opaque. This becomes clear in the elements themselves: fire has light in its nature, although its light does not become apparent to us unless through some nature that differs from fire by way of density. However, air and water, less formal elements, are diaphanous media. And earth, the most material element, is opaque.

Light Is an Active Quality

It is impossible for light [*lumen*] to be a body. This is evident for two reasons. The first depends on a consideration of place. The place of any body is different from the place of another body, because it is not naturally possible for two bodies, of whatever kind they may be, to be present at the same time in the same place, for a contiguous being demands its own distinctive position. Secondly, the same thing is evident from the character of motion. If light were a body, the act of illuminating would be the motion of a body in place. Now, no local motion of a body can occur instantaneously, because everything that moves in place has to pass through the middle of a given distance before it reaches the extremity. But illumination is accomplished instantaneously. Nor can it be said that it is accomplished in an imperceptible extent of time; for the time required for a short distance might be elusive, but for a great distance, say from east to west, the time required could not escape us. In fact, as soon as the sun rises to the horizon, the whole hemisphere is illuminated, right to the opposite point. And there is another matter to be considered from the viewpoint of motion. Every body has some definite natural motion, but the act of illuminating moves in every direction, no more in a circle than in a straight line. So, it is obvious that illumination is not the local motion of any body.

Thirdly, the same point is clear from a consideration of generation and corruption. If light were a body, then when air grows dark through the absence of light, the luminous body would corrupt and its matter would take on another form. This is not so, unless a person claims that darkness is also a body. Nor is it clear from what matter such a body, one that fills the intervening hemisphere, could be produced each day. Moreover, it is ridiculous to say that such a body

Summa of Theology, I, 67, 2 and 3, c. Trans. V.J.B.

might be corrupted simply because of the absence of a luminary. If someone claims that it is not corrupted but that it rises and moves around with the sun, then what could he say about the fact that when some body is placed over a candle, the whole house becomes dark? It does not seem that the light is gathered in around the candle, for no more brightness is observable there after than before. Since all these points oppose not only reason but also sense experience, we have to say that light cannot be a body. . . .

Some people have claimed that light has no physical existence in the air, as color does on a wall, but only intentional being like the similitude of color in the air. But this is impossible for two reasons. First of all, light affects the air in a manner that can be named: in fact, the air actually becomes luminous. Now, color does not so affect it: air is not said to be colored. Secondly, light has a physical effect: bodies are heated by the rays from the sun. Now, thoughts do not cause physical changes.

Others have said that light is the substantial form of the sun. However, this seems impossible for two reasons. First, no substantial form is directly perceptible to the senses, for "that which is" is an object of the intellect, as is stated in the treatise *On the Soul* (III, 6, 430b28). But light is directly visible in itself. Second, it is impossible for that which is a substantial form in one thing to be an accidental form in another thing, because it is the function of a substantial form to establish something in a species and it is always and in all instances present in this species. Light, then, is not the substantial form of air, otherwise when it goes away the air would corrupt. Consequently, it cannot be the substantial form of the sun.

Therefore, we have to say that just as heat is an active form associated with the substantial form of fire, so light is an active quality associated with the substantial form of the sun, or with any other body that is of itself productive of light, if there be any other such. Some indication of this is found in the fact that light rays from various stars have different effects, according to the different natures of their bodies.

How to Form an Opinion on a Debatable Point

As to the number of motions proper to the planets, we shall now state what the astronomers say on this point, so that we may become more interested in these things with a view to forming some conception of their number, when we have made up our minds. For the remainder of the story, which will not be found in their statements, we shall have to seek it out ourselves. Or we may be persuaded by the people who have investigated this point and see if anything becomes evident later from the information that is now given by those who study such things.

However, in the acceptance or rejection of opinions, a man should not be influenced by love or hate for the person who has the opinion but rather by the desire to ascertain the truth. So, Aristotle says that we ought to love both sides, those whose opinion we follow and those whose opinion we reject. For, both parties are striving to discover the truth and they have helped us in this task. Yet, we should be open to conviction by the more certain side: that is, to follow the opinion of those who have arrived at the truth on a more certain basis. . . .

Just as in the law courts no man can pass judgment who does not listen to the arguments from both parties, so must the person whose task is to study philosophy place himself in a better position to reach a judgment by listening to all the arguments, as if they came from undecided litigants.

Exposition of Aristotle's Metaphysics, XII, Lect. 9, n. 2566; III, Lect. 1, n. 342. Trans. V.J.B.

RECOMMENDED READINGS

CROMBIE, A. C. *Augustine to Galileo: The History of Science, A.D. 400–1650.* Cambridge: Harvard University Press, 1953.

KOREN, H. J. *Introduction to the Philosophy of Nature.* Pittsburgh: Duquesne University Press, 1960.

McWILLIAMS, J. A. *Physics and Philosophy.* Washington: American Catholic Philosophical Association, 1945.

MARGENAU, H. *Thomas and the Physics of 1958: A Confrontation.* Milwaukee: Marquette University Press, 1958.

MARITAIN, J. *The Philosophy of Nature.* New York: Philosophical Library, 1951.

MAZZEO, J. A. "Light Metaphysics," *Traditio,* XIV (1955), 196–198.

NOGAR, R. "Toward a Physical Theory," *New Scholasticism,* XXV (1951), 397–438.

SMITH, V. E. *The General Science of Nature.* Milwaukee: Bruce, 1959.

VAN MELSEN, A. G. *The Philosophy of Nature.* Pittsburgh: Duquesne University Press, 1953.

III. Man and Psychology

Foreword

OF COURSE, THOMAS AQUINAS WAS NOT an experimental psychologist. His account of man and his behavior owes elements to the Bible and earlier Christian teaching (notably to Augustine of Hippo), and to his own experience and reflection. But much of the method and terminology of his treatise on man in the *Summa of Theology* (Part I, questions 75 ff.) is from Aristotle. Here, again, Aquinas adapts Aristotelianism to his own purpose. Man is described as a creature of God, endowed with a soul capable of everlasting existence after separation from the body at death, possessed of all the essential capacities of brute animals plus intellect and will. On all these points, Aquinas has significantly modified the psychology of Aristotle's *De Anima*.

When he is commenting on Aristotle's remarkable discussion of soul as the principle of life in any living thing, Aquinas rarely differs from his author. His appreciation of the technique employed in framing the Aristotelian definition of soul is evident. Like Aristotle, Aquinas is convinced that it is not easy to discover the precise nature and activities of man's immaterial part. There is no suggestion that a person can simply look within himself and see his soul. Instead, the vital actions and passions that can be observed in sense experience are taken as the primary data. Yet, there is some personal experience of the functions of understanding and willing. These immaterial functions form the basis of a difficult and lengthy reflection on the kind of being that is able to think in terms of general meanings, to express such thoughts in language, and to desire and love universal goods.

The study of man is regarded as, in one sense, a part of the philosophy of nature. As a bodily substance, man is a mobile being, subject to the same general laws and explanations that we may discover for other bodies. But because man engages in certain nonmaterial activities (intellection and volition), there is a level of his being that transcends the philosophy of physical beings. Man lives on the borderline between the brutes and the angels. He is the most complicated of creatures. The study of the immaterial part of man's being actually belongs in First Philosophy, in metaphysics, because man's rational soul is capable of separation from matter. Unlike an angelic being, the human soul is not a complete nature, a full representative of its species, when it exists after death without matter. Yet, it is so separable; and in this separated condition, it is not in any sense an object of the philosophy of nature.

In spite of his full awareness of these complexities and difficulties inherent in the philosophy of human nature, Aquinas thinks that man is able to achieve a good understanding of himself. The traditional definition of man, as a rational animal, is not taken as an empty formula but as one of the few instances of definitive knowledge of a real being. Thus, anthropology forms a sort of transitional science between the philosophy of nature and metaphysics.

Introduction to the Study of the Soul

In the present treatise on the soul we find, first, an Introduction in which the author does the three things that should be done in any Introduction. For in writing an Introduction one has three objects in view; first, to gain the reader's good will; secondly, to dispose him to learn; thirdly, to win his

Exposition of Aristotle on the Soul, I, Lect. 1. Trans. Foster and Humphries, *Aristotle's de Anima with the Commentary of St. Thomas Aquinas,* pp. 44-47.

attention. The first object one achieves by showing the reader the value of the knowledge in question; the second by explaining the plan and divisions of the treatise; the third by warning him of its difficulties. And all this Aristotle does here. First, he points out the high value of the science he is introducing. Secondly, at "We seek then . . ." he explains the plan of the treatise. Thirdly, at "To ascertain anything reliable . . ." he warns of its difficulty. Under the first point he explains, first, the dignity of this science, and then, at "Indeed, an acquaintance . . ." its utility.

As regards, then, the said dignity we should note that, while all knowledge is good and honourable, one science can surpass another in this respect. All knowledge is obviously good because the good of anything is that which belongs to the fulness of being which all things seek after and desire; and man as man reaches fulness of being through knowledge. Now of good things some are just valuable, namely, those which are useful in view of some end—as we value a good horse because it runs well; whilst other good things are also honourable; namely, those that exist for their own sake; for we give honour to ends, not means. Of the sciences some are practical, others speculative; the difference being that the former are for the sake of some work to be done, while the latter are for their own sake. The speculative sciences are therefore honourable as well as good, but the practical are only valuable. Every speculative science is both good and honourable. . . .

Now this science of the soul has both merits. It has certainty; for everyone knows by experience that he has a soul which is his life-principle. Also it has a high degree of nobility; for among lower things the soul has a special nobility. This is what Aristotle means here when he says, "Holding as we do that knowledge," i.e. speculative science, "is good and honourable." And one science is better and nobler than another in two ways; either, as we have seen, because it is more certain—hence he says "more certain"—or because it is about "more excellent" things, i.e. things that are good in themselves, and "more wonderful things," i.e.

things whose cause is unknown. "For both these reasons," he goes on to say, "we give a primary place to an enquiry about the soul." He uses the term "enquiry" because he is going to discuss the soul in a general way, without attempting, in this treatise, a thorough examination of all its properties. As to the words "a primary place," if they are taken as applying to the whole of Natural Science, then they refer to superiority in dignity and not to priority in order; but if they refer to the science of living things only, they mean priority of order.

Then, with "Indeed an acquaintance etc.," he gains the reader's good will by showing the utility of this science. Some knowledge of the soul, he says, would seem to be very useful in all the other sciences. It can be of considerable service to philosophy in general. In First Philosophy it is impossible to attain knowledge of the divine and highest causes except through what we can acquire by actualising our intellectual power; and if we know nothing about the nature of this power we should know nothing about the immaterial substances, as the Commentator remarks à propos of Book XI of the *Metaphysics*. Again, as regards Moral Philosophy: We cannot master the science of morals unless we know the powers of the soul; thus in the *Ethics* the Philosopher assigns the virtues to the different powers. So, too, it is useful for the Natural Scientist, because many of the things he studies are animate things, all of whose movements originate in the soul: "for it is," says Aristotle, "as it were, the principle of living things": the phrase "as it were" does not express a comparison; it is descriptive.

Next, at "We seek then," he states the plan of his treatise, saying that we are "to consider," i.e. by way of outward symptoms, and "to understand," i.e. by way of demonstration, what the soul really is in its nature and essence; "and then whatever qualities belong to it" or affect it. But in the latter a diversity appears, for while some of the soul's modifications, such as understanding and speculative knowledge, seem to belong to the soul of and in itself, others, such as pleasure and pain, the senses and imagination, though they depend on some soul or other, seem to be common to all animals.

Then at "To ascertain," he introduces the difficulty of this study; and this from two points of view. It is hard, first, to know the essence of the soul, and secondly to know its accidents or characteristic qualities. As to the essence, there is a double difficulty: first, as to how it ought to be defined, and then as to the elements of the definition (this point comes at "Perhaps the first thing needed").

He remarks, therefore, that while knowledge of the soul would be valuable, it is not easy to know just what the soul is. Now this is a difficulty in studying anything; for the question about substance and essence is common to the study of soul and of many other things; the first difficulty being that we do not know what method to use; for some say we should use deductive demonstration, others the method of elimination, others one of comparison. Aristotle himself preferred the method of comparison.

What Life Means

We can grasp the difference between the kind of beings whose proper characteristic is to live and those whose character is not to live, from those things that are obviously alive. Now, to live is obviously appropriate to animals; this is stated by Aristotle (*On Plants*, 7, 260a28); "Life is manifest in animals." Hence, on this basis, we should distinguish living things from the nonliving, according to the way that animals are said to live. This is the sphere in which life is primarily in evidence and in which it ultimately endures.

Now, first of all, we say that an animal is living when it begins to have movement from itself. And as long as such motion is apparent in it, the animal is judged to be alive.

Summa of Theology, I, 18, 1 and 2, c. Trans. V.J.B.

However, when it no longer has any motion from itself but is only moved by something else, at that point the animal is said to be dead, to have lost its life. From this it is plain that those beings that move themselves according to any kind of motion are living beings. . . .

Indeed, the name "life" is derived from an externally apparent fact about a thing, the fact that it is moving itself. Yet, this name is not imposed to signify this fact, but rather to designate the substance to which self-motion, or the activation of itself in any way so as to operate, belongs by virtue of its own nature. Thus, to live is nothing else than to exist as such a nature. "Life" signifies this fact, expressed abstractly, just as the noun "race" signifies abstractly the action of running. Hence, "the living" is not an accidental but a substantial category.

The Soul Is Known Through Its Activities

Since the forms of artifacts are accidents, and since, as far as we are concerned, they are better known than substantial forms because they are closer to sense, he quite appropriately explains the meaning of soul (which is a substantial form) by comparing it with accidental forms. In like fashion, also, the parts of the soul or its potencies are more evident to us than is the soul itself. So, we proceed in our knowledge of the soul from the objects to the acts, and from the acts to the potencies, and the soul itself becomes known through them. Thus, its essential character [*ratio*] is made evident in an appropriate manner through its parts.

Exposition of Aristotle on the Soul, II, Lect. 2, n. 235. Trans. V.J.B.

The Process of Defining Soul

It should be noted that, according to the teaching of Book VII of the *Metaphysics* (1; cf. VI, 1, 1025b30), there is this difference between defining substance and defining accidents, that in the former case nothing *extrinsic* is included: every substance is defined in terms merely of its material and formal principles; but in the latter case something extrinsic to the thing defined is referred to, i.e. the subject of the accidents in question—as when one defines snubness as "curvature of the nose." The reason is that a definition must express what a thing is, and while substance is something complete in its being and kind, accidents have being only in relation to a substance. In the same way no *form* as such is complete in kind; completeness in this sense belongs only to the substance composed of form and matter; so that the latter's definition is complete without reference to anything else, whilst that of the form has to include a reference to its proper subject which is matter. Hence, if the soul is a form its definition will not be complete without reference to its subject or matter.

So, in the first part of this section, he makes certain distinctions, first in view of the work of defining the soul's *essence*, and then, at "Bodies especially seem to be substances," in view of defining its *subject*. As regards the former point he alludes to three distinctions, of which the first is that of being into the ten categories; this he hints at when he says that substance is reckoned to be "one of the kinds of things that are."

The second distinction alluded to is that of substance into matter, form and the compound of both. Matter is that which is not as such a "particular thing," but is in mere potency to become a "particular thing." Form is that by

Exposition of Aristotle on the Soul, II, Lect. 1; Trans. Foster and Humphries, *Aristotle's de Anima with the Commentary of St. Thomas Aquinas*, pp. 166-172.

which a "particular thing" actually exists. And the compound is "the particular thing" itself; for that is said to be a "particular thing" (i.e. something you can point to) which is complete in being and in kind; and among material things only the compound is such. For although immaterial substances are not compounds of matter and form, still they are particular things, having actual existence in themselves, and being complete in their own nature. Not so the rational soul; for though it has the existence in itself which belongs to a "particular thing," it is not a complete nature by itself; it is rather a *part* of a specific nature. Hence it is not in all respects a "particular thing."*

Matter, then, differs from form in this, that it is a potential being; form is the "entelechy" or actuality that renders matter actual; and the compound is the resulting actual being.

Thirdly, he distinguishes two senses of the term "act." In one sense knowledge is an act, in the other thinking is an act; and the difference can be understood by relating

---

*EDITOR'S NOTE: To clarify this important step in the definition of "soul," we might remind the reader that *substance* has two meanings, for Aristotle and Aquinas. These meanings are given in the following text from St. Thomas' *Disputed Questions on the Power of God*, IX, 1, c:

"In one usage, substance means the ultimate subject which is not predicated of any other thing: this is the particular individual in the genus of substance. In another usage, substance means the form or nature of the subject.

"Now the reason for this distinction lies in the fact that several subjects may share in one nature, as several men do in the nature of man. As a result, we have to keep that which remains one distinct from that which is capable of being many. Indeed, the common nature is what a definition signifies, when it indicates what a thing is. So, this common nature is called the essence or quiddity. Whatever is present in a thing as belonging to its common nature is included under the meaning of essence; but this is not true of all

these acts to their potencies. Before one acquires the grammatical habit and becomes a grammarian, whether self-taught or led by another, one is only potentially so; and this potency is actualised by the *habit*. But once the habit is acquired one is still in potency to the *use* of it, so long as one is not actually thinking about grammar; and this thinking is a further actualisation. In this sense, then, knowledge is one act and thinking another.

Then at "Bodies especially" he alludes to three distinctions which are presupposed by his enquiry into the meaning of the definition of the soul, so far as the *subject* endowed with soul is concerned. The first is the distinction between corporeal and incorporeal substances. Now the former are the most evident to us: for, whatever the latter may be in themselves, they do not impinge on our senses, but are only discoverable by an exercise of the reason. Hence he says that "bodies especially seem to be substances."

The next distinction is between physical or natural bodies and artificial bodies. Man and wood and stone are natural

----

that is present in the individual substance. For, if whatever is present in the individual substance were to belong to the common nature, then no distinction among substances of the same nature would be possible.

"Now, what is present in the individual substance, in addition to the common nature, is the individual matter which is the principle of individuation; as a consequence, the individual accidents which characterize this matter are also present.

"Hence the essence is related to the individual substance as its formal part, as humanity stands in relation to Socrates. Thus, in the case of things composed of matter and form, their essence is not completely identical with their substance-as-subject and so it is not predicated of the subject. We do not say that Socrates is humanity as one item.

"However, in the case of simple substances, there is no difference between their essence and their substance, since individual matter as individuating the common nature is not present in them. Rather, their essence is identical with their subsistence."

bodies, but a house or a saw is artificial. And of these the natural bodies seem to be the more properly called substances, since artificial bodies are made out of them. Art works upon materials furnished by nature, giving these, moreover, a merely accidental form, such as a new shape and so forth; so that it is only in virtue of their matter, not their form, that artificial bodies are substances at all; they are substances because natural bodies are such. Natural bodies therefore are the more properly called substances, being such through their form as well as through their matter.

Thirdly, he distinguishes between living and non-living natural bodies; and the living are those which of themselves take nutriment and grow and decay. Note here that this is said by way of example rather than definition. For, besides growth and decay, living things may exhibit sensation and intellectual knowledge and other vital activities. Immaterial substances, as is proved in the *Metaphysics* (XII, 7, 1072b1), have the life of intellect and volition, though they cannot grow and do not take food. But because, in the sphere of the things that are born and die, the plant-soul (the principle of nutrition and growth) marks the point where life begins, this soul is here taken as the type of all living things. However, life is essentially that by which anything has power to move itself, taking movement in its wide sense so as to include the "movement" or activity of the intellect. For we call those things inanimate which are moved only from outside.

After this, at "Therefore every animal body," he begins to define the soul, presupposing the distinctions already made. And his enquiry here has three parts: (*a*) he enquires into the elements of the definition taken separately; (*b*) at "If, then, there is any one generalisation," he states his definition; and (*c*) at "Hence it is unnecessary," he uses it to refute an objection. As to (*a*) he first deals with the elements that refer to the soul's *essence*, and then to those that refer to its *subject*, at "Such a body will be organic," and in the part that concerns the essence he considers first the statement that the soul is an "act," and then, at "Now this can mean one of two things," that it is a "primary act."

Aristotle's first conclusion, then, in line with what has been said already, is that if physical bodies are substances in the fullest sense, all living bodies are substances too, for they are physical bodies. And as each living body is an actual being, it must be a compound substance. But just because to say "living body" is to imply two things, the body itself and that modification of body by which it is alive, it cannot be said that the element in the composition referred to by the term body is itself the principle of life or the "soul." By soul we understand that by which a living thing is alive; it is understood, therefore, as existing *in* a subject, taking "subject" in a broad sense to include not only those *actual* beings which are subjects of their accidental modifications, but also bare matter or potential being. On the other hand the body that receives life is more like a subject and a matter than a modification existing in a subject.

Since, then, there are three sorts of substance: the compound; matter; and form; and since the soul is neither the compound—the living body itself; nor its matter—the body as the subject that receives life; we have no choice but to say that the soul is a substance in the manner of a form that determines or characterises a particular sort of body, i.e. a physical body potentially alive.

Note that he does not say simply "alive," but "potentially alive." For by body actually alive is understood a living compound; and no compound as such can enter into the definition of a form. On the other hand the matter of a living body stands to the body's life as a potency to its act; and the soul is precisely the actuality whereby the body has life. It is as though we were to say that shape is an actuality; it is not exactly the actuality of an actually shaped body—i.e. the compound of body and shape—but rather of the body as able to receive a shape, of the body as in potency to an actual shape.

But lest it be thought that soul is an actuality in the manner of any merely accidental form, he adds that it is a substantial actuality or form. And since every form has the matter proper to it, the soul must actualise just this special sort of body.

The difference between accidental form and substantial

form is that whereas the former does not make a thing simply be, but only makes it be in this or that mode—e.g. as quantified, or white—the substantial form gives it simple being. Hence the accidental form presupposes only potentiality to existence, i.e. bare matter. That is why there cannot be more than one substantial form in any one thing; the first makes the thing an actual being; and if others are added, they confer only accidental modifications, since they presuppose the subject already in act of being.

We can therefore reject the view of Avicebron (in the Book called *Fons Vitae*) that according to the way in which any given thing can be divided into genera and species so it can be divided into substantial forms. Thus an individual man would have one form that made him a substance, another that gave him a body, another that gave him life, and so on. But what our premisses compel us to say is that it is one and the same substantial form that makes a man a particular thing or substance, and a bodily thing, and a living thing, and so on. For the higher form can give to its matter all that a lower form gives, and more; the soul gives not only substance and body (as a stone's form does) but life also. We must not think, therefore, of the soul and body as though the body had its own form making it a body, to which a soul is super-added, making it a living body; but rather that the body gets both its being and its life from the soul. This is not to deny, however, that bodily being as such is, in its imperfection, material with respect to life.

Therefore, when life departs, the body is not left specifically the same; the eyes and flesh of a dead man, as is shown in the *Metaphysics* (VII, 10, 1035b15), are only improperly called eyes and flesh. When the soul leaves the body another substantial form takes its place; for a passing-away always involves a concomitant coming-to-be.

Then, at "Now this can mean," he examines the second term in the definition. He observes that there are two kinds of actuality, as we explained above, the kind that is like knowledge and the kind like thinking. And clearly the soul is of the former kind; for it is due to the soul that an animal is able to be both awake and asleep; and while waking is similar to thinking (for it is a use of the exterior senses just as thinking is a use of knowledge already possessed), sleep is more like the knowledge which lies dormant in the mind so long as it is not actually being used; for in sleep an animal's faculties are quiescent.

Now, of these two actualities, knowledge comes first in the order of coming-to-be in the same person; for it stands to thinking as potency to act. But in the order of nature or essence act is prior to potency (see the *Metaphysics*, IX, 8, 1049b5) as the end and complete perfection of potency. And even in the temporal order of coming-to-be, act, in a quite general sense, is prior; for the potential is actualised only by something already in act. But in this or that particular thing considered in itself potentiality may come first; the thing may be actualised by degrees. Hence his remark that "knowledge . . . is prior [i.e. to thinking] in the order of generation in one and the same thing."

So he concludes that soul is the primary act of a physical body potentially alive, where act means the same sort of actuality as knowledge. He says *primary* act, not only to distinguish soul from its subsequent activities, but also to distinguish it from the forms of the elements, for these retain their own proper activities, unless impeded.

Next, at "Such a body," he examines that part of the definition which has to do with the soul's *subject*, observing that the "physical body" referred to is any organic body, i.e. any body equipped with the various organs required by a living body in consequence of the life-principle's various vital activities. For from this principle [the soul] which is the richest of embodied forms, spring many different activities, so that it requires, in the matter informed by it, a full equipment of different organs. Not so the less perfect forms of inanimate things.

Now plants, the least perfect of animate things, exhibit less organic diversity than animals. That is why Aristotle chooses plants to illustrate his assertion that every animate body is organic, saying that even plants have organically diversified parts. But these parts are very simple, i.e. like to one another; they lack the differentiation that we find in animals. Thus the foot of an animal is made up of different parts, flesh, nerves, bones and so forth, but the organs of plants are composed of less diverse sets of parts.

The organic character of the parts of plants is displayed in their diverse functions. Thus a leaf functions as a covering for the pericarp or fruit-bearing part, i.e. for the part in which the fruit is born. The pericarp, again, protects the fruit itself. So too the roots have a function in a plant similar to that of the mouth in an animal; they draw in the nourishment.

Next, at "If, then," he gathers all these observations into one definition, saying that if any definition covers all types of "soul" it will be this: *the soul is the primary actuality of a physical bodily organism.* He does not need to add "having life potentially"; for this is implied in "organism."

The Psychic Powers of Man

A power as such is spoken of in relation to an act. Hence a power must be defined by its act, and powers in turn distinguished from one another inasmuch as their acts are different. Now acts derive their species from their objects, because, if they are acts of passive powers, their objects are active. However, if they are the acts of active powers, their objects are as ends. Now the species of an operation must be considered in both of these ways. For the act of heating and that of making cold are distinguished from one another, because the principle of the former is heat, and that of the latter, cold. Besides, both are terminated in similar ends. For an agent acts in order that it may cause something similar to itself to exist in another. It follows, therefore, that the distinction between the powers of the soul is based on a difference [i.e., a specific diversity] of objects.

Disputed Question on the Soul, 13, c. Trans. Rowan, *The Soul*, pp. 165-170.

Now it is necessary to consider the difference between objects in this way and in this way alone, namely, that objects specifically differentiate the actions of the soul. For a species is differentiated in any genus only by the [specific] differences which essentially divide the genus. The species of "animal," for instance, are not distinguished by white and by black, but by rational and non-rational. Furthermore, it is necessary to consider three grades in the actions of a soul. For the action of a soul transcends that of the nature operating in inanimate things. But this occurs in two ways. First, with respect to the manner of acting; secondly, with respect to what is produced by the action. Now with respect to the manner of acting, every action of a soul must transcend the operation or action of an inanimate nature. For every operation of a soul must proceed from some intrinsic agent, because an action of a soul is a vital action (moreover, every living thing is one that moves itself to operation). However, so far as the effect produced is concerned, not every action of a soul transcends an action of the nature of an inanimate thing. For the effect produced, that is, a natural mode of existing [*esse naturale*], and the things necessary for it, must be present in the case of inanimate bodies just as they are in the case of animate ones. But in the case of inanimate bodies, the effect is brought about by an extrinsic agent, whereas in the case of animate bodies, it is caused by an intrinsic agent. The actions to which the powers of a vegetal soul are directed, are of this sort. For the generative power is directed to giving existence to the individual thing; the augmentative power, to giving the thing its proper size; and the nutritive power, to preserving the thing in existence. But in inanimate things these effects are brought about only by an extrinsic agent. For this reason the aforementioned powers of a soul are said to be natural.

However, there are other higher actions of a soul which transcend the actions of natural forms, and also the effects produced by them, seeing that all things are disposed by nature to exist in the soul with an immaterial existence. For the human soul, in a certain respect, is all things by sensing and understanding. Moreover, there must be different grades

of such immaterial existence. For there is one grade inasmuch
as things exist in the soul without their proper matter, but
with the singularity and individuating conditions which are
the result of matter. This is the grade of sense, which is
receptive of individual species without matter, yet receives
them in a bodily organ. Now the intellect which receives
species completely abstracted from matter and material conditions, and without [the aid of] a bodily organ, constitutes
a higher and more perfect grade of immateriality. Furthermore, just as a thing has a natural inclination toward something, and has movement and action in order to pursue that
toward which it is inclined through its natural form, so also
does the inclination toward a thing apprehended by sense
or by intellect, follow upon the apprehension of a sensible
or intelligible form. This inclination belongs to the appetitive
power. And again, as a consequence of this, there must be
some movement by which the thing [having sense or intellect]
attains the thing desired. This pertains to the motive power.

Moreover, five things are required for the perfect sense
knowledge which an animal should have. First, that sense
receive species from sensible things, and this pertains to the
proper sense. Secondly, that the animal make some judgment
about the sensible qualities received, and distinguish them
one from another, and this must be done by a power to which
all sensible qualities are related. This power is called the
common sense [*sensus communis*]. Thirdly, that the species
of sensible things which have been received be retained. Now
an animal needs to apprehend sensible things not only when
they are present, but also after they have disappeared. And
it is necessary that this also be attributed to some power.
For in corporeal things there is one principle that receives,
and another that retains, because things which are good
recipients are sometimes poor retainers. This power is called
imagination or "phantasy" [*phantasia*]. In the fourth place,
the animal must know certain intentions which sense [i.e., the
external sense] does not apprehend, such as the harmful,
the useful, and so on. Man, indeed, acquires a knowledge of
these by investigation and by inference, but other animals,

by a certain natural instinct. For example, the sheep flees naturally from the wolf as something harmful. Hence in animals other than man a natural estimative power is directed to this end, but in man there is a cogitative power which collates particular intentions. This is why it is called both particular reason and passive intellect. In the fifth place, it is necessary that those things which were first apprehended by sense and conserved interiorly, be recalled again to actual consideration. This belongs to a memorative power, which operates without any investigation in the case of some animals, but with investigation and study in the case of men. Therefore in men there is not only memory but also reminiscence. Moreover it was necessary that a power distinct from the others be directed to this end, because the activity of the other sentient powers entails a movement from things to the soul, whereas the activity of the memorative power entails an opposite movement from the soul to things. But diverse movements require diverse motive principles and motive principles are called powers.

Now because the proper sense, which is first in the order of sentient powers, is changed immediately by sensible objects, it was necessary for it to be divided into different powers in accordance with the diversity of sensible modifications. For the grade and order of modifications by which the senses are altered by sensible qualities, must be considered in relation to immaterial modifications, because sense is receptive of sensible species without matter. Hence, there are some sensible objects whose species, although they are received immaterially in the senses, still cause a material modification in sentient animals. Now qualities which are also principles of change in material things are of this sort, for instance, hot and cold, wet and dry, and the like. Hence, because sensible qualities of this kind also modify us by acting upon us, and because material modification is made by contact, it was necessary that such sensible qualities be sensed by making contact with them. This is the reason why the sensory power experiencing such qualities is called touch. However, there are some sensible qualities which do not, indeed, change us materially, although their mutation has a material change connected with it. This occurs in two ways. First, in this way, that the material change affects the sensible quality as well as the one sensing. This pertains to taste. For, although the taste of a thing does not change the sense organ by making it the tasted thing itself, nevertheless this modification does not occur without some change taking place in the thing tasted as well as in the organ of taste, and particularly as a result of moisture. Secondly, in this way, that the material change affects the sensible quality alone. Now change of this sort is caused either by a dissipation and alteration of the sensible object, as occurs, for instance, in the sense of smell, or by a local change only, as occurs in the case of hearing. So it is that hearing and smell sense not by contact with an object, but through an extrinsic medium, because they occur without a material change on the side of the one sensing, although material change does take place in the sensible object. However, taste alone senses by contact, because it requires a material modification in the one sensing. Furthermore, there are other *sensibilia* which modify a sense without a material change being involved, such as light and color, and the sense which apprehends these in sight. Hence, sight is the noblest of all the senses and extends to more objects than the other senses do [*universalia*], because the sensible qualities perceived by it are common both to corruptible and incorruptible bodies.

Similarly the appetitive power, which follows the apprehension of the senses, must be divided twofoldly. For a thing is appetible either because it is delightful and suitable to the senses, and the concupiscible power is directed to this; or because the capacity of enjoying things delightful to the senses is made possible through it, which sometimes occurs together with something that is displeasing to sense. For instance, when an animal by fighting makes possible the enjoyment of something properly delightful by driving away anything that hinders this. The irascible power is directed to this end.

Moreover, since the motive power is directed to local movement, it is diversified only with respect to different [local] movements. These movements may differ for different animals, since some of them are able to crawl, some to fly, some to walk, and some to move in other ways; or they may differ for different parts of one and the same animal, because the particular parts of the body have their own movements.

Again, the grades of intellectual powers are similarly distinguished into cognitive and appetitive. Moreover, movement is common to sense and to the intellect, for the same body is moved by each of these powers through one and the same movement. Again, intellectual cognition requires two powers, namely, the agent intellect and the possible intellect, as is clear from the previous articles.

Consequently it is obvious that there are three grades of powers in the soul, namely, the vegetal, sentient, and rational. Moreover, there are five genera of powers, i.e., the nutritive, sentient, intellective, appetitive, and locomotive, and each of these contains many powers under itself, as has been pointed out.

Man's Soul and Its Potencies

After the consideration of spiritual and corporeal creation, we must now consider man, who is composed of a spiritual-corporeal substance: first, of the nature of man himself, second, of his production. Now, it is the work of the theologian to consider the nature of man in regard to his soul but not in regard to his body, except as the body has a relation to the soul. So, the first consideration will deal with the soul.

Is the soul corporeal? (75: 1)

In order to investigate the nature of the soul, we should

take it as given that soul means the first principle of life in those things that live in our environment. In fact, we call animated things living, while inanimates are without life. Now, life is chiefly manifested by two operations: knowledge and motion. The ancient philosophers, unable to rise above their imagination, claimed that some body is the source of these operations; for, they said that bodies alone exist and what is not a body is nothing. According to this view, they said that the soul is a body.

Although the falsity of this opinion may be shown in many ways, we shall use one which shows with greater generality and certitude that the soul is not a body. It is obvious that not every principle of a vital operation is a soul, for then the eye would be a body because it is a sort of principle of seeing, and the same thing would be said of the other instruments of the soul. Instead, we say that the soul is the first principle of life. Now, though a body could be some sort of principle of life (as the heart is a principle of life in an animal), yet, a body cannot be the first principle of life. Indeed, it is clear that to be a principle of life, or living, is not proper to a body from the very fact that it is a body—otherwise every body would be living, a principle of life. So, it is appropriate to a certain body to be living, and also a principle of life, from the fact that it is a certain kind of body. Now, that which is actually of a certain kind possesses this qualification from some principle that is called its act. The soul, then, which is the first principle of life, is not a body but the act of a body— as heat, which is the principle of the action of heating, is not a body but an act of a body.

Does the human soul subsist? (75: 2)

We have to say that the principle of intellectual operation, which we call the soul of man, is some sort of incorporeal and subsistent principle. Indeed, it is manifest that man is able to know the natures of all bodies through his intellect. Now, whatever can know such things must have nothing of them in its nature, for what is present in it naturally would impede the knowing of other things. We observe, for example, that a sick person's tongue, infected with a choleric and bitter humor, is unable to perceive something sweet; instead, everything seems bitter to it. So, if the intellectual principle had the nature of any body within it, it would not be able to know all bodies. Every body has a definite nature. Hence, that the intellectual principle be a body is an impossibility.

It is likewise impossible that it understand through a corporeal organ, for, again, the definite nature of this corporeal organ would prohibit the knowing of all bodies. For instance, if some precise color is not only in the pupil but also in a glass vase, the liquid that is poured in seems to be of this same color.

Therefore, this intellectual principle called mind or intellect has an operation by itself which it does not share with the body. Now, nothing can operate by itself unless it subsists by itself. For, to operate is only characteristic of being in act, and, consequently, a thing operates in the same manner that it exists. For this reason, we do not say that heat heats but that a hot thing does. The conclusion remains, then, that the human soul which we call intellect or mind is something incorporeal and subsistent.

1. We can understand "complete substantial entity" [*hoc aliquid*] in two ways: first, as anything that subsists; second, as a complete subsistent within the nature of any species. The first way excludes inherence as an accident and as a material form. The second way excludes the imperfection of a part. Thus, a hand could be called a *hoc aliquid* in the first way but not in the second. So, since a human soul is a part of the human species, it can be called a *hoc aliquid* in the first way but not in the second, for that is the way in which the composite of soul and body is called a *hoc aliquid*. . . .

3. The body is required for the action of the intellect not as an organ whereby this action is exercised but from the

standpoint of an object, for phantasms are related to the intellect as color to sight. To need the body in this way does not prevent the intellect from being subsistent; otherwise, an animal would not be something subsistent because it needs external sense qualities in order to sense.

Is the soul composed of matter and form? (75: 5)

The soul does not have matter. This can be looked at in two ways; first, from the meaning of soul in general. Indeed, it belongs to the meaning of soul that it be the form of a body. It is, then, either form by virtue of its entirety or because of one of its parts. If it is so by virtue of its entirety, one of its parts cannot be matter, provided matter means a being that is only in potency, because a form, as form, is an act. Now, what is only in potency cannot be a part of an act, since potency is repugnant to act, in the sense that it is distinguished as contrary to act. But if it is form by virtue of one of its parts, we will call that part the soul, and the matter of which it is first of all act we will call the primary animated thing.

Second, we can look at it in a specific way, from the meaning of the human soul, as intellectual. In fact, it is obvious that everything that is received in another is received in it according to the mode of the receiver. Thus, whatever is known is present in the knower as its form. Now, the intellectual soul knows a thing in its absolute nature, for example, a stone insofar as it is stone absolutely. So, the absolute form of a stone is in the intellectual soul according to its own formal meaning [secundum propriam rationem formalem]. Hence, the intellectual soul is simply a form, not something composed of matter and form. For, if the intellectual soul were composed of matter and form, the forms of things would be received in it as individuals, and so it would only know the singular, as do the sense powers which receive the forms of things in a corporeal organ, for matter is the individuating principle of forms. We may conclude, then, that the intellectual soul and every intellectual substance that knows absolute forms is lacking in the composition of form and matter.

Is the human soul corruptible? (75: 6)

We have to say that the human soul, the intellectual principle, is incorruptible. Indeed, something is corrupted in two ways: [1] essentially [*per se*]; [2] accidentally [*per accidens*]. Now, it is impossible for a subsistent thing to be generated or corrupted accidentally, that is, by something else that is generated or corrupted. In fact, the fact that a thing is generated or corrupted belongs to it in the same way that its act of being [*esse*] does, for this is what is received through generation and lost through corruption. Hence, whatever has an act of being essentially must be generated or corrupted essentially; while, things that do not subsist, such as accidents and material forms, are said to come into being and to be corrupted through the generation and corruption of the composite.

Now, it was shown above that the souls of brutes are not essentially subsistent, but only the human soul is. Hence, the souls of brutes are corrupted when their bodies are corrupted; while, the human soul is not able to be corrupted, unless it be essentially corrupted. Now, the latter is quite impossible not only in regard to it but also in the case of any subsistent that is simply a form. Indeed, it is apparent that what belongs essentially to anything is inseparable from it. To be essentially belongs to a form which is an act. Hence, matter acquires actual being by the very fact that it acquires a form; while, corruption occurs in it by the very fact that the form is separated from it. Now, it is impossible for a form to be separated from itself, so it is impossible for a subsistent form to cease to be.

Granted, even, that the soul were composed of matter and form, as some have said, it would still be necessary to assert that it is incorruptible. For corruption is found only where there is contrariety: generations and corruptions take place from contraries and to the contrary. . . . Now, there cannot be any contrariety in the intellectual soul. It receives according to the mode of its being [*esse*]; the things that are received in it are without contrariety, because even the intelligible principles of contraries are not contraries in the intellect; instead, there is one knowledge of contraries. So, it is impossible for the intellectual soul to be corruptible.

An indication of this point can be taken from the fact that everything naturally desires to be in its own way. Now, in knowing things, desire is a consequence of knowledge. The sense power knows being [*esse*] only under the guise of the here and now; while the intellect apprehends being without qualification and in regard to every time. Hence, every being possessed of intellect naturally desires to be always. But a natural desire cannot be unfulfilled. Therefore, every intellectual substance is incorruptible. . . .

2. Just as the possibility of being created does not suggest passive potency but only the active potency of the Creator, Who is able to produce something from nothing, so, when it is said that a thing is changeable into nothing, this does not mean a potency toward nonbeing in the creature but a potency in the Creator to refrain from conveying being. But something is called corruptible because there is present in it a potency toward nonbeing.

Is the soul the substantial form of man? (76: 1)

It is necessary to state that the intellect, which is the principle of intellectual operation, is the form of the human body. Indeed, that whereby a thing is primarily put into operation is the form of that to which the operation is attributed. For example, that whereby a body is primarily healed is health, and that whereby a soul primarily knows is knowledge: hence health is a form of the body, and knowledge of the soul. Now, the reason for this is that nothing acts except as it is in act; hence, a thing acts by virtue of the same principle whereby it actually exists. Now, it is apparent that the primary item whereby the body lives is the soul. And since life is indicated by various operations in various levels of living things, that by which we primarily perform each of these vital operations is the soul. In fact, the soul is the primary principle whereby we perform acts of nutrition and sense, and move about in place; likewise, by it we primarily understand. So, this principle whereby we primarily understand, whether it be called intellect or intellectual soul, is the form of the body. Now, this is Aristotle's argument in the second book *On the Soul* (II, 1, 412b10). . . .

Therefore, the only way that remains is that which Aristotle took as his position: that a given man understands because the intellectual principle is his own form. In this way, then, it is apparent from the very working of the understanding that the intellectual principle is united to the body as a form.

The same can be shown from the rational meaning of the human species. Of course, the nature of anything is manifested from its operation. Now, the proper operation of man, as man, is to understand; indeed, he rises above all else by this operation. Hence, Aristotle, in the *Ethics* (X, 7, 1177a17), places ultimate happiness in this operation as in what is proper to man. Therefore, man must be placed in his species by that which is the principle of this operation. Now, each being receives its species through its proper form. So, the conclusion is that the intellectual principle is the proper form of man.

Are there other forms in man besides the intellectual? (76: 4)

If one took the position that the intellectual soul is not united with the body as a form but merely as a mover, as the Platonists claimed, then it would be necessary to say that there is another substantial form in man by which the body would be established in being as movable by the soul. However, if the intellectual soul is united with the body as a substantial form (as we have already said above), it is impossible for any other substantial form apart from it to be found in man.

To show this, we should consider that a substantial form differs from an accidental form in that the accidental form does not confer being without qualification, but only a certain kind of being: as heat makes its subject to be hot but not unqualifiedly to be. When an accidental form comes in, we do not say that a thing comes into being or is generated simply, but only in a qualified sense. Now, a substantial form confers being simply, and so, as a result of its entry, something is said simply to be generated, and, as a result of its departure, simply to be corrupted.

Because of this, the ancient natural philosophers (who claimed that matter is the first actual being: for instance, fire or air, or something like that) said that nothing is generated or corrupted in the unqualified sense but that every becoming is but an alteration, as is said in the *Physics* (I, 4, 187a30). If this were the case, that some other substantial form whereby the subject of the soul would be an actual being pre-existed in matter beside the intellectual soul, it would follow that the soul does not confer being in an unqualified way and, consequently, it would not be a substantial form. Moreover, the entry of the soul would not be generation unqualifiedly but only in a restricted sense. All of these are clearly false.

Hence, we must say that there is no other substantial form in man than the intellectual soul, and that it, as the virtual container of the sensitive and nutritive souls, also virtually contains all the lower forms, and it does by itself alone whatever the more imperfect forms do in other beings. And we have to say the same about the sensitive soul in brutes, and the nutritive in plants, and universally about all more perfect forms in relation to the imperfect ones. . . .

3. Various grades of perfection are observed in matter, such as *to be, to live, to sense,* and *to understand.* Now, the item which follows is always more perfect than the prior one [in this enumeration]. Therefore, the form which confers only the first level of perfection on matter is most imperfect; but

the form that confers the first, second, third, and so on, is most perfect—yet it belongs to matter without any intermediary.

If the soul is united with the body as a form (as we have already said), it cannot be united to it by means of an intermediary body. The reason is that a thing is called one on the same basis that it is a being. Now, the form by itself makes the thing to be in act, since the form is essentially act and it does not through any medium confer the act of existing. Hence, the unity of a thing composed of matter and form is from the form itself, which of itself is united to the matter as its act. Nor is there anything else that unifies, except the agent which makes the matter actually to be, as is said in the *Metaphysics* (VII, 6, 1045b21).

Operative powers are not identical with essence of soul (77: 1)

The soul in its essence is an act. So, if this essence of the soul were the immediate principle of operation, then what possesses a soul would always have the activities of life, just as the possessor of a soul is always alive. As a form, act is not ordered to a further act; instead, it is the ultimate terminus of generation. Hence, to be still in potency to another act does not belong to a subject by virtue of its essence, as a form, but by virtue of its potency.

So, the soul itself as the subject of its potency is called first act, ordered to second act. Now, we find that the possessor of a soul is not always in act in regard to the activities of life. Consequently, even in the definition of the soul, it is called "The act of a body possessing life in potency, which potency does not exclude the fact that it is a soul, however" (*On the Soul*, II, 1, 412b25). Hence, the conclusion is that the essence of the soul is not its potency, for as act nothing is in potency, insofar as it is act. . . .

3. Action pertains to the composite, just as the act of being does; indeed, to act is a function of the existent. Now, the

composite possesses the act of being substantially through
the form; it operates through the power which results from the
substantial form. Hence, the potency of the soul is related to
the soul in the same way that the active accidental form is
related to the substantial form of the agent; for instance, as
heat is to the form of fire.

Diversification of the soul's potencies (77: 3)

Potency, inasmuch as it is potency, is directed to act.
Hence, the meaning [ratio] of potency must be taken from
the act to which it is directed and, consequently, the diversification of the meaning of potency depends on the diversification of the meaning of act. Now, the meaning of act is
diversified by the diverse meanings of object.

Indeed, every action belongs either to an active or passive
potency. The object is related as a principle and moving
cause to the act of a passive potency; insofar as it moves the
power of sight, color is the principle of vision. But the object
is related as a term and end to the act of an active potency;
thus, the object of the power of growth is perfect size, which
is the end of the growing thing. Now, action receives its
species from these two, either from the principle or from the
end or term. In fact, heating differs from cooling in that the
former proceeds from a hot thing, that is, an active one, to
a heated thing, while the latter proceeds from a cold thing to
a cooled one. Hence, potency must be diversified by virtue
of act and object.

Yet, we must keep in mind that items, that are accidentally so, do not diversify the species. The fact that a certain
coloration occurs in an animal does not mean that the species
of animals is diversified by the difference of color but by
a difference that applies essentially [per se] to the animal, by
the difference, namely, of the sensitive soul which is sometimes found along with reason and sometimes apart from
reason. Hence, rational and irrational are differences which
distinguish animals, being constitutive diversities of species.

Thus, not every diversity of objects diversifies the potencies of the soul, but rather the difference of that to which the potency is directed of itself. For example, the sense potency is essentially directed to changeable quality, which is essentially divided into color, sound, and the like. So, there is one sense potency for color—namely, sight; and another for sound—namely, hearing. However, it is accidental to changeable quality, to the colored thing, to be musical or grammatical, large or small, man or stone. So, with differences of this kind, the potencies of the soul are not distinguished.

1. Though act is posterior to potency in actual being, act is, however prior in intention and in its function as the end of the agent. And the object, though extrinsic, is nevertheless the principle or end of the action. Those things that are intrinsic to the thing are proportioned to the principle and the end.

The ordering of the soul's powers (77:4)

Three orders are observed among them. Two of these are observed as the dependency of one potency on another; the third is taken on the basis of the order of the objects.

Now, the dependency of one potency on another can be taken in two ways: first, according to the order of nature, insofar as the perfect are naturally prior to the imperfect; second, according to the order of generation and time, in the sense that there is a process from the imperfect to the perfect. The intellectual powers are prior to the sense powers, on the basis of the first ordering of potencies; as a consequence, they direct them and command them. Similarly, in this ordering the sense powers are prior to the potencies of the nutritive soul.

However, the reverse holds according to the second ordering. The potencies of the nutritive soul are prior to the powers of the sensitive soul in the process of generation, and so they prepare the body for the activities of the latter. And the same is true of the sense powers in relation to the intellectual ones.

Now, on the basis of the third ordering, the sensitive powers are ordered in relation to each other—namely, sight, hearing, and smell. For, the visible is naturally prior, since it is common to the higher [celestial] and lower bodies. Audible sound is produced in air which is naturally prior to a mixture of the elements from which odor arises.

There are three potencies of the vegetative part. The vegetative, as we have said, has as its object the body that lives by means of the soul. Now, three operations are necessary to this body: by one, it acquires the act of existing [*esse*]; to this the generative potency is directed. By another, the living body acquires a due size; to this the augmentative potency is ordered. By another, the body of the living being is maintained both in being and in its due size; and to this the nutritive power is directed.

The five external senses (78:3)

The potencies are not for the sake of the organs but the organs are for the potencies. So, there are not different potencies because there are different organs; instead, nature has established a diversity of organs so that they would be suitable to the diversity of potencies. Likewise, nature has provided various media for the diverse senses, according as it was appropriate to the acts of the potencies.

Now, it is not the function of sense but of intellect to know the natures of sensible qualities. Therefore, the plan of the numbering and distinguishing of the exterior senses must be taken on the basis of what pertains to sense properly and essentially. Sense is a passive potency brought into being in order to undergo immutation from the exterior sense object. So, the exterior object productive of such immutation is that which is essentially perceived by sense power, and the sense potencies are distinguished on the basis of diversity of it.

There are two kinds of immutation: natural and spiritual. By the natural, the form of the cause of immutation is received in the subject of immutation as it physically exists; thus is heat received in the heated thing. On the other hand, by spiritual immutation the form of the cause of immutation is received in the subject of immutation as it spiritually exists; thus, the form of color is in the pupil of the eye, which does not thereby become colored. The working of the sense power requires a spiritual immutation whereby the *intention* of the sensible form is produced in the sense organ. Otherwise, if the mere natural immutation sufficed for sensing, all natural bodies would sense whenever they underwent alteration.

But in some senses there is found only spiritual immutation, as in the case of sight. In others there is also a natural immutation along with the spiritual, either on the side of the object only, or also on the part of the organ. On the side of the object, we find a natural immutation in place in the case of sound, which is the object of hearing; for, sound is produced by percussion and the movement of air. In the case of odor, which is the object of smell, it is by alteration, for a body has to be altered by a hot thing in order to give off an odor.

On the part of the organ, there is a natural immutation in the case of touch and taste; for the hand touching a hot thing is heated and the tongue is moistened by the liquidity of the object of taste. However, the olfactory and auditory organs suffer no natural immutation in sensing, unless it be accidental.

Now, sight, being without natural immutation of organ and object, is most spiritual and perfect of all the senses, and it applies to more objects. After it come hearing and then smell, which have a natural immutation on the part of their objects. Local motion is more perfect and is naturally prior to alteration, as is shown in the *Physics* (VII, 2, 260a28). Touch and taste are most material; we will speak later of their distinction. That is why the other three senses do not function through contact, lest some natural change penetrate the organ, as does happen in these two senses. . . .

4. The sense of taste, according to Aristotle, is a certain kind of touch situated in the tongue only. It is not generically different from touch, but only from touch of the kind that is spread throughout the whole body.

If, in fact, touch is but one sense because of one common character of its object [*ratio objecti*], we will have to say that taste is distinguished from touch by a characteristic difference of the immutation. Touch is subject to natural immutation and not simply a spiritual one, in regard to its organ in accord with the quality that is properly presented to it. While, taste is not necessarily subject to a natural immutation by the quality that is properly presented to it. Thus, the tongue may become sweet or bitter, but by means of a previously presented quality in which the object of taste is based, that is, by virtue of the humor that is an object of touch.

The differentiation of the interior senses (78:4)

Since nature is not deficient in necessary things, there must be as many actions of the sensitive soul as are required for the life of a perfect animal. Now, if these actions cannot be traced back to one principle, they require a diversity of potencies—for, a potency of the soul is simply the proximate principle of an operation of the soul.

However, we must keep in mind that it is requisite for the life of a perfect animal that he be able to perceive a thing in the case not only of its sensible presence but also of its absence. Otherwise, when animal movement and action follow upon perception, the animal would not be motivated to seek after some absent thing. The contrary to this is very obvious in the case of perfect animals, for they are moved forward by successive motions. In fact, they are moved toward an object that is perceived as absent. So, an animal through its sensitive soul must not only take in the species of sense objects when it is stimulated by them during their presence, but it must also keep and retain them. Now, to take in and to retain are attributed to different principles in the case of bodily things, for wet things are good at receiving impressions but bad at retaining them, and the contrary is so of dry objects. Consequently, since a sensitive potency is the act of a bodily organ, there must be a different potency to receive the species of sensible things and to keep them.

Again, we must consider that if an animal were moved only because of pleasure and pain in the sense order, it would not be necessary to posit in the animal anything more than the perception of forms within the grasp of sensation, in which forms it would delight or experience horror. But it is necessary for an animal to seek after, or flee from, things not only because they are agreeable or disagreeable in the sensory process but on account of other advantages and utilities, or on account of their harmful aspects. Thus, a sheep, seeing a wolf approaching, runs away as if from a natural enemy and not because of the unsuitable coloring or shape. Likewise, a bird collects straw not because it is a sense pleasure but because it is useful for building a nest. So, it is necessary for an animal to perceive meanings [*intentiones*] of this kind, and external sense does not perceive them. There must be some other principle for this sort of perception, because the perception of the forms of sensible objects arises from an impression from the sensible thing but not the perception of the meanings that have been mentioned.

So, the proper and common sense powers are directed to the reception of sensible forms, and the distinction of these powers will be stated later. The fancy, or imagination, a sort of treasure house of forms taken in by sensation, is directed to the retention or preservation of these forms. The estimative power is directed to the apprehension of the meanings [*intentiones*] that are not taken in by sensation. While, the memorative power, which is a sort of treasure house for such meanings, is for their retention. The mark of this is that the principle of remembering is produced in animals out of some meaning of this kind; for example, that something is harmful or suitable. And this notion of the past on which memory concentrates is numbered among meanings of this kind.

It should be borne in mind that as far as sensible forms are concerned, there is no difference between a man and other animals: they are stimulated in quite the same way by external sense objects. But there is a difference in regard to these meanings that have been mentioned, for the other animals perceive these intentions by some natural instinct only, while man does so by some sort of inference. And so, that which is called the natural power of estimation in the case of the other animals is called the cogitative power in man, for it discovers these meanings by some kind of inference. Hence, it is also called the particular reason, and the medical doctors assign a definite organ to it, that is, the middle section of the head. Indeed, it makes inferences of individual meanings, just as the intellective reason does for universal meanings.

In the area of the memorative power, man has not only memory, for the sudden recall of past items, just like the rest of the animals, but he also has reminiscence, something like a memory for searching out, in a syllogistic way, things of the past in terms of individual meanings.

As a matter of fact, Avicenna posited a fifth potency, midway between the estimative and the imaginative powers, and it combined and separated forms in the imagination; for instance, when we compose one form of a golden mountain (which we have never seen) out of the imagined form of gold and the imagined form of mountain. But this operation is not evident in other animals than man, and in his case the imaginative power is enough for this. In fact, Averroes (in a book that he wrote on *Sense and Its Object*) assigns this action to it.

So, it is necessary to posit but four interior powers in the sensitive part: namely, common sense, imagination, and the estimative and memorative powers.

That understanding is a potency of the human soul (79: 1)

We have to say, in accord with what has been previously established, that understanding is a potency of the soul and not the very essence of the soul. Indeed, the very essence of an operative reality is only the immediate principle of its operation when this operation is its act of being [*esse*]. For, since potency is related to operation as to its act, so is essence related to the act of being. Now, it is only in God that the act of understanding is the same as that of being. Hence, in God alone is understanding His essence; in the case of other intellectual beings who are creatures, the understanding is a power of the intellectual agent.

Is there a passive potency of understanding? (79: 2)

[Three meanings of passivity are explained. The first is the undergoing of an action which removes something from the passive subject that is natural to it. The second meaning is a little broader: here the passive subject undergoes an action that removes something from the subject, but this something may be either suitable or unsuitable to the nature of the passive subject.] Thirdly, a subject is said to undergo a passion, in a broad sense, from the very fact that what is in potency to something receives that to which it was in potency, without losing anything. In this sense, everything that goes from potency to act can be said to undergo a passion, even when it is made perfect. And it is in this sense that our act of understanding is a case of undergoing a passion.

Now, this is evident from this reasoning. The understanding, as has been said, performs an operation in regard to universal being. It may be considered, then, whether the intellect is in act or in potency by considering how the intellect stands in regard to universal being. In fact, there is an intellect which is related to universal being as the act of the entire range of being: this is the divine intellect, for it is the essence of God in which the entirety of being pre-exists originally and virtually, as in a first cause. So, the divine intellect is not in potency but is pure act.

However, no created intellect can be related as act to the whole universal being, for if it were, it would be an infinite being. Hence, every created intellect, by the very fact that it is such, is related to intelligible objects as potency is to act and is not the act of all intelligible things. . . .

The human intellect, which is the lowest kind of intellect, is in potency in regard to intelligible things and initially is "like a blank slate on which nothing is written," as the Philosopher says in the third book, *On the Soul* (4, 430a1). This is quite clear from the fact that in the beginning we are only potentially intelligent, while later on we become actually intelligent. And so, it is apparent that our understanding is a sort of undergoing of a passion, according to the third meaning of passion. Consequently, intellect is a passive potency.

Must man also have an agent intellect? (79: 3)

[After explaining that if we supposed with Plato that there is an actual world of intelligible forms, then there would be no need for an agent intellect, Aquinas proceeds.] However, since Aristotle did not suppose that the forms of natural beings subsist without matter, and since forms existing in matter are not actually intelligible, it followed that the natures or forms of sensible things, which we do understand, would not be actually intelligible.

Now, nothing is brought from potency to act except by means of some being that is in act. So, we have to grant some power on the side of the intellect which would make things actually intelligible, by the abstraction of species from their material conditions. This is the reason why we must posit an agent intellect.

Does each soul have an agent intellect? (79: 4)

[After criticizing earlier theories that there is but one higher agent intelligence in which all men must participate in order actually to understand, Aquinas says that there must be some power in the soul whereby sense objects are made actually intelligible, through an illumination of images retained in the imaginative power.] And we know this from experience, when we perceive ourselves abstracting universal forms from their particular conditions: this is to make things actually intelligible. Now, no action belongs to a thing unless by virtue of some principle formally inhering in it, as we said above in the treatment of the potential intellect. So, the power which is the principle of this act must be something in the soul. Thus, Aristotle compared the agent intellect to a light, that is something received in the air. On the other hand, Plato compared the separate intellect making impressions on the soul to the sun, as Themistius says in his commentary to the third book, *On the Soul* (c. 5).

But the separate intellect, according to the writings of our faith, is God Himself, the Creator of the soul, in Whom alone we shall find happiness, as will be clear later. Hence, the human soul participates in intellectual light coming from Him, according to Ps. 4: 7: *The light of thy countenance, O Lord, is signed upon us.*

Is memory another power of intellect? (79: 7)

The potencies of the soul are distinguished according to the different rational characteristics of their objects [*rationes objectorum*], in the sense that the rational character of each potency lies in its relation to that to which it is directed, and this is its object.

It was stated earlier that if any potency be ordered, in its proper character, to any object according to the general intelligibility of that object, then that potency will not be diversified on the basis of particular differences. For example, the potency of sight, which looks to its object on the basis that it is colored, is not diversified because of the characteristics of white and black. Now, the intellect looks to its object on the basis of common being, in the sense that the possible intellect is that which becomes all things. Hence, the possible

intellect is not subdivided into different powers because of
any differences pertaining to beings.

Of course, the potency of the agent intellect is different
from that of the possible intellect, because, in regard to the
same object, one principle which makes that object actual
must be an active potency, while another which is moved by
the actually existing object must be passive. Thus, the active
potency is related to its object as actual being is to potential
being; while, the passive potency is related in the contrary
way to its object, as potential being is to actual being.

And so, there can be no other difference of potencies in
the understanding than the possible and the agent. Hence,
it is clear that memory is not a different potency from the
understanding; in fact, it is proper to the character of a passive
potency to retain, just as much as to receive.

Is reason a different potency from intellect? (79: 8)

Reason and intellect cannot be different potencies in man.
This is clearly known from a consideration of their respective
acts. To understand is to apprehend intelligible truth, without any qualification. To reason is to proceed from one item
of understanding to another, in order to know intelligible
truth. . . . So, it is evident that reasoning is compared to
understanding as movement is to rest, or as acquisition is to
possession; one of these terms pertains to the imperfect, the
other to the perfect. And since motion always proceeds from
the immobile and terminates in something that is at rest, as
a consequence human reasoning in the way of investigation or
discovery proceeds from certain simply understood things,
that are first principles; and again, in the way of judgment,
it returns to first principles by an act of resolution in which
it examines what has been discovered.

Now, it is plain that to be at rest and to be moved cannot
be based on different potencies but only on one and the same
power, even in the case of natural things, for something is

moved to a place and rests in the place by virtue of the same nature. Therefore, for all the greater reason, do we understand and reason through the same potency. Thus, it is evident that reason and intellect are the same potency in man.

Are the speculative and practical intellects different potencies? (79: 11)

The practical and speculative intellects are not different potencies. The reason for this, as has been said, is that what is accidentally related to the rational character of an object, which a potency is directed to, does not produce a diversity of potencies. It is accidental to a colored object that it is a man, or large or small; hence, all things of this kind are apprehended by the same visual potency.

Now, it is accidental to something apprehended by the intellect that it be ordered toward operation, or not so ordered. However, the speculative and practical intellect differ in this way. For, the intellect is speculative when it does not order what it apprehends toward operation but to the consideration of truth alone; while, the intellect is called practical when it orders what it apprehends toward operation. This is what the Philosopher says in the third book, *On the Soul* (10, 433a14): "The speculative differs from the practical by the end." Hence, both are named from their ends: one is indeed speculative, the other is in fact practical, that is, operative.

Is appetite a special potency of the soul? (80: 1)

It is necessary to grant an appetitive potency in the soul. To make this clear, we must consider that some inclination follows upon any form whatever. Thus, fire is inclined from its form toward a higher place, and also to the production of something like itself. Now, form is present in a more exalted way in things that share in knowledge than in those that lack knowledge. Indeed, in things that lack knowledge, form is found determining each thing to one act of being appropriate to it, and this is also natural for each thing. So, a natural inclination follows upon this form and it is called a natural appetite. On the other hand, in beings that have knowledge, each one is so determined to its proper and natural act of being by its natural form that it is nevertheless receptive of the species of other things. Thus, sense receives species from all sensibles and intellect from all intelligibles, so that in this way man's soul knows all things somehow, on the basis of sensation and understanding. By this fact, knowing beings somehow draw near to God's likeness, "in which all things pre-exist," as Dionysius says (*On Divine Names*, c. 5).

Just as forms exist in a higher way in beings possessed of knowledge than the forms of physical things, so there must be in them an inclination higher than a physical inclination which is called a natural appetite. Now, this higher inclination belongs to the appetitive force of the soul, whereby an animal can desire things which it apprehends and not merely those to which it is inclined by its natural form. And so, it is necessary to place an appetitive power in the soul.

Are sensory and intellectual appetites different potencies? (80: 2)

We must say that intellectual appetite is a different potency from the sensory one. In fact, appetitive potency is a passive potency, disposed from its origin to be moved by something that is apprehended; hence, "an apprehended object of appetite is an unmoved mover, while appetite is a moved mover," as is stated in the third book, *On the Soul* (10, 433b16) and in the *Metaphysics* (XI, 7, 1072a26).

Now, passive and mobile things are distinguished by the distinction of their agents and movers, because a moving agent must be proportionate to its moved object, and the active to the passive. So, passive potency itself must get its own character from its relation to its agent. Therefore, since what is apprehended by the intellect is of a different genus from what is apprehended by the sense, it follows that intellectual appetite is a different potency from the sensitive one.

The distinction of irascible and concupiscible appetites (81: 2)

The sensitive appetite is generically one power which is called sensuality but it is subdivided into two potencies that are species of sensitive appetite, that is, the irascible and the concupiscible.

For clarification of this, it should be considered that in the sphere of corruptible natural things there must be not only an inclination toward the attainment of agreeable objects and an inclination to flee from harmful objects but also an inclination to resist corrupting and contrary things that offer an impediment to agreeable objects and provide occasions for harm. Thus, fire has a natural inclination not only to draw away from a lower place that is unsuitable for it and tend toward a higher place that is suited to it, but it also resists corrupting and impeding objects.

Therefore, since sensitive appetite is an inclination that follows upon sense apprehension (as natural appetite is an inclination that follows upon a natural form), it is necessary that there be two appetitive potencies in the sensory area. One enables the soul to be simply inclined to pursue things that are sensibly agreeable and to avoid those that are harmful, and this is called the *concupiscible* potency. The other enables the animal to resist attacking agents that oppose its beneficial objects and favor its harmful ones, and this power is called the *irascible*. Hence, it is said that its object is the difficult, because its tendency is to overcome opposed things and to rise above them.

Now, these two inclinations are not reducible to one princi-

ple, because at times the soul applies itself to painful objects,
against its concupiscible inclination, so that it may fight
against opposition in accord with its irascible inclination. So,
too, the passions of the irascible power are observed as strug-
gling against the passions of the concupiscible—for a height-
ened concupiscible feeling diminishes anger and a rising
feeling of anger decreases concupiscence, in most instances.
From this it is also evident that the irascible is in a sense the
battler and defender for the concupiscible, when it rises up
against impediments to the agreeable objects that the concupiscible desires, and against harmful agents from which the
concupiscible flees. For this reason, all irascible passions take
their start from concupiscible passions and also terminate in
them. Thus, anger is born from a painful experience and, when
this has been overcome, it terminates in joy. For this reason,
also, animals' fights are concerned with concupiscible objects,
with food and sexual matters, according to a statement in the
eighth book, *On the History of Animals* (1, 589a2).

Volitional Activity and Necessity

Necessity has many meanings. Indeed, the necessary is that
which cannot not be. Now, this may apply to a thing in one
way because of an intrinsic principle: either a material one,
as when we say that everything composed of contraries is
necessarily corruptible; or a formal one, as when we say that
it is necessary for a triangle to have three angles that equal
two right angles. Now, this is physical [*naturalis*] and absolute necessity.

In another way, necessity may apply to something that
cannot not be because of an extrinsic factor, either an end
or an agent. It is because of the end, for example, when an
agent cannot attain, or properly attain, a certain end without

Summa of Theology, I, 82, 1, c, reply to Obj. 3. Trans. V.J.B.

a given means; in this sense, food is said to be necessary to life, and a horse to a journey. This is termed *necessity of the end;* sometimes, it is also called utility. On the other hand, it is applicable to a thing, because of the agent, when someone is forced by an agent, so that he is not able to do the contrary. This is called *necessity of coercion.*

So, this necessity of coercion is completely repugnant to the will. We speak of the violent as that which is against the inclination of a thing. Now, the movement of the will is an inclination toward something. And so, just as we call something natural because it is in accord with an inclination of nature, so do we call something voluntary because it is in accord with an inclination of the will. Therefore, just as it is impossible for something to be both violent and natural, so is it impossible for something to be simply coerced, or moved by violence, and also voluntary.

On the other hand, necessity from the end is not repugnant to the will, even when it is possible to attain the end in one way only. For instance, from willing to cross the sea there arises in the will a necessity to will a boat. Likewise, even natural necessity is not repugnant to the will. In point of fact, the will must of necessity adhere to the ultimate end, which is beatitude, just as the intellect of necessity adheres to first principles; for the end functions in the sphere of operations just as a principle does in the realm of speculation, as is said in the second book of the *Physics* (9, 200a21). Indeed, what naturally and inalterably belongs to something must be the basis and principle of all its other aspects, because the nature of a thing is first in each instance and every motion proceeds from something immobile.

3. [It is objected that we control our acts by our will and yet we cannot control what is necessary; so a will-act cannot arise from necessity.] To this we must say that we are in control of our acts in the sense that we are able to choose this or that. Now, choice does not apply to the end but to "things that are for the end," as is said in the *Ethics* (II, 9, 1111b27). Hence, appetition for the ultimate end is not one of the acts that we control.

Has Man Free Choice?

We must say that man is possessed of free choice; otherwise, advice, exhortations, precepts, prohibitions, rewards, and punishments would be useless. To make this evident, we ought to consider that some things act without judgment; for instance, a stone moves downward, and likewise all noncognitive agents.

Again, other things act from judgment, but not free judgment; for example, brute animals. The sheep judges when it sees a wolf, by natural and not free judgment, that it ought to flee; for it so judges by natural instinct and not as a result of inference. The same is true of any judgment made by brute animals.

However, man acts with judgment, since he judges by means of the cognitive power that something should be avoided or attained. Instead, because this judgment does not issue from a natural instinct for a particular kind of activity but from rational inference, he therefore acts with free judgment, being able to incline toward different objectives. In fact, reasoning about contingent matters is open to opposite ways, as is evident in dialectical syllogisms and rhetorical arguments. Now, particular activities are contingent matters, and so, rational judgment on them is open to different possibilities and is not determined to one objective. And so, man must be possessed of free choice, by the very fact that he is rational.

5. [The objection is that we are the kind or quality of men that we find ourselves to be, as a result of our nature: it is natural and not free for us to seek a given end.] The quality of a man is twofold: one is natural, the other is adventitious. Now, natural quality can be understood either on the intellectual level or on the level of the body and its associated powers. So, from the fact that a man has a certain natural

Summa of Theology, I, 83, 1, c, reply to Obj. 5. Trans. V.J.B.

quality on the intellectual level, he naturally desires his ultimate end, happiness. Of course, this appetitive desire is natural and not subject to free choice, as has already been made clear.

On the level of the body and its associated powers, a man can be of a certain kind by virtue of a natural quality, inasmuch as he has a certain physical constitution, or disposition, arising from some sort of influence from corporeal causes. These latter cannot make an impression on the intellectual part because it is not the act of any body. And so, depending on the kind of person that each man is in his bodily quality, so will the end appear to him—because man is inclined to choose or repudiate something, as a result of this kind of disposition. However, these inclinations are subject to rational judgment, to which the lower appetite is obedient, as we said. Hence, this does not prejudice freedom of choice.

Moreover, adventitious qualities are items like habits and passions, and a person is more inclined to one thing than to another by them. Yet, these inclinations are also subject to rational judgment. And qualities of this kind are also subject to it because it is in our power to acquire such qualities, either by causing them or disposing ourselves to them, and also we may rid ourselves of them. So, there is nothing here that is opposed to freedom of choice.

The Union of Soul and Body

Since matter exists for the sake of form and not vice versa, we must discover, on the side of the soul, the reason why the body should be united to it. Hence it is said, in the *De anima*, that the soul is not only the form and mover of the body but also its end. Moreover, it is evident, from the preceding *Disputed Questions*, that it is natural for the human soul to be united to the body. For, although the soul is lowest in the

Disputed Question on the Soul, 8. Trans. Rowan, *The Soul*, pp. 98-102.

order of intellectual substances (as primary matter is lowest
in the order of sensible things), it does not have intelligible
species naturally impressed on it, as superior intellectual
substances have, whereby it can perform its proper operation
of intellection; but is in potency to them because it is like a
wax tablet on which nothing is written, as is said in the *De
anima*. For this reason it must receive its intelligible species
from external things through its sensory powers, which cannot perform their proper operations without bodily organs.
Consequently it is necessary for the human soul to be united
to a body.

Therefore, if the human soul is capable of being united to
a body, because it needs to receive intelligible species from
things through the intermediary of the senses, then the body,
to which the rational soul is united, must be one which can
most adequately present to the intellect those sensible species
from which are derived the intelligible species existing in
the intellect. Hence the body to which the rational soul is
united must be best disposed for sensory operation. But
although there are several sensory powers, still there is one
which is the basis of the others, namely, touch, in which every
sensible nature is principally rooted. For this reason it is also
said in the *De anima*, that an animal derives its name from
this sense. This is the reason why, when this sense is unmoved,
as occurs during sleep, all other senses are unmoved. Again,
not only are all the other senses rendered inactive by an
excess of their proper sensible [objects], as sight, for instance,
is made inoperative by very bright objects, and hearing by
too intense sounds, but so also is the sense of touch rendered
incapable of performing its proper operation [*solvuntur*] by
an excess of its sensible object, for example, excessive warmth
or cold. Therefore, since the body to which the rational soul
is united must be best disposed for a sentient nature, it must
have the most competent organ of touch. And so it is said in
the *De anima*, that among all animals we have this sense to
a greater degree, and also that one man is more adept than
another in intellectual operations as a result of this sense. For

we see that those who have tender flesh (those who are of good touch) are well-endowed mentally.

Now, since the organ of any sense must not possess actually any of the contraries of which a sense is perceptive, but must be in potency to them in order that it may be able to receive them (because the recipient must be deprived of the thing received), the case must be otherwise for the organ of touch than it is for the organs of the other senses. For the organ of sight, that is, the pupil of the eye, is deprived completely of white and of black, and of every kind of color whatever. It is similar in the case of hearing and smell. But this cannot occur in the case of the sense of touch, for touch is capable of experiencing those qualities which the animal body must be composed of, namely, hot and cold, wet and dry. For this reason it is impossible for the organ of touch to be deprived completely of its sensible objects; rather must it be reduced to a mean, because in this way it is in potency to contraries. Therefore, since the body to which the rational soul is united must be best disposed for the sense of touch, it must be brought in the fullest measure to an intermediate state by the harmonious combination [of its constituent elements and their qualities].

In this way it is evident that the total operation of an inferior nature reaches its highest peak in man as a most perfect being. For we see that the operation of nature ascends progressively from the simple elements, by blending them, until it reaches the most perfect mode of combination, which is the human body. Consequently this disposition of the human body, to which the rational soul is united, must exist in order that the body may possess the most tempered combination.

Moreover, if any one also wishes to examine the particular dispositions of the human body, he will find them ordered to this end, that man may have the best sense. Therefore man, in proportion to his size, has a larger brain than any other animal, because a good disposition of the brain is necessary for the good condition of the internal sentient powers, namely, the imagination, the memory, and the cogitative power. And in order that his operation may be freer, he has his head placed on high. For man is the only erect animal, the others, indeed, are bent over. Furthermore, in order to have this erectness and to preserve it, there must exist in the heart an abundance of heat (by which many spirits are generated) so that the body may be maintained erect by this copious amount of heat and spirits. The fact that a man stoops over when he is old is a sign of this, because his natural heat is diminished.

In the light of what is stated above, the nature of a disposition of the human body must be determined in relation to the particular [dispositions] proper to man. However, we must take into consideration that in those things which are constituted of matter, some dispositions exist in the matter itself, and that on account of these a definite matter is chosen for a definite form. There are also some dispositions which proceed from the necessary character of matter, and not from the choice of the agent; for instance, when an artisan chooses hardness in iron to make a saw in order that it may be useful for sawing. But the fact that sharpness can be given to iron, and that it can rust, results from the necessary character of matter. For the artisan would rather choose a matter in which defects are not present, if it could be found. But because it cannot be found, the artisan does not neglect to work with the available matter of this kind simply because of the defects intrinsic to such matter. This also occurs in the human body, for, likewise, whatever is combined and disposed according to parts in order that such a body may be best fitted for sentient operations, is selected in this matter by the Maker of man. But that this body is corruptible, that it may become fatigued, and have defects of this kind, follows from the necessary character of this matter. For the body, as a mixture of contraries, must be subject to such defects. Nor can any objection be raised in view of the fact that God could make it otherwise, because we do not investigate what God could make in the establishment of nature, but what the nature of things undergoes as made, as Augustine says in the *Super Genesim ad litteram*.

Moreover, it must be recognized that when God remedied these defects in man at his creation, He employed the help of original justice whereby the body was made subject completely to the soul and the soul to God, so that neither death nor passion nor any defect could affect man unless the soul were first separated from God. But when the soul turned away from God through sin, man was deprived of this gift, and is subject to the defects which are intrinsic to the nature of matter.

Incorruptibility of the Human Soul

It must necessarily be granted that the human soul is incorruptible. In proof of this we must take into consideration the fact that whatever belongs to a thing in virtue of its very nature [*per se*], cannot be taken away from it; for example, animality cannot be taken away from man, nor can the even and odd be taken away from number. Moreover it is evident that the act of existing in itself is a result of a form, for everything has its act of existing from its proper form; wherefore its act of existing can in no way be separated from its form. Therefore things composed of matter and form are corrupted by losing the form that gives them their act of existing. Moreover a form itself cannot be corrupted in itself [*per se*], but is corrupted accidentally as a result of the disintegration of the composite, inasmuch as the composite, which exists in virtue of its form, ceases to exist as a composite. This, indeed, is the case if the form is one that does not have an act of existing in itself, but is merely that by which a composite exists.

Now if there is a form having an act of existing in itself, then that form must be incorruptible. For a thing having an act of existing [*esse*] does not cease to exist unless its form

Disputed Question on the Soul, 14. Trans. Rowan, *The Soul*, pp. 181-183.

is separated from it. Hence if the thing having an act of existing is itself a form, it is impossible for its act of existing to be separated from it. Now it is evident that the principle by which a man understands is a form having its act of existing in itself and is not merely that by which something exists. For, as the Philosopher proves in the *De anima*, intellection is not an act executed by any bodily organ. The main reason why there is no bodily organ capable of receiving the sensible forms of all natural things, is that the recipient must itself be deprived of the nature of the thing received; just as the pupil of the eye does not possess the color that it sees. Now every bodily organ possesses a sensible nature. But the intellect, by which we understand, is capable of apprehending all sensible natures. Therefore its operation, namely, understanding, cannot be carried out by a bodily organ. Thus it is clear that the intellect has an operation of its own in which the body does not share. Now a thing operates in accordance with its nature [*quod est*], for things that exist of themselves have an operation of their own, whereas things that do not exist of themselves have no operation of their own. For example, heat in itself does not produce warmth, but something hot. Consequently it is evident that the intellective principle, by which man understands, has its own mode of existing superior to that of the body and not dependent upon it.

It is also evident that an intellective principle of this sort is not a thing composed of matter and form, because the species of things are received in it in an absolutely immaterial way, as is shown by the fact that the intellect knows universals, which are considered in abstraction from matter and from material conditions. The sole conclusion to be drawn from all this, then, is that the intellective principle, by which man understands, is a form having its act of existing in itself. Therefore this principle must be incorruptible. This indeed agrees with the Philosopher's dictum, that the intellect is something divine and everlasting. Now it was shown in preceding articles (Articles II and V), that the intellective principle, by which man understands, is not a substance existing apart from man but is something formally inhering in him which is either the soul or a part of the soul. Thus, from the foregoing considerations we conclude that the human soul is incorruptible.

Now all those who held that the human soul is corruptible missed some of the points we have already made. Some of these people, holding that the soul is a body, declared that it is not a form in its entirety, but a thing composed of matter and form. Others held that the intellect does not differ from the senses, and so they declared that the intellect does not operate except through a bodily organ; that it does not have a higher mode of existence than that of the body, and, therefore, that it is not a form having an act of existing in its own right. Still others held that the intellect, by which man understands, is a separate substance. But the falsity of all these opinions has been demonstrated in preceding articles. It therefore remains that the human soul is incorruptible.

RECOMMENDED READINGS

ALLERS, R. "Intellectual Cognition," *Essays in Thomism*. New York: Sheed and Ward, 1942, pp. 39-62.

BAKER, R. R. *The Thomistic Theory of the Passions and Their Influence on the Will*. Notre Dame: University of Notre Dame, 1941.

BRENNAN, R. E. *Thomistic Psychology*. New York: Macmillan, 1941.

DONCEEL, J. *Philosophical Psychology*. Milwaukee: Bruce, 1948.

KLUBERTANZ, G. P. *The Discursive Power*. St. Louis: The Modern Schoolman, 1952.

———. *Philosophy of Human Nature*. New York: Appleton-Century-Crofts, 1953.

NAUS, J. E. *The Nature of the Practical Intellect*. Rome: Gregorian University, 1959.

PEGIS, A. C. *St. Thomas and the Problem of the Soul in the Thirteenth Century*. Toronto: Institute of Mediaeval Studies, 1934.

RENARD, H. *The Philosophy of Man*. Milwaukee: Bruce, 1948.

RYAN, E. J. *The Role of the 'Sensus Communis' in the Psychology of St. Thomas*. Carthagena, Ohio: Messenger Press, 1951.

THOMAS, I. "Introduction," to *Aristotle's de Anima with the Commentary of St. Thomas Aquinas*. New Haven: Yale University Press, 1951, pp. 5-37.

IV. Reality and First Philosophy

Foreword

THE METAPHYSICS OF THOMAS AQUINAS represents an effort to understand reality on a higher level than that achieved in the philosophy of nature. All things that exist have at least that fact in common: they are. What does it mean, to exist, to be something? As Aquinas says, the first philosophers of Greece thought that *to be* means *to be a body*. Many people still think so today.

However, Aquinas suggests that there is a radical difference between *what* a thing is, and *that* it is. The former is a question of essence, the latter of existence. They are not even known in the same way: one conceives essences (dogs, wood, water); it is even possible to conceive an essence (say, a horse with fifty legs) without being bothered about whether it exists or not. On the other hand, one judges that a given thing exists, or that it does not. If we do not attend to what exists, there is only one meaning for existence, that is, *to be*. Now, it can be argued, as Aquinas does, that to be is not restricted to any class of things, not even to the class of all material things. This is the famous "judgment of separation" which is discussed in the *Exposition* of Boethius' little treatise *On the Trinity*. The judgment separates the meaning of "to be" from materiality. It is an important foundation stone in Thomistic metaphysics, because it opens the way to the consideration of beings that may be real but not material.

If being does not have to be material, there are certain characteristics that it must have in all its instances. These are the aspects of being that transcend all classifications into

143

distinct species or genera. In all cases, a being is one, true, and good. This theory of the transcendental properties of being in general is investigated especially in the questions *On Truth*.

Another key development in Aquinas' first philosophy is the theory of potency and act. Whatever *is* exists actually, in act. The correlative of this existential act is the potency or capacity to be. Essences are such potencies. On another level of analysis, whatever *is done* is an action, or operative act, and its correlative is operative potency. These two principles, act and potency, are used to explain the constitution and activities of immaterial as well as material beings. God, however, is regarded as Pure Act: He cannot exist more fully than He does, and so He contains no potency for further actuation in the order of existence. But God exercises activities and man thinks of Him as endowed with operative potencies. It is in the questions *On the Power of God* that this point is studied.

The theory of causality is also raised to the metaphysical level by Aquinas. He uses the Aristotelian four causes (material, formal, efficient, and final) but places special emphasis on final causality. The finality of beings is thoroughly treated in the opening chapters of the third book of *Summa contra Gentiles*.

The analogy of being is another cardinal teaching. It is developed in the *Exposition of the Metaphysics* and at many points in the *Summa of Theology*. In some sense, all beings, from the highest to the lowest, are alike in the fact that they are. However, beings differ in their essences and as individuals. Since every finite being is the actualization of some essence, we may think of what is common in all beings as the real relation between essence and existence. These relations vary, because many different essences exist, but they are not entirely dissimilar. A dog's existence fits a dog's essence; a man's existence fits a human essence. Being, then, is analogical; it represents a widely varying plurality of *ratios* (of essence to existence), which are in turn related to each other in some understandable proportion. God is the limit case; His essence is related to His existence by way of identity. This is being at its fullest.

There is little question that Aquinas' metaphysics is difficult and complex. It is not identical with the first philosophy of Aristotle, though it does derive important notions from Aristotelianism. It well repays close study, for Thomas Aquinas made one of the greatest human efforts to penetrate the mysteries of ultimate reality and existence.

An Introduction to Metaphysics

All sciences and arts are directed in an orderly way toward one thing, that is, to the perfection of man which is his happiness. That is why one of them must be the ruler of all the others. It is justified in taking the name *wisdom;* for it is the function of the wise to rule others.

Now, it is possible to consider what this science is, and what are its objects, if one takes a careful look at the way in which anyone is suited to be a ruler. Men with strong bodies and weak intellects are naturally fitted for obedience, but men of powerful understanding are naturally the rulers and masters of others. So, too, that science should be the ruler of the others which is most intellectual. This is the science that deals with the greatest objects of understanding.

Things may be considered to be the greatest objects of understanding from three points of view. The first is in relation to the process of understanding. Here, the greatest objects of understanding are the first causes; for, those things are greater in the order of intelligibility which are principles from which a scientist may reason to true conclusions, known with certitude. The knowledge of the highest causes is, then, wisdom. This is the knowledge that is the ruler of the other sciences.

Another way of getting at the meaning of the greatest objects of the intellect is to compare the objects of the intel-

Exposition of Aristotle's Metaphysics, Prologue. Trans. V.J.B.

lect with those of the senses. The objects of sense knowledge are particulars; those of intellectual knowledge are
universals. But there are degrees of universality. The highest
intellectual knowledge considers the most universal principles.
Now, these are: being, and the items that are associated
with it, such as one and many, potency and act. It is not
right for these to be left undetermined; a full knowledge of
the objects of the special sciences requires that we first
understand these most universal principles.

Moreover, they should not be treated in any one of the
special sciences; for, since each and every genus of things
requires these universal principles in order to be known,
they might with equal right be treated in every particular
science. The point is that they should be treated in one
general science, which is the ruler of the other sciences, because it is the most intellectual.

Finally, we can grasp the character of the greatest objects
of the intellect by considering intellectual knowledge itself.
The more a thing is separated from matter, the more understandable it is. Indeed, the object and the power of understanding must be brought into proportion, they must become
members of one genus, since the understanding and what is
understood are one in act.

The greatest objects of understanding, then, are those
most separated from matter. Some intelligible objects are
only separated by intellectual abstraction from their signate
matter. That is to say, the intellect of the natural scientist
considers many of the physical qualities and the quantitative
aspects of bodies—only prescinding from their individual
differences which, in the concrete, defy understanding and
science. Other intelligible objects, those of the mathematical
scientist, are separated in reasoning from their complex
physical qualities but not from their quantitative properties,
nor from the imaginative representations which are the quasi-
material objects of the mathematician. But there is a third
kind of intelligible object: some beings exist apart from
matter. These are God and intellectual beings. The science

that considers these beings is obviously the most intellectual one; it is thus the leader and ruler of the other sciences.

Now, the consideration of these three kinds of objects [existentially immaterial substances, the most universal aspects of being, and the first causes] should be assigned to one science, not to diverse ones. For, the separate substances that we mentioned are the universal and primary causes of existing being. It is the function of the same science to consider the appropriate causes for each genus and also the genus itself; the natural philosopher, for instance, considers the principles of any natural body. Hence, the consideration of separate substances and of being in general (which functions as the genus for which the aforementioned are the common and universal causes) must belong to the same science.

It is evident from this that although this science considers these three items, it does not think of each of them as its subject; its subject is simply being in general. For, the subject is that within a science whose causes and general properties we investigate. The causes that we search after, in any class, are not the subject matter. Rather, the knowledge of the causes of any kind of things is the end toward which scientific consideration is directed. Now, although the subject of this science is being in general, the science as a whole is concerned with those things that are existentially, or as a result of rational effort, separated from matter. Those things are called separated, in being and in reason, not only if they are the sort of things that could never be in matter (such as God and the intellectual substances), but also if they could exist without matter, as is the case with being in general. Of course, this would not be so, if their very existence depended on matter.

So, there are three names suggesting the perfection of this science; and they are distinguished according to the aforementioned three objects. It is called *divine science* or *theology*, because it deals with the separated substances. It is called *metaphysics*, because it considers being and its properties. These properties that transcend physical classifications are

discovered in the process of analysis, in which the more
general comes after the less general. Again, it is called *first
philosophy*, because it deals with the primary causes of
things. Thus, we see what is the subject of this science, and
by what name it is designated.

What Are the Subjects of First Philosophy?

For the clarification of this question it is necessary to know
which science ought to be called divine science. It is to be
noted that if every science considers some generic subject,
then it should consider the principles of this genus; because
science is only brought to perfection by the knowledge of
principles. This is evident from the Philosopher, at the
beginning of his *Physics* (I, 1, 184a12).

But there are two kinds of principles. There are some
that are both complete natures in themselves and also, in
spite of this, principles of other beings. Thus, the celestial
bodies are principles for lower bodies, and simple [elemental]
bodies are principles for bodies composed of the elements.
So these principles are not only considered in the sciences as
principles, they are also considered as existing things in
themselves. For this reason, they are treated not only in the
science that deals with the things for which they function
as principles, but they also occupy an essentially separate
science—just as there is a certain division of natural science
for the celestial bodies, apart from the section in which
bodies composed of the elements are treated.

Then, there is another type of principles that are not
complete natures in themselves but are only principles for
natures: as unity for number, a point for a line, and form
and matter for a physical body. As a consequence, principles
of this kind are treated only in the science that is concerned
with the things for which they function as principles.

Now, just as there are certain common principles for each

Exposition of Boethius on the Trinity, V, 4, c. Trans. V.J.B.

definite genus which apply extensively to all the principles of a given genus, so also do all beings, by virtue of their sharing in being, have certain principles that are principles for all beings. In fact, according to Avicenna in his *Sufficiencies (Physics, I, 2, fol. 14r), these principles can be called common in two senses. One way is by predication (for instance, I may say: form is common to all forms because it is predicable of any of them); the other way is by causality (thus, we may say that the sun is numerically one principle for all things subject to generation). There are, then, for all beings principles that are common not only in the first way (which the Philosopher cites in the *Metaphysics*, XII, 4, saying that all beings have the same principles analogically) but also in the second way, in the sense that there are certain things existing in their own numerical identity that are principles for all things. Thus, for example, the principles of accidents are reducible to the principles of substance, and the principles of corruptible substances are reducible to incorruptible substances. And so, in a given level and order, are all beings reducible to certain principles.

Now, since that which is the principle of actual being for all things must be a greatest being (as is said in the *Metaphysics*, II, 1, 993b25), therefore principles of this kind have to be most perfect. For this reason, they must be in act in the fullest manner, such that they have nothing or the very minimum of potency; because act is prior to, and more important than, potency (as is said in the *Metaphysics*, IX, 8–9, 1049b5–1051a4). Again for this reason, they must exist without matter, for it is potential, and without motion, for it is the actuation of something that is still in potency. Now, principles like this are divine things, "for if the divine exists anywhere it must be in such a nature," because "exists" applies in the most proper sense to the immaterial and immobile, as is stated in the sixth book of the *Metaphysics* (1, 1026a20).

Therefore, divine things of this kind, because they are principles for all beings and yet are complete natures in themselves, can be treated from two points of view: first, in that they are common principles for all beings; second, as they are things in themselves. Now, although these first principles are most knowable in themselves, nevertheless our understanding stands in relation to them as the eye of a nocturnal animal to the light of the sun (as is stated in the *Metaphysics*, II, 1, 993b9). So, we are not able to attain to them by the light of the natural reason, except when we are drawn up to them by means of their effects. The philosophers have reached them in this way, as is clear from Rom. 1:20: *For the invisible things of God are clearly seen, being understood through the things that are made.* Hence, divine things of this kind are only treated by the philosophers insofar as they are the principles of all things. Therefore, they are investigated in that teaching in which items that are common to all beings are placed, for it has as its subject being insofar as it is being. Now, this science is called the divine science by them.

However, there is another way of knowing these things, not as they are manifested through their effects but as they manifest themselves. The Apostle [Paul] in I Cor. 2:11-12 describes this way *the things that are of God, no man knoweth, but the Spirit of God;* and again in the same place (2:10): *But to us God hath revealed them by His Spirit.* So, divine things are studied in this way, according as they subsist in themselves and not merely as they are the principles of things.

And so, theology or divine science is of two kinds. One, in which divine things are considered not as the subject of the science but as principles of the subject, is the kind of theology that the philosophers seek. The other, which considers these divine things themselves in their own right as the subject of a science, is the kind of theology that is handed down in sacred Scripture.

Now, both deal with things that are separate from matter and motion as far as their act of being is concerned; but they do it differently, according to the two possible ways that something can be separated in being from matter and motion. One way is such that it is proper to the character of the thing called separate that it could in no way exist in matter and motion; thus are God and the angels said to be separate from matter and motion. The other way is such that it is not essential to the character of the thing that it be in matter and motion, though sometimes it may be found in matter and motion. In this way, being, substance, potency, and act are separate from matter and motion; because they do not depend for their actual being on matter and motion, as mathematical objects have customarily depended since they never can exist except in matter, although they could be understood apart from sensible matter. So, philosophical theology studies things that are separate in the second way as its subjects, but it treats things that are separate in the first way as principles of its subject. On the other hand, sacred Scripture treats things that are separate in the first way as its subjects, even though some things that are in matter and motion are discussed in it, to the extent that the explanation of divine things requires.

How Natural Philosophy Precedes Metaphysics

Although the divine science [i.e., metaphysics] is primary among all sciences, still, in the order of nature as far as we are concerned, the other sciences are prior. Indeed, as Avicenna says at the beginning of his *Metaphysics*, the order proper to this science is that it be learned after the natural sciences, in which many points that this science uses are determined; for example, the process of generation and corruption, motion, and similar items. Likewise, it must come after mathematics. For the knowledge of substances that exist apart from matter, this science needs to know the number and ordered relations of the celestial orbs; this is not possible without astronomy, for which the entire mathe-

Exposition of Boethius on the Trinity, V, 1, reply to Obj. 9. Trans. V.J.B.

matics is a prerequisite. The other sciences, like musical theory and morals, and the like, are required for its full development.

Nor does this necessarily imply a vicious circle, in the sense that it is based on conclusions proved in the other sciences and yet it proves the principles of the other sciences. In fact, the principles that another science, say, natural philosophy, takes from first philosophy do not prove the points which the first philosopher takes from the natural philosopher; rather, they are proved by means of different principles that are self-evident. Likewise, the first philosopher does not prove the principles that he hands over to the philosopher of nature by means of principles that he gets from him, but by means of other self-evident principles. Thus, there is no circle involved in its definition.

Furthermore, the events perceptible to the senses, from which natural-philosophy demonstrations come, are more easily known by us in the beginning. But when we have reached the knowledge of the primary causes by means of them, then from these causes it will become apparent to us what is the essential explanation for these events on which factual demonstrations were based. And thus, natural science contributes something to divine science, and yet its own principles come to be known by means of the latter. That is the reason why Boethius puts divine science last, because it is last in relation to us.

Being, Essence, and the Act of Existing

It should be known that being by itself is spoken of in two ways, as the Philosopher says in the fifth book of the *Metaphysics*. In the first way it is divided into the ten categories; in the second way it signifies the truth of propositions. The difference between the two is that in the

---

On Being and Essence, Ch. 1. Trans. Maurer, *On Being and Essence*, pp. 26-29.

second sense we can call everything being about which we can form an affirmative proposition, even though it may posit nothing in reality. Thus, we call even privations and negations beings, for we say that affirmation *is* opposed to negation, and that blindness *is* in the eye. But, in the first sense, only that can be called being which posits something in reality. In this sense of the word, then, blindness and the like are not beings.

So, the term *essence* is not taken from being in the second sense of the word. For, as it is clear in the case of privations, in that sense we call some things beings which do not have an essence. Essence is rather taken from being in the first sense. That is the reason why the Commentator declares in the same place that being in the first sense of the word is that which signifies the essence of a thing.

And because, as we have said, being in this sense is divided into the ten categories, essence must signify something common to all natures, through which natures different beings are placed in different genera and species. For example, humanity is the essence of man, and so with other things.

Moreover, since that by which a thing is constituted in its proper genus and species is what is signified by the definition expressing what the thing is, philosophers have taken to using the word *quiddity* for the word *essence*. The Philosopher frequently calls this the *what a thing was to be,* in other words, that by which a thing is a *what.* It is also called *form,* inasmuch as form signifies the determination of each thing, as Avicenna says in the second book of his *Metaphysics.* Furthermore, it is called by another name, namely, *nature,* using nature in the first of the four senses given by Boethius in the treatise *De Duabus Naturis.* In this sense every being which the intellect can in any way grasp is called a nature; for a thing is intelligible only by its definition and essence. Thus the Philosopher, too, declares in the fifth book of the *Metaphysics* that every substance is a nature. In this sense of the word, however, nature seems to mean the thing's essence as ordered to its proper activity, for nothing is without its proper activity. The term *quiddity*, on the other hand, is derived from what the definition signifies, while essence means that through which and in which a being has its act of existing [*esse*].

Now, being is predicated absolutely and primarily of substances; it is predicated secondarily and as in a qualified sense of accidents. For this reason essence is truly and properly in substances, but in accidents it is present in a certain manner and in a qualified sense.

Some substances, furthermore, are simple and some composite, and essence is in both. But, in simple substances it is present more truly and excellently, inasmuch as they also have the act of existing [*esse*] in a more excellent way; for they are the cause of composite substances—at least this is true of God, the first of the simple substances. But, because the essences of the simple substances are more hidden from us, we ought to begin with the essences of composite substances, so that, beginning with easier matters, we may advance more suitably in knowledge.

Importance of the Act of Being

This act of being [*esse*] that I am talking about is the most perfect of all things; and this is obvious from the fact that act is always more perfect than potency. Now, no signate form whatever is actually understood unless by virtue of the fact that actual being [*esse*] is given. For, humanity, or the form of fire, can be considered as existing in the potency of matter, or even as in the power of an agent, or even as present in understanding—but the fact that it has actual being [*esse*] makes it actually existent.

Hence, it is clear that this item that I call actual being [*esse*] is the actuality of all acts, and for this reason is the perfection of all perfections. Nor should this be understood

Disputed Questions on the Power of God, VII, 2, reply to Obj. 9. Trans. V.J.B.

to mean that to this item that I call actual being there is something added that is more formal than it, determining it as act does potency. For actual being, in this sense, is essentially different from that to which an addition is made for the sake of determination. Nothing can be added to the act of being [*esse*] that is extraneous to it, since nothing is extraneous to it except nonbeing, and that can be neither form nor matter.

Hence, the act of being is not so determined by something else, as act is by potency. Indeed, in the very definition of forms their appropriate matter is included, in place of specific differences, as for instance when we speak of the soul as the act of an organic physical body.

It is in this way that this act of being is distinguished from that act of being, such and such a nature. This is why Dionysius says (*On Divine Names*, c. 5) that although living things are more important than those which merely exist, still, to be is more noble than to live; for, living things do not merely possess life: right along with life they also have actual being.

Essential Natures: Universal or Individual?

Since that which has the nature of a genus, species or difference is predicated of this particular designated thing, the essence, expressed as a part (for instance, by the word *humanity* or *animality*), cannot possibly have the nature of a universal, that is, of a genus or species. Thus, Avicenna declares that rationality is not a difference, but the originative source of a difference. For the same reason humanity is not a species nor animality a genus. Similarly, we cannot say that essense has the nature of a genus or species, if, as the Platonists held, essence is something existing outside particular things, because then the genus and species would not

On Being and Essence, Ch. 3. Trans. Maurer, *On Being and Essence*, pp. 39–42.

be predicated of the particular individual. For we cannot say that Socrates is something separated from himself. What is more, something separated would be of no help in knowing the particular being. We conclude, therefore, that the essence has the nature of a genus or species insofar as it is expressed after the manner of a whole, for instance, by the word *man* or *animal*, as containing implicitly and indistinctly everything that is in the individual.

If nature or essence is understood in this sense, we can consider it in two ways. First, we can consider it according to its proper meaning, which is to consider it absolutely. In this sense, nothing is true of it except what belongs to it as such; whatever else is attributed to it, the attribution is false. For example, to man as man belong rational, animal and whatever else his definition includes, whereas white or black, or anything of this sort, which is not included in the concept of humanity, does not belong to man as man. If someone should ask, then, whether the nature so considered can be called *one* or *many*, neither should be granted, because both are outside the concept of humanity and both can be added to it. If plurality were included in the concept of humanity, it could never be one, although it is one inasmuch as it is present in Socrates. Similarly, if unity were contained in its concept, then Socrates' and Plato's nature would be one and the same, and it could not be multiplied in many individuals.

Nature or essence is considered in a second way with reference to the act of existing [*esse*] it has in this or that individual. When the nature is so considered, something is attributed to it accidentally by reason of the thing in which it exists; for instance, we say that man is white because Socrates is white, although whiteness does not pertain to man as man.

This nature has a twofold act of existing, one in individual things, the other in the mind; and according to both modes of existing, accidents accompany the nature. In individual beings, moreover, it has numerous acts of existing corresponding to the diversity of individuals. Yet, the nature itself, considered properly—that is to say, absolutely—demands none of these acts of existing. It is false to say that the nature of man as such exists in this individual man, because, if existing in this individual belonged to man as man, it would never exist outside this individual. Similarly, if it belonged to man as man not to exist in this individual, human nature would never exist in it. It is true to say, however, that it does not belong to man as man to exist in this or that individual, or in the intellect. Considered in itself, the nature of man thus clearly abstracts from every act of existing, but in such a way that none may be excluded from it. And it is the nature considered in this way that we predicate of all individual beings.

Yet, we cannot say that universality belongs to the nature so considered, because unity and community belong to the notion of a universal. Now, neither of these belongs to human nature considered absolutely. If community were included in the notion of man, in whatever being humanity were found, community would be found. This is false, because we do not find any community in Socrates; everything in him is individuated. So, too, we cannot say that human nature as it exists in individual men has the character of a genus or species. We do not find human nature in them with a unity such that it constitutes one essence belonging to all, which the notion of a universal requires.

Human nature, then, can have the character of a species only as it exists in the intellect. Human nature itself exists in the intellect in abstraction from all individual conditions, and it thus has a uniform relation to all individual men outside the intellect, being equally the likeness of all and leading to a knowledge of all insofar as they are men. And from the fact that the nature has such a relation to all individual men, the intellect forms the notion of species and attributes it to the nature. That is why the Commentator asserts, in his exposition on the first book of the *De Anima*, that it is the intellect which causes universality in things. Avicenna also says this in his *Metaphysics*. And although the nature existing in the intellect has the character of a uni-

versal from its relation to things outside the intellect, since
it is one likeness of them all, nevertheless, as it exists in this
or that intellect, it is a certain particular species apprehended
by the intellect. The Commentator was thus clearly in error
in his exposition on the third book of the *De Anima,* for he
wanted to conclude that the intellect is one in all men from
the universality of the form in the intellect. For, the universality of that form does not come from the existence which
it has in the intellect, but from its relation to things whose
likeness it is. In the same way, if a material statue represented
a great number of men, it is agreed that the statue's image
or likeness would have an individual and proper act of existing
as it existed in this particular matter, but it would have
community inasmuch as it would be the common representative of many men.

Demonstration of God's Existence from Motion

In reference to the unity of the divine essence, we must first
show that God exists. This is obvious on the basis of reason.
For, we see that all things that are moved are moved by
others, lower things by higher ones. The elements, for instance, are moved by the celestial bodies, and among the
elements, the stronger move the weaker. Even among the
celestial bodies, the lower ones are moved by the higher ones.

Now, this procedure cannot go on to infinity. Since everything that is moved functions as a sort of instrument of the
first mover, if there were no first mover, then whatever
things are in motion would be simply instruments. Of course,
if an infinite series of movers and things moved were possible,
with no first mover, then the whole infinity of movers and
things moved would be instruments. Now, it is ridiculous,
even to unlearned people, to suppose that instruments are

Compendium of Theology, Part I, Ch. 3. Trans. V.J.B.

moved but not by any principal agent. For, this would be like supposing that the construction of a box or bed could be accomplished by putting a saw or a hatchet to work without any carpenter to use them. Therefore, there must be a first mover existing above all—and this we call God.

The Cause of Existing: God

Now, whatever belongs to a being is either caused by the principles of its nature, as the capability of laughter in man, or it comes to it from some extrinsic principle, as light in the air from the sun's influence. But it is impossible that the act of existing be caused by a thing's form or its quiddity (I say *caused* as by an efficient cause); for then something would be the cause of itself and would bring itself into existence— which is impossible. Everything, then, which is such that its act of existing is other than its nature must needs have its act of existing from something else. And since every being which exists through another is reduced, as to its first cause, to one existing in virtue of itself, there must be some being which is the cause of the existing of all things because it itself is the act of existing alone. If that were not so, we would proceed to infinity among causes, since, as we have said, every being which is not the act of existing alone has a cause of its existence. Evidently, then, an intelligence is form and act of existing, and it has its act of existing from the First Being which is simply the act of existing. This is the First Cause, God. . . .

There is a being, God, whose essence is His very act of existing. That explains why we find some philosophers asserting that God does not have a quiddity or essence, because His essence is not other than His act of existing. From this it follows that He is not in a genus, for the quiddity of anything in a genus must be other than its act of existing, since

On Being and Essence, Ch. 4-5. Trans. Maurer, *On Being and Essence*, pp. 47, 50-51.

the different beings within a genus or species have the same
generic or specific quiddity or nature, whereas their act of
existing is different.

If we say, moreover, that God is purely and simply the
act of existing, we need not fall into the mistake of those
who assert that God is that universal existence whereby each
thing formally exists. The act of existing which is God is
such that no addition can be made to it. Consequently, in
virtue of its very purity it is the act of existing distinct from
every act of existing. . . .

Similarly, although God is simply the act of existing, it is
not necessary that He lack the other perfections or excellences. On the contrary, He possesses all perfections of all
genera of beings; so He is said to be unqualifiedly perfect, as
the Philosopher and Commentator assert in the fifth book of
the *Metaphysics*. But He possesses these perfections in a
more excellent way than other things, for in Him they are
one, while in other things they are diversified. The reason
for this is that all these perfections are His according to His
simple act of existing. So, too, if someone through one
quality could perform the operations of all the qualities, he
would in that one quality possess all the qualities. In the
same way, God possesses all perfections in His very act of
existing.

Being as One, True, and Good

Among these four first items, being is most especially the
first, and so it should be positively predicated. Indeed,
negation or privation cannot be the first that is conceived
by the intellect, since *what* is negated or deprived is always
needed for the understanding of the negation or privation.

Now, the other three must add to being something that
does not contract being; for, if they were to contract being,

Disputed Questions on the Power of God, IX, 7, reply to Obj. 6. Trans.
V.J.B.

they would not in that case be first. Of course, this is impossible unless they add something according to reason only. Now, this is either a negation (which one does add, as has been said), or a relation, or something that is originated in order to be referred universally to being. Such is either the intellect, to which the *true* implies a relation, or the appetite, to which the *good* implies a relation, for the good is what all desire, as is said in the first book of the *Ethics*.

Being and Good: Qualified and Unqualified

Although a good thing and a being are the same in reality, yet something is not in the same way called "being" without qualification [*simpliciter*] and "good" without qualification, because they differ in meaning. Since being means that something is properly in act, and since act has properly an ordered relation to potency, in this sense something is called being without qualification by virtue of the fact that it is first distinguished from that which is merely in potency. Now, this is the substantial act of being of any sort of thing; consequently, anything whatever is called a being without qualification, by virtue of its substantial act of being [*esse*].

On the other hand, something is said to be in a qualified way [*secundum quid*] because of further added acts. For instance, to be white means to be in a qualified way; indeed, to be white does not remove the condition of being simply in potency, because it occurs to a thing that is already in actual, previous existence.

However, good implies the essential notion of something perfect, that is an object of appetite, and consequently, it suggests the character of something that is ultimate. Hence, that which is ultimately perfect is called good in the unqualified sense. Something that does not possess the ultimate perfection that it ought to have, even though it possess some

Summa of Theology, I, 5, 1, reply to Obj. 1. Trans. V.J.B.

perfection by virtue of the fact that it actually exists, is nevertheless not called perfect without qualification, or good in an unqualified sense, but only in a qualified way.

And so, something is called a being in the unqualified sense but a qualified good, by virtue of the first act of being, which is the substantial one; but by virtue of ultimate act, a thing is called a qualified being but an unqualified good. Thus, Boethius' statement that "in the realm of things, it is a different matter for them to be good, and for them to be" (*De Hebdomadibus*, PL 64, 1312) should be related to the act of being good and the unqualified act of being, because something is a being without qualification on the basis of first act, while it is good without qualification according to ultimate act. And yet, it is somewhat good by virtue of its first act and something of a being by virtue of its ultimate act.

On Physical and Moral Evil

According to Augustine (*Enchiridion*, 1), God is so good that He would never permit anything evil to occur, unless He were powerful enough to be able to draw good from every instance of evil. Hence, the fact that evils appear in the world is due neither to impotence nor ignorance on the part of God. Rather, it is due to the ordering of His wisdom and the magnitude of His goodness, from which proceeds the multiplication of the various degrees of goodness in things, many of which would be lacking if He permitted no evil to occur. There would not be the good of patience, unless the evil of persecution occurred; nor would there be the good of the maintenance of life in the lion, unless there were the evil of the destruction of animals on whom he lives. . . .

If effects are related to their proper causes, evil is but rarely found. This is apparent among things in nature. Some wrong or evil does not occur in natural activity, unless be-

Disputed Questions on the Power of God, III, 6, reply to Obj. 4, 5. Trans. J.B.

cause of an impediment interfering with the agent cause. Now, this happens in few cases, such as monsters in nature, and the like.

In the sphere of voluntary actions, evil seems to occur more frequently in deeds than in the making of things; because art does not fail, except in rare instances, for it imitates nature. But in the case of actions with which virtue and vice are concerned, there are two appetites as movers, the rational and the sensory. And what is good in relation to one appetite may be evil in relation to the other. For example, to seek pleasures is good in regard to sensory appetite, as concupiscent, but may be evil in relation to rational appetite. Now, since more people depend on sensation than on reason, the result is that more evil men are found than good. Yet, in the case of a person who follows his rational appetite, most of his actions turn out well and only a few evil.

Analogy in Predication and in Being

It is impossible for something to be predicated of God and creatures univocally, because every effect that is not equal to the power of the agent-cause receives the likeness of the agent not according to the same ratio but in a deficient manner. Thus, what is present in the effects in a divided and multiple fashion, in the cause is found simply and in the same way. The sun, for example, through one power produces many types and varieties of forms in things here below. Similarly, as was said above, all the real perfections that are present in things in a divided and multiple manner pre-exist in God in a unified way.

So, too, when any name pertaining to perfection is predicated of a creature, it signifies this perfection as distinct on the basis of a principle of distinction from other things. For instance, when the word "wise" is predicated of man, we mean some perfection distinct from the essence of man,

Summa of Theology, I, 13, 5, c, reply to Obj. 1. Trans. V.J.B.

and from his potency and his act of being, and from all such items. However, when we predicate this name of God, our purpose is not to signify something distinct from His essence, or power, or act of being. Thus, when this name "wise" is predicated of man, in some fashion it circumscribes and includes in its intelligibility the thing that is signified; this is not so when it is predicated of God; instead, it leaves the reality that is signified as not comprehended and as exceeding the meaning of this name. It is consequently obvious that this name "wise" is not predicated of God and of man according to the same intelligibility [*ratio*]. The same explanation applies to other names. Hence, no name is univocally predicated of God and creatures.

Yet, it is not a case of pure equivocation, as some thinkers have asserted. If it were, nothing could be known about God from the side of creatures, nor could any demonstration be made. Instead, the fallacy of equivocation would always occur. Now, this is both contrary to the Philosopher, who proves many things demonstratively concerning God, and also against the Apostle, who says, Rom. 1:20, *The invisible things of God are clearly seen being understood by the things that are made.*

Therefore, we have to say that names of this kind are predicated of God and creatures by analogy, that is, proportion. Now, this occurs in the case of names in two ways: either because many things have a proportional relation to one item (as "healthy" is predicated of medicine and urine, insofar as both have a direct relation and proportion to animal health, of which the latter is a sign, while the former is a cause); or because of the fact that one item has a proportional relation to the other (as "healthy" is predicated of medicine and an animal, in the sense that medicine is the cause of the health that is found in the animal). In this latter way, some things are said about God and creatures analogically, and not merely equivocally, and not univocally.

Indeed, we cannot name God unless from creatures, as was said before. And so, whatever is said about God and creatures is expressed on the basis of some orderly relation of the creature to God, as to a principle and a cause in which all the perfections of things pre-exist in an eminent manner. Now, this way of being common is midway between pure equivocation and simple univocity. In fact, in the case of analogical predications, there is neither one intelligibility [*ratio*], as happens in univocal predications, nor is there complete diversity, as in the case of equivocal predicates. Instead, the name that is so predicated plurally signifies different proportional relations to some one item; for example, "healthy" as predicated of urine signifies the mark of animal health, but predicated of medicine it signifies the cause of the same health.

In answer to the first objection, it should be said that although equivocal predications should be reduced to univocal ones, nevertheless in the order of actions the nonunivocal agent necessarily precedes the univocal agent. In fact, a nonunivocal agent is the universal cause of the generation of all men. A univocal agent is not the universal agent cause of the whole species, otherwise it would be the cause of itself, for it is contained within the species; instead, it is the particular cause in relation to this individual which it establishes as a participant in the species. Therefore, the universal cause of the whole species is not a univocal agent. Of course, a universal cause is prior to a particular one.

Now, this universal agent, though not univocal, is not wholly equivocal, for then it would not make a product like to itself. Rather, it can be called an analogical agent, just as all univocal predications are reduced to one that is primary, not univocal but analogical, and it is being.

Proportion and Analogy

Proportion is nothing but a relation of two items that are in mutual agreement in some point, on the basis of their further agreement or disagreement. Now, to be in agreement

Exposition of Boethius on the Trinity, I, 2, c, reply to Obj. 3. Trans. V.J.B.

can be understood in two ways. One way depends on the fact that they agree within the same genus of quantity or quality; for example, the relation of surface to surface, or of number to number, insofar as one exceeds the other or equals it, or also of one instance of heat to another case of heat. Now, there can be no proportion between God and creature in this way, since they do not agree within any genus.

In a second way, agreement can be understood in the sense that they agree in a certain order; it is thus that a proportion is observed between matter and form, the maker and his product, and other pairs like these. Such a proportion is required between a cognitive power and its knowable object, since the object stands as the act of the knowing potency. So, too, is the proportion of the creature to God, as an effect is to its cause and a knower to his object. However, because of the infinite transcendence of the Creator over the creature, there is no proportion of the creature to the Creator, such that it might receive His influence according to full strength, or might know Him perfectly as He has perfect knowledge of Himself.

Analogy Between God and Finite Beings

It is impossible to say that something is predicated univocally of a creature and God because in all univocal predication the nature signified by the name is common to those of whom the univocal predication is made. Hence, from the point of view of the nature signified by the predicate, the subjects of the univocal predication are equal, even though from the point of view of its real existence one may take precedence over another. For example, all numbers are equal from the point of view of the nature of number, even though, by the nature of things, one number is naturally prior to another. No matter how much a creature imitates God, however, a point cannot be reached where something would belong to it for the same reason it belongs to God. For things which have the same formal characters but are in separate subjects are common to the same subjects in regard to substance or quiddity but distinct in regard to the act of being. But whatever is in God is His own act of being; and just as His essence is the same as His act of being, so is His knowledge the same as His act of being a knower. Hence, since the act of existence proper to one thing cannot be communicated to another, it is impossible that a creature ever attain to the possession of something in the same manner in which God has it, just as it is impossible for it to attain the same act of being as that which God has. The same is true of us. If *man* and *to exist as man* did not differ in Socrates, man could not be predicated univocally of him and Plato, whose acts of existing are distinct.

Nevertheless, it cannot be said that whatever is predicated of God and creatures is an equivocal predication; for, unless there were at least some real agreement between creatures and God, His essence would not be the likeness of creatures, and so He could not know them by knowing His essence. Similarly, we would not be able to attain any knowledge of God from creatures, nor from among the names devised for creatures could we apply one to Him more than another; for in equivocal predication it makes no difference what name is used, since the word does not signify any real agreement.

Consequently, it must be said that knowledge is predicated neither entirely univocally nor yet purely equivocally of God's knowledge and ours. Instead, it is predicated analogously, or, in other words, according to a proportion. Since an agreement according to proportion can happen in two ways, two kinds of community can be noted in analogy. There is a certain agreement between things having a proportion to each other from the fact that they have a determinate distance between each other or some other relation to each other, like the proportion which the number two has to unity in as far as it is the double of unity. Again, the agreement is occasionally noted not between two things which have a proportion between them, but rather between two related proportions—for example, six has something in common with four because six is two times three, just as four is two times two. The first type of agreement is one of proportion; the second, of proportionality.

We find something predicated analogously of two realities according to the first type of agreement when one of them has a relation to the other, as when being is predicated of substance and accident because of the relation which accident has to substance, or as when healthy is predicated of urine and animal because urine has some relation to the health of an animal. Sometimes, however, a thing is predicated analogously according to the second type of agreement as when sight is in the mind as sight is in the eye.

In those terms predicated according to the first type of analogy, there must be some definite relation between the things having something in common analogously. Consequently, nothing can be predicated analogously of God and creature according to this type of analogy; for no creature has such a relation to God that it could determine the divine perfection. But in the other type of analogy, no definite relation is involved between the things which have something in common analogously, so there is no reason why some name cannot be predicated analogously of God and creature in this manner.

But this can happen in two ways. Sometimes the name implies something belonging to the thing primarily designated which cannot be common to God and creature even in the manner described above. This would be true, for example, of anything predicated of God metaphorically, as when God is called lion, sun, and the like, because their definition includes matter which cannot be attributed to God. At other times, however, a term predicated of God and creature implies nothing in its principal meaning which would prevent our finding between a creature and God an agreement of the type described above. To this kind belong all attributes which include no defect nor depend on matter for their act of existence, for example, being, the good, and similar things.

Potency and Act in Various Compositions

Now, the composition of matter and form is not to be explained in the same way as that of substance and the act of being, even though both be compositions of potency and act.

First of all, this is so because matter is not substance itself, for then it would follow that all forms are accidents, as the ancient natural philosophers thought. Rather, matter is a part of substance.

Secondly, it is so because the very act of being [*ipsum esse*] is not the proper act of matter but of the whole substance. That, of which we can say that it is, is the item whose act is to be. Now, we do not predicate *to be* of matter but of the whole. Hence, matter cannot be called that which is; instead, substance itself is that which is.

It is clear, then, that the composition of act and potency has greater extension than the composition of form and matter. Consequently, matter and form are divisions of material substance, while potency and act are divisions of common being. For this reason, whatever concomitants potency and act have, as such, are common to both material and immaterial created substances; for instance, to receive and to be received, to perfect and to be perfected. However, whatever characteristics are proper to matter and form as such, as, for instance, to be generated and corrupted, and the like, these are peculiar to material substances and in no way appropriate to immaterial created substances.

Summa Against the Gentiles, II, 54. Trans. V.J.B.

How Various Acts Are Distinguished

(*Article 1, c.*) It is impossible for an angel's action, or that of any other creature, to be its substance. For action is properly the actuality of a perfected power [*virtutis*], just as the act of being [*esse*] is the actuality of substance or essence. Now, it is not possible that something which is not pure act but contains some admixture of potency be its own actuality, because actuality is contrary to potentiality. Only God, of course, is pure act. Hence, only in God is His substance His act of being and His action.

Moreover, if an angel's act of understanding were its substance, the angel's act of understanding would have to be subsistent. Now, there can be but one subsistent act of understanding, as is true of any abstract item that is subsistent. Hence, the substance of one angel could be distinguished neither from the substance of God, which is the very subsistent act of understanding, nor from the substance of another angel. So, if an angel itself were its own act of understanding, there could not be various, more and less perfect, degrees of understanding, for this variety depends on a variable participation in the very act of understanding itself.

(*Article 2, c.*) The angel's action is not its act of being [*esse*]; nor is the action of any other creature. There are two kinds of action, as is said in the ninth book of the *Metaphysics*. One passes over into something external, bringing a passion to it; for instance, the actions of burning and sawing. The second kind of action does not pass over into an external thing but instead remains within the agent itself; for instance, the actions of sensing, understanding, and willing. But in this latter kind of action, no change is produced in an external thing; instead, the action is done entirely within the agent.

As for the first kind of action, it is obvious that it cannot be the agent's act of being, for the agent's act of being means something within it, while this sort of action is a flowing out to an act caused by the agent. The second kind of action, however, in its essential character possesses infinity, either absolutely or with qualification. If it be absolutely, as in the case of understanding, whose object is the true, or willing, whose object is the good (both of these objects are convertible with being), then in this case the acts of understanding and willing are open to all objects and both receive specification from the object. If it be with qualification, then the act of sensing is infinite because it is open to all sensible objects, as vision is to all visible things. But the act of being of any creature is determined to one objective, generically and specifically. Only God's act of being is absolutely infinite, including all within itself, as Dionysius says in the fifth chapter *On the Divine Names*. Hence, only the divine act of being is identical with its act of understanding and its act of willing.

(*Article 3, c.*) Neither in an angel, nor in any creature, is a perfected power or an operative potency the same as its essence. This is clear from the following. Since potency gets its meaning from act, the diversification of potencies must depend on the diversity of acts. This is why it is said that the appropriate act corresponds to the appropriate potency. Now, in every created thing, essence differs from its act of being and is related to it as potency to act, as is clear from what has been said.

The act to which operative potency corresponds is operation. Now, the acts of understanding and of being are not the same in an angel; nor is any other operation, either in the angel or in any other kind of creature, identical with its act of being. Consequently, an angel's essence is not its intellectual potency, nor is the essence of any created being its operative potency.

Active and Passive Operative Potencies

Indeed, an active power is not distinguished from a passive power because it has an activity, for since every power of the soul, active as well as passive, has some activity, every power would be active.

We learn the distinction between the two by comparing the power to its object. For, if the object relates to the power as that which undergoes and is changed, the power will be active. If, on the other hand, it relates as agent and mover, the power is passive. Hence it is that all the powers of the vegetative soul are active, because in nutrition, growth, and generation food is changed through the power of the soul. On the other hand, all the sensitive powers are passive, because they are set in motion and come into act through sensible objects. In our understanding, however, there is an active and a passive power, because through intellect the intelligible in potency becomes intelligible in act. This is the activity of the agent intellect, and our understanding is, thus, an active power. The thing actually intelligible also makes the understanding in potency understanding in act, and in this way the possible intellect is a passive power.

Disputed Questions on Truth, XVI, 1, reply to Obj. 13. Trans. Mulligan, McGlynn, and Schmidt, Truth, vol. II, p. 307.

Potency, Act, and God

To clarify this question, we should note that potency is spoken of in relation to act. Now, there are two kinds of act: namely, first, which is form, and second, which is operation. As is apparent from men's common understanding, the name "act" was first attributed to operation, for this is the way that nearly all men understand act. In the second place, it

Disputed Questions on the Power of God, I, 1, c. Trans. V.J.B.

was transferred from this usage to form, because form is the principle and end of operation.

Consequently and on the same basis, there is a double meaning for potency. In one sense, it is *active*, and the act that is operation corresponds to this meaning. It seems that the name "potency" was first ascribed to this sense. The other is "passive potency," to which primary act, which is form, corresponds. It seems that the name "potency," was secondarily applied to this usage.

Now, just as nothing undergoes an action unless by virtue of passive potency, so nothing acts unless by virtue of primary act, which is form. It has been said that the name "act" first came from action. Now, it is appropriate for God to be pure and first act. Consequently, to act in the fullest sense is proper to Him, and also to diffuse His likeness into other beings. So, active potency belongs to Him in the fullest sense, for potency is called active because it is the principle of action.

However, we should also note that our intellect strives to form an expression of God as something that is most perfect. And since it is impossible to reach up to Him, unless by analogy from His effects, and since it can find among creatures no highest perfect reality that is altogether without imperfection, therefore an effort is made to describe Him from the various perfections that are found in creatures, even though something is lacking in each of these perfections. Yet, whatever item of imperfection accompanies any of these perfections is in this way entirely set apart from God. For example, "to be" signifies something complete and simple but not subsistent, while "substance" means something subsistent but subjected to something else.

Therefore, we attribute substance and actual being [*esse*] to God, but substance in the sense of subsistence and not of a substratum, and the act of being in the simple and complete sense, but not in the sense of inherence whereby it inheres in some other item. Likewise, we attribute operation to God, in the sense of an ultimate complement and not in the sense of that into which an operation passes over. So, we attribute potency by virtue of the fact that it endures and is the principle of operation, but not in the sense that it is perfected by operation.

Four Kinds of Causes

We must consider, in order to clarify this, that although there are four kinds of causes, matter is not a principle of action but stands as the subject receiving the effect of the action. On the other hand, the end, agent, and form do function as the principle of action, but in a certain order.

The first principle of action is the end, for it moves the agent. The second is the agent; while the third is its form because it is applied to the action by the agent, even though the agent itself acts by virtue of its own form. This is illustrated clearly in the case of artifacts. The artist is, in fact, moved to action by the end, which is the thing produced, for example, a box or a bed; and he uses the hatchet in the action, for it cuts by means of its own sharpness.

Summa of Theology, I, 105, 5, c. Trans. V.J.B.

Interrelations of the Four Causes

Since the good is that which all desire, and this has the rational character of an end, it is obvious that the good implies the rational character of an end. Yet, the meaning of the good is based on the prior character of the efficient cause and of the formal cause. Indeed, we see that what is first in the process of causing is last in the caused product. For, fire first becomes hot before it takes on the form of fire, yet the heat in fire follows upon the substantial form.

Now, in the process of causing, we find first the good and end which motivates the efficient cause; secondly, the action of the efficient moving toward the form; thirdly comes

Summa of Theology, I, 5, 4, c. Trans. V.J.B.

the form. The converse must be so in the caused product: first, there is its form, by which it is a being; secondly, the efficient power whereby it is perfected in actual being may be considered in it—for, "each thing is then perfect when it can make a product like itself," as the Philosopher says in the *Meteorology* (IV, 3, 380a12); thirdly follows the character of the good whereby perfection is established in being.

Forms: Substantial and Accidental

We must say that something comes under a common item in two ways: one, as the individual under the species; another, as the species under the genus. So, whenever there are many individuals under one common species, the distinction of many individuals is due to individual matter which stands apart from the nature of the species. And this is so in created things. However, when there are many species under one genus, it is not necessary for the forms whereby the species are distinguished from each other to be different in reality from the form of the common genus. Indeed, a given individual is placed within the genus *substance*, and within the genus *body*, and so on to the *most specific species*, by one and the same form. If this individual were to owe the fact that it is a substance to a certain form, then of necessity other additional forms by which it is placed within lower genera and species would be accidental forms.

This is evident from the following. An accidental form differs from a substantial one because the substantial form makes a substantially existing individual [*hoc aliquid*]; whereas, an accidental form comes to a thing that is already existing as a substantial individual. Therefore, if the first form, by which it is placed within a genus, makes the individual to be an individual substance, then all the other forms will come to an actually subsisting individual, and so they will be accidental forms.

Disputed Question on Spiritual Creatures, 1, reply to Obj. 9. Trans. V.J.B.

It will also follow that through the advent of the later forms whereby the thing is placed in the most specific or subalternate species, generation and corruption by way of removal will not occur in an unqualified sense but only in a qualified way. For, since generation is a change into real being, that which unqualifiedly becomes a being from a condition of nonactual but merely potential being is what is said to be generated without qualification. So, if something is made from an actual pre-existent, it will not be generated as a being in the unqualified sense but only as this being. The same reasoning applies to corruption.

Therefore, it should be stated that the forms of things are ranked in order, and that one adds to the other by way of perfection. This is apparent by what the Philosopher says in the *Metaphysics* (VIII, 3, 1043b33); that the definitions and species of things are like numbers, in which species are made many by adding one. Then, too, this becomes apparent by induction, for the species of things are pluralized on different levels by virtue of the perfect and the imperfect.

And so, this explanation refutes the position of Avicebron in the *Fons Vitae* (tr. IV, c. 1), that prime matter, considered as wholly lacking in form, first of all receives the form of substance. When this has taken place, it then receives in some division of itself another form beside the form of substance, and by this it becomes a body, and so on until the last species. Now, in that division in which the bodily form is not received, it remains an incorporeal substance, and some people call the matter of something that is not subject to quantity spiritual matter. However, he says that the matter that is already perfected by the form of substance which is the subject of quantity and the other accidents is the key to the understanding of incorporeal substances.

Indeed, that one individual is an inanimate body and another an animate body is not due to the fact that the animate individual possesses a certain form to which the substantial form of body is subordinated. Rather, it is because this animate individual possesses a more perfect form whereby it is enabled not only to subsist and be a body but also to live

—while the other individual has a more imperfect form whereby it does not attain life but only bodily subsistence.

Every Agent Acts for an End

In the case of agents that manifestly act to some end, we call that the end to which the effort of the agent tends. Gaining that, he is said to gain his end; and missing that, he is said to miss his intended end. Nor on this point does it make any difference whether the end be tended to with knowledge or not: for as the target is the end of the archer, so is it also the end of the path of the arrow. The effort of every agent tends to some certain end. Not any and every action can proceed from any and every power. Action is sometimes terminated to some product, sometimes not. When action is terminated to some product, the effort of the agent tends to the same. When action is not terminated to any product, the effort of the agent tends to the action itself. Every agent therefore must intend some end in his action, sometimes the action itself, sometimes something produced by the action. . . .

Actions are open to criticism only so far as they are taken to be done as means to some end. It is not imputed as a fault to anyone, if he fails in effecting that for which his work is not intended. A physician is found fault with if he fails in healing, but not a builder or a grammarian. We find fault in points of art, as when a grammarian does not speak correctly; and also in points of nature, as in monstrous births. Therefore both the natural agent, and the agent who acts according to art and with a conscious purpose, acts for an end. . . .

To the agent that did not tend to any definite effect, all effects would be indifferent. But what is indifferent to many things, does not do one of them rather than another: hence from an agent open to both sides of an alternative there does not follow any effect, unless by some means it comes to be

Summa Against the Gentiles, III, 2. Trans. J. Rickaby, *On God and His Creatures*, pp. 185-186.

determined to one above the rest: otherwise it could not act at all. Every agent therefore tends to some definite effect, and that is called its end.

Still, there are actions that do not seem to be for any end, as things done for sport, and acts of contemplation, and things done without advertence, as the stroking of the beard and the like: from which instances one may suppose that there is such a thing as an agent acting not for any end. But we must observe that though acts of contemplation are not for any other end, they are an end in themselves: as for things done in sport, sometimes they are their own end, as when one plays solely for the amusement that he finds in play; sometimes they are for an end, as when we play that afterwards we may resume work more vigorously: while things done without advertence proceed not from the understanding, but from some phantasy or physical principle; yet even these acts tend to certain ends, though beyond the scope of the intellect of the agent.

Finality Depends on Intelligence

Indeed, every agent acts for the sake of an end, for all things desire the good. Now, in order that it be adapted to an end, the action of an agent must be disposed and made proportionate to it, and this cannot be accomplished without the help of some intellect which knows the end and the intelligible character [ratio] of the end, and also the orderly relationship of the end and that which is for the sake of the end. Otherwise, the agreement of the action to the end would be a matter of chance.

However, the intellect that confers this prior ordering to the end is sometimes joined to the agent or mover, as in the case of man in regard to his actions, and sometimes it is separated, as in the example of the arrow which tends toward

Disputed Questions on the Power of God, I, 5, c. Trans. V.J.B.

a definite end not by means of an intellect joined to the arrow but by the intellect of the man who aims it.

Now, it is not possible for that which acts from the necessity of nature to determine its end for itself. For, such a thing would be an agent of its own accord, and that which is acting or moved by itself has the ability to act or not to act, to be moved or not to be moved (as is said in the *Physics*, VIII, 4, 254b15), and this cannot be appropriate to what is moved necessarily since it is determined to one alternative.

For since everything that acts, acts as a result of the necessity of its nature it must be, then, that the end is determined by something that is intelligent. For this reason, it is said by the philosophers that the work of nature is the work of intelligence. Hence, if at times a natural body be conjoined to an intellect, as clearly occurs in the case of man, then, in regard to those actions whereby the intellect determines his end, nature obeys the will, as is evident in the motion of man in place. But, in regard to those actions in which he does not determine the end for himself, there is no obedience [to will], for instance, in the act of nutrition and growth.

The conclusion of these arguments, then, is that whatever acts from the necessity of its nature cannot be a first agent, since the end is determined for it by another being.

RECOMMENDED READINGS

ANDERSON, J. F. *An Introduction to the Metaphysics of St. Thomas Aquinas*. Chicago: Regnery, 1953.

GILSON, E. *Being and Some Philosophers*. Toronto: Pontifical Institute of Mediaeval Studies, 1949.

———. *Elements of Christian Philosophy*. New York: Doubleday, 1960.

HART, C. A. *Thomistic Metaphysics*. Englewood Cliffs, N. J. Prentice-Hall, 1959.

HENLE, R. J. *Method in Metaphysics*. Milwaukee: Marquette University Press, 1951.

KLUBERTANZ, G. P. *Introduction to the Philosophy of Being*. New York: Appleton-Century-Crofts, 1955.

KREYCHE, R. J. *First Philosophy*. New York: Holt, 1959.

MARITAIN, J. *Preface to Metaphysics*. New York: Sheed & Ward, 1939.

——. *St. Thomas and the Problem of Evil*. Milwaukee: Marquette University Press, 1942.

OWENS, J. *St. Thomas and the Future of Metaphysics*. Milwaukee: Marquette University Press, 1957.

PHELAN, G. B. *St. Thomas and Analogy*. Milwaukee: Marquette University Press, 1941.

REITH, H. *The Metaphysics of St. Thomas Aquinas*. Milwaukee: Bruce, 1958.

SMITH, G. *General Metaphysics*. New York: Macmillan, 1960.

——. *Natural Theology*. New York: Macmillan, 1951.

V. Moral Life and Ethics

Foreword

THE MORAL THINKING OF AQUINAS is developed in many of his works, from the early *Exposition of the Sentences* (Book III) and *Summa contra Gentiles* (Book III) to the *Exposition* of the *Nicomachean Ethics* and the lengthy considerations in both divisions of the *Summa of Theology*, Part II. Of the disputed questions, those *On Evil* are most important in this chapter.

Both in ethics and moral theology, his position is teleological. Morally good action is that which is conducive to man's attainment of his ultimate end, final happiness, the everlasting contemplation of the Perfect Good. He is convinced that all men naturally incline toward this final end, and that the chief area of difficulty in the moral life lies in the prudent selection and use of the proper means (that is, actions) whereby such an end may be reached.

Since God has created the universe and men, and since He continues to exercise providential care over all things that go on in creation, Aquinas believes as a theologian that there is an eternal law which is the highest and ultimate standard of moral good and evil. However, Aquinas did not claim that men on earth know this eternal law directly, as it is in the Mind of God. Part of it is revealed to man in the form of the divine positive law found in Scripture. The ten commandments given to Moses are precepts of such divine law. It is in the third book of the *Summa contra Gentiles* that moral problems are handled from the point of view of this divine law.

181

Apart from revelation, there is another way in which men come to know some part of the eternal law as it applies to their moral actions. The natural moral law is a rational participation in the eternal law, based on natural experience and the understanding of man's nature and its relations to the natures of other things in man's environment. This law is natural in the way in which it is promulgated—made known —to men. All peoples, Aquinas felt, have a sufficient awareness of what is good and bad for human beings to enable them to live in a manner that is suitable to their nature.

Practical understanding starts to reason from a very general proposition (the rule of synderesis) to the effect that *good should be done and evil avoided.* This is the primary precept of natural law but it is not by itself an adequate guide for human action, because it does not specify as to what is good or bad. Further moral reasoning consists in determining certain general types of "goods" and "evils" for men. Some kinds of actions are judged generally good, because they tend to perfect man's being and powers, and because they contribute to the public welfare. (It will be noted that Aquinas' ethics shares affinities with self-perfectionism and with social utilitarianism.) Other types of actions are self-abusive, brutish, selfish, and so, evil. In establishing these differences between types of good and evil actions, Aquinas engages in careful and lengthy processes of reasoning. Specific precepts of natural moral law are developed as conclusions to such reasonings. An example included in this chapter is the consideration of the evil of fornication. The reader will see that the argument is almost naturalistic or pragmatic. He is concerned about the influence of such activity on the welfare of the children that may be produced from such irregular unions. Aquinas is quite ready to use comparisons with the observed behavior of dogs and birds, in order to set up a higher ideal for human behavior.

General moral rules, even when made rather definite, are not concrete reasons for doing or avoiding a proposed action. Moral knowledge must be applied to the decision of a concrete problem by the judgment of conscience. There is no special mental power that is conscience; it is simply a rather definite practical judgment made by human understanding. Such a conscience does not guarantee good action. It is always possible for a man to act in violation of his conscience. Such an act, contrary to an honest judgment of conscience, is evil. There is a further moment in consciousness, in which the agent judges that he *will* act (the judgment of choice) and then he chooses to do so. The external bodily act thus becomes part of a total moral action, because it is controlled or commanded by the agent using his intellect and will. Much the same is said about the omission of action. It will be seen, then, that Aquinas considers bodily actions to have moral significance—but only to the extent that they are subject to voluntary control.

Moral virtues play an important role in Thomistic moral theory. As habits of the intellect, will, or the two sensory appetites, they make the agent capable of doing what is good, more easily, more promptly, and more accurately. Vices are also moral habits, but bad ones. As habits, these qualities are not automatic mechanisms but perfectants of their respective powers. They do not reduce awareness or responsibility but increase man's capacities, for good or ill. Hundreds of moral virtues, with their typical actions and opposed vices, are discussed in the second division of Part II of the *Summa of Theology*. The basic virtues on the natural level are, of course, prudence, temperance, fortitude, and justice, the traditional cardinal virtues. There are also supernatural virtues, which God more directly produces in man. Faith, hope, and charity are the theological virtues.

Moral reasoning about one's individual problems is not moral science but belongs in the area of prudence—or imprudence. It is possible to teach moral science but prudence must be acquired by personal effort. That is why there is always something general about Thomistic moral conclusions. Personal thinking about one's own moral actions is not a part of the study of either ethics or moral theology.

The Subject Matter of Moral Philosophy

As the Philosopher says at the beginning of his *Metaphysics* (I, 2, 982a18), the function of the wise man is to order. The explanation for this is that wisdom is the highest perfection of reason and to know order is proper to reason. For, though the sense powers may know certain things in isolation from all else, it pertains to understanding or reason alone to know the orderly relation of one thing to another.

Now, two types of order are found among things. One belongs to the parts as related to each other within a whole, or within some plurality of items; it is thus that the parts of a house are ordered to each other. The other type is the order of things toward an end. This second kind of order is more important than the first. In fact, as the Philosopher says in the *Metaphysics* (XII, 10, 1075a15), the order of the parts of an army among themselves depends on the ordering of the whole army in relation to its leader.

Order is related to reason in four ways, however. There is one sort of order which reason does not produce but only observes; this is the orderly relation of things in nature. There is a second kind of order which reason, as a result of thinking, produces in its own action; for instance, when it orders its concepts in relation to each other, and its signs to the concepts (for signs are meaningful words). Then there is a third sort of order which reason, as a result of thinking, produces in the operations of the will. And the fourth kind of order is that which reason, as a result of thinking, produces in extra-mental things of which it is the cause; for instance, in a box or a house.

Now, since rational thinking is perfected by means of a habit, there are different habits of science for these diverse orders that reason thinks about properly. It is the province of natural philosophy to think of the order in things, which

Exposition of Aristotle's Ethics, I, Lect. 1, nn. 1-3. Trans. V.J.B.

reason observes but does not make. In this sense, even metaphysics is included under natural philosophy. However, the order that reason produces, as a result of thinking, in its own action belongs to rational philosophy; for its function is to consider the order of the parts of speech among themselves and the mutual ordering of principles among themselves and to their conclusions.

Next, the order in voluntary actions belongs to the consideration of moral philosophy. While, the order that reason, as a result of thinking, produces in external things that are arranged by human reasoning belongs to the mechanical arts. And so, to moral philosophy (which we are now treating) it is proper to think about human actions, as they are ordered among themselves and in relation to their ends.

Now, I say human operations, those which issue from man's will according to the ordering of reason. For, if some operations occur in man that are not subject to will and reason, they are not properly called human but physical. An example is found in the workings of the vegetative soul; these in no way fall under the consideration of moral philosophy. Just as the subject matter of natural philosophy is motion, or mobile reality, so the subject matter of moral philosophy is human action as ordered to an end, or even man as he is acting voluntarily for the sake of an end.

The Young and the Study of Moral Science

Aristotle shows that generation or alteration do not occur in the acquisition of science. For, whatever comes to a person simply by means of a quieting or settling down of certain disturbances or movements does not owe its advent to generation or alteration. But science (that is, speculative knowledge) and prudence (that is, practical reason) do come into the soul by means of a quieting and settling down of bodily motions and of sensory passions. So, science and prudence do not enter animate beings by means of generation or alteration. . . .

He says that this sort of thing happens when a person acquires science originally. It seems that this is accomplished by virtue of a quieting and a settling down of disturbance, that is, of disordered motions, that are present in boys, both in regard to the body (for their whole nature is in a condition of change resulting from growth) and also in regard to the sensory part of the soul, because passions are dominant in them.

Consequently, what he says about "quieting" can be related to the turmoil of bodily motion which becomes quiet in a nature returning to its normal condition. And his statement about "settling down" can be applied to the passions of the sensory part of the soul, which do not completely grow quiet but settle down from their removal of rational thinking and they do not rise to the point of actual disturbance of reason. Similarly, we speak of settling down in the case of fluids, when the impure dregs fall to the bottom, leaving the upper part pure.

So, this is the reason why the young [*juvenes*] cannot learn by grasping what they are told by others. Neither in regard to what they hear through their internal senses, nor in regard to any items that present themselves in their knowledge, are they able to make a judgment as well as their elders, or *presbyters*, which means the same. For *presbyter* in Greek has the same meaning as elder [*senex*] in Latin.

This is so because there is much disturbance and motion within themselves, in the case of young people, as has been said. Of course, disturbance of this kind is entirely removed, or at least diminished, sometimes by nature, when the state of old age in which these motions grow quiet is reached—and sometimes as a result of other causes, such as practice and the acquisition of habits. Then they can learn well and also form a judgment.

What It Means to Act Voluntarily

There must be a voluntary character in human acts. To make this clear we should consider that the principle of some acts is within the agent, or within that which is moved, while the principle of other movements or actions is outside. When a stone is moved upward, the source of this movement is outside the stone; but when it is moved downward, the principle of this motion is in the stone itself. Now, some of the things that are moved by an internal principle move themselves; others do not. Since every agent or moved thing acts, or is moved, because of an end, as we said before, those things perfectly moved by an inner principle, in which there is some internal principle such that they are not merely moved but are moved toward their end. Now, for something to be done for the sake of an end, some knowledge of the end is needed. So, whatever kind of agent acts or is moved in such a way by an internal principle that it possesses some knowledge of the end, this agent has within itself not only the principle of its action that enables it to act but also to act for the sake of its end. In regard to the one that has no knowledge of its end, even though there be within it a principle of action or movement, there is not really within it a principle of action or motion; instead, it is in another being by which the principle of its movement toward the end is impressed upon it. Hence, things of this kind are not said to move themselves but to be moved by other agents.

On the other hand, those beings that do possess a knowledge of their end are said to move themselves, for there is a principle in them, not simply so that they may act but so that they may act for the sake of their end. Therefore, since both factors come from an inner principle, namely, that they act, and that they act for the sake of an end, the movements and actions of these agents are called voluntary. In fact, this is

Summa of Theology, I-II, 6, 1, c. Trans. V.J.B.

the meaning of the term "voluntary": *that movement and act be from a thing's own inclination.* . . . Hence, when a man knows the end of his work to the fullest extent and moves himself, then the voluntary character of his acts is present to the greatest degree.

Voluntary Action and Free Choice

The genus of the act of choice is the voluntary, because it is always predicated of choice and of more than that. Hence, Aristotle says, first of all, that every act of choice is something voluntary; but choice and the voluntary are not wholly the same, for the voluntary is of greater extension. He proves this by two arguments. . . .

Children and the other animals share in voluntary action, in the sense that they operate by their own spontaneous motion. Yet, they do not share in the act of choice, because their actions are not performed as a result of deliberation, which is a prerequisite for choice. Therefore, voluntary action includes more than choice. . . .

We call those actions that we perform suddenly voluntary, because their source lies within us; but they are not said to occur by choice, because they are not done deliberately. So, the voluntary includes more than the act of choice. . . .

Aristotle says, first of all, that choice is also distinct from the act of wishing, although it may seem to be close to wishing. In fact, both belong to the one potency, the rational appetite which is called the will. However, wishing is the name of the act of this potency, when the act is referred to the good without qualification. Choice, on the other hand, names the act of the same potency as referred to the good that pertains to our action whereby we are directed toward some definite good. . . .

Exposition of Aristotle's Ethics, III, Lect. 5, nn. 434-436, 443-446. Trans. V.J.B.

Indeed, choice is not said to apply to impossible things, because it has reference to our own action. If a person said that he was choosing something impossible, he would appear to be stupid. The voluntary, however, looks to the good without qualification and it can apply to any sort of good, even if it be impossible. Thus, one may wish not to die, which is impossible according to the condition of this corruptible life. Therefore, choosing and wishing are not the same. . . .

A person's wish can center on actions that are not performed by himself. An example is the man who is watching a duel: he may wish that one of the contestants will win, by identifying himself with this contestant; he may wish to enter the fray, as if he were a combatant even though he is not, or even that one of the true athletes may win. But no one chooses actions that are accomplished by another person; one can choose only actions that he thinks he can do himself. Therefore, choice is different from wishing. . . .

Aristotle says that wishing refers to the end, rather than to what is done for the sake of the end, because we will the means to the end for the sake of the end. Now, if one thing is for the sake of another, this other is more important. But choice is solely concerned with the means to the end and not with the end itself, because the end is taken as the basis, as already predetermined. The means to the end are investigated by us, in order to adapt them to the end. For example, we chiefly *wish* health as the end of medical treatment; but we *choose* the medicines by means of which we may be made healthy. Likewise, we wish to be happy, which is the ultimate end, and we say that we wish it. But it is not appropriate to say that we choose to be happy. Therefore, choice is not the same act as wishing. . . .

Aristotle then states the root of the entire difference to which all the preceding distinctions may be reduced. He says that choice may be seen to deal with things that are within our power. This is the reason why it applies neither to impossibilities, nor to actions performed by others, nor to the end which for the most part is pre-established for us by nature.

The Ultimate End of Man Is Happiness

We must again come back to the good that is the subject of
our inquiry, that is, to happiness, so that we may investigate
what it is. The first point to be considered is that different
things seem to be aimed at, as a good, in different actions
and arts. Thus, in the art of medicine the good that is intended
is health, while in the military art the intended good is victory,
and in the other arts there is some other good.

If we ask what is the good intended in any art or any undertaking, it should be noted that it is that for the sake of which
all the other things are done. In medicine, of course, everything is done for the sake of health. In the military art, all
activities are for the sake of victory. In building, all efforts
are for the sake of constructing the house. And similarly, in
every sort of undertaking, there is some other thing that is
the intended good, for the sake of which all the rest of the
things are done. Now, this good that is intended in every
action or choice is called an end. For an end is simply that
for the sake of which other things are done.

So, if some end suddenly presented itself to which all
human arts and activities directed their operations, then such
an end would be the good that is worked for, without any
qualification. It would be what is intended in all human
activities. If, on the other hand, many goods so presented
themselves as objectives toward which the different ends of
the various arts were directed, then our rational investigation
would have to rise above this plurality until it reached the
objective itself, some other item that is one. Indeed, the
ultimate end of man as man must be one, because of the
unity of human nature. In the same way, the end of a medical
doctor as a doctor is one, because of the unity of the medical
art. So, this ultimate end of man is called the human good,
and it is happiness.

Exposition of Aristotle's Ethics, I, Lect. 9, nn. 104-106. Trans. V.J.B.

Perfect Happiness as the Contemplation of God

Felicity or happiness consists in an operation and not in a habitual state, as the Philosopher proves in the *Ethics* (I, 8, 1098b30). So, happiness can be related to a potency of the soul in two ways. One way is as the object of the potency; and in this sense, happiness is chiefly related to the will. Indeed, happiness is the name of the ultimate end of man and of the highest good itself. Now, the end and the good are the object of the will.

Another way is as act to potency; and in this sense, happiness basically and substantially consists in an act of the intellect; formally and as a complement, it consists in an act of the will, for it is impossible for the very act of the will to be the ultimate end of the will. The ultimate end of man is what is primarily desired. Now, it cannot be that what is primarily willed is the act of the will. As a matter of fact, a potency must be brought to bear upon its object before it is directed toward its own act. Thus, the act of any potency is understood before the reflection upon that act is; for the act terminates in the object and so, in each case, the potency is directed toward its object before it is directed to its own act. For example, sight first sees a color before it sees that it is seeing a color. So, too, the will wishes some good before it wills its act of wishing. Thus, the act of the will cannot be the primary object of desire, and consequently, it cannot be the ultimate end.

However, every time that some external good is desired as an end, that act of ours is for us like an internal end; and when it is accomplished, we then attain the objective itself. We say, for example, that eating is the end and happiness of the person who regards food as his end; similarly, possession is the objective of the person who makes money his end.

Quodlibetal Questions, VIII, 9, 19, c. Trans. V.J.B.

Now, the end of our desires is God; hence, the act whereby we are primarily joined to Him is basically and substantially our happiness. But we are primarily united with God by an act of understanding; and therefore, the very seeing of God, which is an act of the intellect, is substantially and basically our happiness. However, since this action is most perfect and most appropriate to its object, it is therefore followed by the greatest enjoyment, which adorns and perfects this operation, as beauty does youth, to quote the *Ethics* (X, 4). As a result, this joy which belongs to the will is a formal complement of happiness. Thus, the ultimate basis of happiness lies in the vision, while its complement consists in the fruition.

Moral Good and Evil Specified by the End

Actions differ in species according to a diversity of forms which are the principles of the actions, even though the agents may not be of different species. Thus, to heat and to cool are specifically different actions, because heat and cold are formally different. Now, the form of the will is the end and the good, which is its object and the thing desired. Therefore, the specific difference among acts of the will must be discovered from the rational character of the end. And since acts belong in the genus moral, because they are voluntary, so the specific difference in the genus of moral acts is based on a diversity of the end.

On the Sentences, II, 40, 1, 1, Response. Trans. V.J.B.

Good and Evil in Rational Agents

Virtue and vice indicate some differences of movement and action, on the basis of whether they are performed well or badly. For, a virtue is that whereby one is related in a good way toward action, while a vice involves a bad way. The same is true of the other habits, whether they be intellectual, as in the case of science, or corporeal, as in the case of health.

Nevertheless, well and badly apply chiefly to a quality in animated things; and especially to those that possess *proairesis*, that is, choice. This is so, because the good has the rational character of an end. Actions done by choice are performed for the sake of an end. Now, to act for an end is especially the function of animated beings. Of course, inanimate things act or are moved for the sake of an end but not as knowers of their end, nor as themselves acting for the end, but rather as directed by another agent who has given them a natural inclination, as an arrow is directed toward an end by the archer.

Of course, irrational animated things know their end and move themselves locally toward the end, as possessors of judgment concerning the end; but the appetite for the end, and for the means to this end, are determined for them as a result of natural inclination. For this reason, they are things acted upon rather than agents. In their case, also, there is no free decision.

However, rational agents, in whom alone is choice found, do know their end, and they know the proper relationship of means to the end itself. So, just as they move themselves toward their end, so also do they toward the desiring of the end, or of the means that are for the sake of the end; and due to this fact, free choice is present in them.

Exposition of Aristotle's Metaphysics, V, Lect. 16, nn. 999-1000. Trans. V.J.B.

On Natural Justice

That is naturally just which has everywhere the same power
and force of inducing toward the good and restraining from
evil. Now, this happens because nature, the cause of this
concrete justice, is everywhere the same in all men. Of
course, the concrete justice that depends on a certain state
or ruler for its establishment is a matter of virtue only for
those who are subject to the jurisdiction of that state or
ruler.

Aristotle explains this concrete justice, secondly, with
reference to its cause, when he says that the naturally
just does not depend on the fact that it seems so, or not; that
is, it does not stem from some human opinion but from nature.
Indeed, just as there are certain naturally known things in
the speculative area, such as the indemonstrable principles
and those judgments that are closely related to them (for
some rules are discovered by human effort and they are the
closely related principles), so also in the operative area are
there certain principles that are naturally known as indemonstrable and also closely related principles. Examples
are: evil is to be avoided; one should not steal; and the
like. Still other principles are thought out through the careful effort of men; these are called legally right things in this
text.

Now, we must bear in mind that the naturally just thing
is that to which nature inclines a man. But nature is observed
to be twofold in man. First, because he is an animal, there
is that which is common to himself and the other animals.
Second, there is the nature of man that is peculiar to him as
a man, that is, insofar as he can distinguish between the
indecent and the decent. Now, the Jurists speak of the
naturally just in terms only of what is connected with a

Exposition of Aristotle's Ethics, V, Lect. 12, nn. 1018, 1019, 1023, 1024,
1029. Trans. V.J.B.

natural inclination common to man and the other animals; for example, the union of male and female, the upbringing of offspring, and similar points. That sort of concrete justice which is associated with an inclination peculiar to human nature, in the sense that man is a rational animal, the Jurists call the law of peoples [*jus gentium*], because all peoples use it; for instance, that agreements are to be kept, that ambassadors are safe with the enemy, and similar rules. Now, both these meanings are included under the naturally just, as the Philosopher uses the term here. . . .

We should also keep in mind, at this point, that what is just, legally or positively, always takes its origin from the naturally just, as Cicero says in his *Rhetoric* (II, 161). But there are two ways in which something may stem from the naturally just. The first is as a conclusion from principles. Now, the just in the positive or legal sense cannot come from the naturally just in this way: that is, given the premises, the conclusion must follow; but since the naturally just thing is so always and everywhere, as we have said, this is not appropriate to the legally or positively just. Hence, whatever follows as a conclusion from the naturally just is an item of natural justice. For example, from the rule *no person is to be harmed unjustly* follows the conclusion *one should not steal*, which of course belongs to natural justice. The second way in which something may stem from the naturally just is by means of a determination. In this sense, all instances of positive or legal justice stem from the naturally just. Thus, the rule *a thief should be punished* is naturally just; but that *he should be punished by this or that penalty* is an item of positive legality.

We should further note that what is legally just stems in two ways from the natural, according to the aforementioned method of determination. One way admits of some admixture of human error, while the second way does not. Aristotle shows this by examples. It is naturally just that a citizen subjected to some hardship through no fault of his own should be assisted. A consequence of this is that a captive should be redeemed. Now, the amount paid for ransom is a question of legal justice and it follows from the preceding instance of natural justice without any possibility of error. It is also naturally just for honor to be shown to a benefactor; but that divine honor must be given to a man, and that a certain sacrifice should be offered him, this is a conclusion due to human error. . . .

However, we should note that since the rational characteristics [*rationes*] of mutable things are themselves immutable, whatever is natural to us, in the sense of pertaining to the rational character of man, is not changeable in any way. An example is the fact that man is an animal. But things that are merely associated with man's nature, like dispositions, actions, and movements, these are changeable in some instances. Likewise, the rules that belong to the essential character of justice itself cannot be changed at all; for example, that one should not steal, because it is an unjust thing to do. However, rules that are associated with justice may be changed in some cases.

How We Know Natural Moral Law

The precepts of the law of nature are related to practical reason in the same way that the first principles of demonstration are to speculative reason. Both are principles that are self-known [*per se nota*]. Now, we speak of something as self-known in two ways: first, in itself; second, in relation to us.

Any proposition is called self-known in itself when its predicate belongs to the intelligible meaning of its subject. However, it is possible for such a proposition not to be evident to a person ignorant of the definition of the subject. Thus, this proposition, *man is rational*, is self-evident in its own nature, since to say man is to say rational; yet, for a person who is ignorant of what man is, this proposition is not self-known.

Summa of Theology, I-II, 94, 2, c. Trans. V.J.B.

Consequently, as Boethius says (*De Hebdomadibus*, PL 64, 1311), there are some axioms or propositions that are in general self-known to all. Of this type are those propositions whose terms are known to all; for example, *every whole is greater than its part*, and *things equal to one and the same thing are equal to each other*. But there are some propositions that are self-known only to the wise, those who understand the meaning of the terms of these propositions. Thus, to one who understands that an angel is not a body, it is self-known that an angel is not present circumscriptively in place. This is not obvious to uninstructed people, who fail to grasp this point.

A definite order is found among items that fall under the apprehension of men. For, that which first falls under apprehension is *being* [*ens*]: the understanding of it is included in all things whatsoever that one apprehends. So, the first indemonstrable principle is: *It is not proper at once to affirm and to deny*. This is based on the intelligible meaning of being and nonbeing. On this principle all others are founded, as is said in the *Metaphysics* (III, 3, 1005b29).

Now, just as "being" is the first item that falls within apprehension without any qualification, so "good" is the first that falls within the apprehension of practical reason, which is directed toward work: *for every agent acts for the sake of an end*, which has the intelligible meaning of good. Thus, the first principle in the practical reason is what is based on the meaning of "good"; and it is: *The good is what all desire*. This is, then, the first principle of law: *Good is to be done and sought after, evil is to be avoided*. On this all the other precepts of the law of nature are based, in the sense that all things to be done or avoided belong to the precepts of the law of nature, if practical reason apprehends them as human goods.

Now, since the good has the rational character of an end, and evil has the contrary meaning, as a consequence reason naturally apprehends all things to which man has a natural inclination as goods and, therefore, as things to be sought

after in working, and their contraries are apprehended as
evils and as things to be avoided.

So, the order of the precepts of the law of nature is in
accord with the order of natural inclinations. First, there is
present in man the inclination toward the good on the level
of the nature which he shares with all substances, inasmuch
as each substance desires the preservation of its own existence
according to its own nature. Now, those things whereby the
life of man is preserved, and whereby its contrary is impeded,
pertain to the natural law according to this inclination.

Second, there is present in man an inclination toward some
more special things, on the level of the nature which he
shares with other animals. And on this level, those things are
said to belong to natural law "which nature teaches to all
animals" (*Corpus Juris Civilis, Digesta*, I, tit. 1, leg. 1), as,
for instance, the union of male and female, the upbringing of
offspring, and similar things.

Third, there is present in man an inclination toward the
good that is in accord with the nature of reason, and this is
proper to him. Thus, man has a natural inclination toward
knowing the truth about God, and toward living in society.
On this level, those things within the scope of this inclination
pertain to the natural law; for instance, that man should
avoid ignorance, that he should not offend those with whom
he must associate, and others of this kind that are concerned
with this level.

[The difficulties mentioned at the beginning of the article
boil down to this: Why are there many precepts of natural
law, when man's nature is one and so is his reason?]

1. All these precepts of the law of nature, insofar as they
are referred to one first precept, do have the rational character
[*ratio*] of one natural law.

2. All inclinations of this kind, of whatsoever parts of
human nature, for instance, of the concupiscible or irascible
powers, belong to the natural law inasmuch as they are
regulated by reason, and they are reduced to one first precept,
as has been said. According to this, there are many precepts

in themselves of the law of nature but they share in one common root.

3. Although reason is one in itself, it is directive of all things that pertain to men. For this reason, all things that can be regulated by reason are contained under the law of reason.

Synderesis: The Understanding of Practical Principles

Since reasoning is somewhat variable, and is in a way mobile, according as it proceeds in its deductions from principles to conclusions, and since deception is possible in this process of reasoning, every act of reasoning must proceed from some knowledge that has a definite uniformity and stability. Such knowledge does not come about by discursive investigation; rather, it is presented all at once to the intellect. Just as reasoning in the speculative area goes deductively from certain self-evident principles (for which the habit is called *understanding*), so also must practical reasoning make its deductions from self-evident principles (for example, that evil should not be done, that the precepts of God will have to be obeyed, and others such); and the habit for these is *synderesis*.

Hence, I say that synderesis is distinguished from practical reasoning not indeed in the substance of the potency but as a habit which is in a way inborn in our mind from the very light of the agent intellect, as is the case with the habit of speculative principles (such as, every whole is greater than its part, and the like). However, we need sense perception and memory to make definite our knowledge of these, as is said in the *Posterior Analytics* (II, 19, 99b20). And so, I say that synderesis designates either simply a habit, or else the potency as developed in us by an innate habit.

On the Sentences, II, 24, 2, 3, c. Trans. V.J.B.

Moral Rules and Natural Law

Moral rules are concerned with those matters that essentially
pertain to good behavior. Now, since human morals are
spoken of in relation to reason (for it is the proper principle
of human acts), those customs that are in conformity with
reason are called good, and those that are in discord with
reason are deemed bad. Just as every judgment of speculative reason proceeds from the natural knowledge of first principles, so, too, does every judgment of practical reason issue
from certain naturally known principles, as we have explained
before.

Now, it is possible to proceed in different ways from these
principles in making judgments on different problems. There
are some cases in human actions that are so explicit that they
can be approved or condemned at once, with very little
thought, by reference to those general and primary principles.
Then, there are other problems for the judgment of which
a good deal of thinking on the different circumstances is required. Careful consideration of such problems is not the
prerogative of just any person but of the wise. In the same
way, it is not the function of all men to consider the conclusions of the sciences but only of the philosophers. Again,
there are still other matters for the judgment of which man
stands in need of help by divine instruction, as is so in the
case of items of belief.

And so, it becomes evident that since moral precepts belong
among the matters that pertain to good behavior, and since
these are items that are in conformity with reason, and since
every judgment of human reason is derived in some fashion
from natural reason, it must be true that all moral rules belong to the law of nature, but not all in the same way.

For, there are some things that the natural reason of every
man judges immediately and essentially as things to be done

Summa of Theology, I-II, 100, 1, c. Trans. V.J.B.

or not done; for example, *Honor thy father and mother,*
and *Thou shalt not kill; Thou shalt not steal.* Precepts of this
kind belong in an unqualified way to the law of nature.

Then, there are other things that are judged by a more
subtle rational consideration, on the part of the wise men,
to be matters of obligation. Now, these belong to the law of
nature in this way: they of course require instruction, by
which less favored people are taught by those who are wise;
for example, *Rise up before the hoary head, and honor the
person of the aged man* (Lev. 19:32), and other injunctions
of this kind.

Finally, there are other matters for the judgment of which
human reason needs divine instruction, whereby we are taught
concerning matters of divinity; for example, *Thou shalt not
make to thyself a graven thing, nor the likeness of any
thing. . . . Thou shalt not take the name of thy God in vain*
(Exod. 20:4, 7).

The Meaning of Moral Conscience

The term "conscience" means the application of knowledge
to something; hence, *conscire* means, in a way, to know along
with something [*simul scire*]. Now, any kind of knowledge
can be applied to something; so, conscience cannot be the
name of any special habit, or of any potency; rather, it
designates the very act which is the application of any kind
of habit, or of any kind of knowledge, to some particular act.

Knowledge is applied to action in two ways: first, when one
considers whether the act is or was being done; second,
when one considers whether the act is right or not. According
to the first way of application, we are said to have the
conscience of an action, in the sense that we know that this
act was done or not. Thus, we say colloquially: This was not
done "to my knowledge" [*de conscientia mea*]; that is, I do
(or did) not know whether this was done. And it is in this

Disputed Questions on Truth, XVII, 1, c. Trans. V.J.B.

way that one understands the passage in Gen. 43:22: *It is not in our consciences, who placed the money in our bags;* and in Eccles. 7:23: *Thy conscience knoweth that thou hast often spoken evil of others.* It is according to this usage that conscience is said to testify to something: Rom. 9:1: *My conscience giving testimony for me.*

But in the second way of application, whereby knowledge is applied to action in order to know whether the act is right or not, there are two possibilities. In one manner, we are directed by means of habitual knowledge to something which is to be done, or not done. In another manner, the act after being done is examined in relation to habitual knowledge, as to whether it is right or not right. These two procedures in the realm of operative knowledge are distinguished according to the two methods used in speculative thinking: the way of discovery and the way of judgment. For, the way in which we look by means of knowledge to see what should be done (that is, when we are as it were taking counsel) is like the process of discovery, whereby we investigate the conclusions by going from the principles. But the way in which we examine and discuss the rightness of things already done is like the way of judgment, in which we resolve conclusions into their principles. Now, we use the name "conscience" for both kinds of application.

When knowledge is applied to the action, as directing it, conscience is said to instigate, or to induce, or to bind. However, when knowledge is applied to the action by way of examining things already done, conscience is thus said to accuse or cause remorse, provided what has been done is found to be in discord with knowledge in the light of which it is examined; and to defend or excuse, when what has been done is found to have proceeded according to the pattern of the knowledge.

One should understand that in the first kind of application of knowledge to the act, with the purpose of knowing whether it was done, this application is a matter of sensory knowledge; of memory, for example, through which we remember what has been done; of sensation, through which we perceive this particular act that we are now doing. However, in the second and third kinds of application, in which we take counsel as to what should be done, or examine what has been done already, the habit of operative reason (called synderesis), the habit of wisdom (by which superior reason is perfected), and the habit of science (by which inferior reason is perfected) are applied to the act. They may be all applied together, or just one or the other of them. For, we examine what we have done in the light of these habits; and we take counsel as to what actions should be done according to them. However, the act of examination is not merely concerned with things that have been done but also with actions to be done; counsel, however, deals solely with things to be done.

How the Morality of an Action Is Judged

Though an action receives its species from the object, it does not receive its species from it considered as a material object but according to the rational character of the object. Thus, the act of seeing a stone is not specified by the stone but by the colored thing which is the essential object of vision. Now, every human action has either the rational character of wrong-doing, or of a meritorious act, inasmuch as it is voluntary. But the object of the will, according to its proper meaning, is the apprehended good; and so, the human act is judged virtuous or vicious according to the apprehended good toward which the will is essentially attracted and not according to the material object of the action.

For instance, if a man kills a stag, believing that he is killing his father, he commits the sin of patricide. On the other hand, if some hunter, thinking to kill a stag and having taken due care, kills his father by chance, he is quite free from the crime of patricide.

Quodlibetal Questions, III, 12, 17, c. Trans. V.J.B.

Specific Differences in Moral Matters
and Circumstances

Since a moral action is an act that issues in a voluntary way from reason, moral action must be specified according to something that is considered objectively as having an ordered relation to reason. Thus, we said in the preceding article that if it be in agreement with reason, the act will be good specifically, but if it be in discord with reason, it will be evil specifically.

Now, what is not in agreement with reason, on the basis of the object that is considered, may specifically differentiate sin in two ways: first, materially, and second, formally. Material diversification arises by opposition to the corresponding virtue, for virtues differ specifically because of the way that reason discovers a mean in various subject matters. For instance, justice exists according to the way that reason establishes a mean in exchanges and distributions and similar activities; temperance works in the area of concupiscent feelings; fortitude in the field of feelings of fear and daring; and likewise for the others.

Nor should it seem unfitting to anyone that the species of the virtues are differentiated according to the various subject matters, because material diversity has usually been taken as distinguishing individuals rather than species; as a matter of fact, even among physical things in nature material diversity produces a difference of species when the diversity of matter requires a diversity of form. So, too, in moral actions specifically different virtues must deal with different subject matters in which reason finds the mean in different ways. Thus, in cases of concupiscence reason discovers the mean by way of restraint; and so the virtue that is set up in these matters is nearer to defect than to excess, as the very name "temperance" indicates. In problems of daring and fear, however,

Disputed Questions on Evil, II, 6, c. Trans. V.J.B.

reason finds the mean by considering not restraint but rather impulsion; and so the virtue that is established in these matters is nearer to excess than to defect, as the name "fortitude" shows. And we can see the same in the other areas.

Thus, by opposition to the virtues, sins are specifically differentiated according to various subject matters, for example, homicide, adultery, and theft. Nor should we say that they differ in species according to the difference of their precepts; rather, on the contrary, the precepts are distinguished on the basis of the diversification of the virtues and vices, because there are precepts so that we may act in accord with virtue and avoid sins. Of course, if there were any sins that were such simply because they were prohibited, then it would be reasonable in their case for the sins to differ specifically according to a difference of their precepts.

But because there is but one virtue for a given subject matter and yet it is possible for sins to be specifically different in regard to it, in the second place we must consider formally the specific differentiation of sins; let us say, insofar as one sins by way of excess or defect, for thus does cowardice differ from presumption, and illiberality from prodigality; or else according to differences of circumstances, and thus the species of gluttony are distinguished according to the items in this verse: *too quickly, too magnificently, too much, too eagerly, too zealously.*

So, then, now that we understand how sins are specifically distinguished, we must consider what a circumstance is. Of course we say that a circumstance is something that circumscribes the act, as something extrinsically considered, outside the substance of the action. Now, this occurs first of all on the side of the cause: either the final one when we consider *why* one acted, or on the part of the principal agent when we consider *who* did it, or on the part of the instrument when we consider *by what* instrumentality he did it or *by what means.* Secondly, it may circumscribe the act by way of measure: for instance, when we consider *where* or *when* he did it. Thirdly, it may relate to the action itself: either we may consider the *manner* of acting, whether he struck lightly or forcefully, frequently or but once; or we may consider the object or matter of the action, for instance, whether he struck his father or a stranger; or also the *effect* produced in acting, for instance, whether in striking he caused a wound or even death. And all these are included in this verse: *who, what, where, by what means, why, how,* and *when,* provided that under *what* we include not only the effect but also the object, so that it covers both *what results* and *on what.*

Is Augustine's Definition of Virtue Suitable?

St. Augustine says: "Virtue is a good quality of the mind, by which we live righteously, of which no one can make bad use; which God works in us, without us." [Cf. *On Free Choice,* II, 19.]

It would seem that this is not a good definition.

Objections:

1. Virtue is a kind of goodness. If, then, it is good, it is so either by its own goodness, or by the goodness of something else. If the latter, we have an infinite process; if the former, virtue becomes the primary good, because only the first good is good *per se.*

2. Further, that which is common to all being should not be placed in the definition of any one thing. But goodness, which is convertible with being, is common to all being. Therefore, it should not be included in the definition of virtue.

3. Further, as good is in moral beings, so is it in natural beings. But good and bad do not vary the species of natural

Disputed Question on the Virtues in General, 2. Trans. Reid, *The Virtues (in General),* pp. 9–13.

things. Neither, therefore, should "good" be placed in the definition of virtue, as though it were the specific difference of virtue.

4. Further, a *differentia* is not included in the definition of its genus. But good is included in the definition of quality, just as being is. Consequently, it should not be added to the definition of virtue, so as to say that: "Virtue is a good quality of the mind, etc."

5. Further, evil and good are opposites. But evil does not constitute any species, since it is a privation; neither, therefore, does good. Thus goodness must not be placed as an essential *differentia* in the definition of virtue.

6. Further, goodness is more universal than quality. Therefore, one quality does not differ from another by its goodness; for which reason goodness should not be placed in the definition of virtue, as though it were the *differentia* of that quality.

7. Further, nothing is made up of two acts. But goodness denotes a certain act, and quality likewise. It is improper, then, to say that virtue is a "good quality."

8. Further, what is predicated in the abstract is not predicated in the concrete; thus whiteness is a color, it is not something colored. But goodness is predicated of virtue in the abstract. Therefore, it is not predicated of it in the concrete; and so it is incorrect to say that virtue is a "good quality."

9. Further, no *differentia* is predicated in the abstract of a species; wherefore, Avicenna says that man is not rationality but rational being. But virtue is goodness. Therefore, goodness is not the *differentia* of virtue; hence we cannot truly say that virtue is a "good quality."

10. Further, a moral evil is called a vice. Therefore, moral good is the same as virtue; and therefore, goodness should not be included in the definition of virtue, or else the same thing would define itself.

11. Further, mind refers to the intellect. But virtue pertains rather to the will [*affectum*]. Therefore, it is wrong to say that virtue is a good quality of the "mind."

12. Further, according to Augustine, mind denotes the higher part of the soul. But there are some virtues in the lower powers. Therefore, it is not suitable to say, in the definition of virtue, "a good quality of the mind."

13. Further, the subject of virtue is a power, and not the essence of the soul. But mind seems to designate the essence of the soul; for Augustine says that in mind there are understanding, memory, and will. Therefore "mind" is not to be placed in the definition of virtue.

14. Further, that which is proper to a species should not be included in the definition of its genus. But righteousness [*rectitudo*] is proper to justice. Hence righteousness should not be placed in the definition of virtue, as it is in Augustine's definition: "a good quality of the mind, by which we live righteously."

15. Further, in living things to live is to be [*vivere viventibus est esse*]. But virtue does not perfect one in being but in acting. Therefore, we should not say "by which we live righteously."

16. Further, whoever takes pride in a certain thing makes a bad use of it. But some are proud of their virtues. Therefore, one can make a bad use of virtues.

17. Further, in his book *De Libero Arbitrio* Augustine says that it is only of the supreme goods that no one makes bad use. But virtue is not one of the highest goods, because the latter are sought for their own sake, which is not so with virtues, since these are desired for the sake of something else, namely for happiness. Therefore, it is improper to say: "of which no one can make bad use."

18. Further, a thing is generated, nourished, and increased by the same cause. But virtue is nourished and increased by our acts, for the diminution of cupidity is the increase of charity. Therefore, virtue is generated by our acts, so that it is incorrect to place in the definition: "which God works in us, without us."

19. Further, that which removes an impediment is regarded as a mover and cause. But, in a certain sense, free

will removes the impediments to virtue. Therefore, free will is, to this extent, the cause of virtue, so that it is not right to say that God works virtue in us, without us.

20. Further, Augustine says: "He who created thee without thee, will not justify thee without thee." Therefore, the conclusion is as above.

21. Lastly, this definition seems to be proper to grace. But virtue and grace are not one and the same thing. Consequently, virtue is not well-defined by Augustine.

I reply:

We must hold that Augustine's is the true definition of virtue, even if the last phrase be omitted; and that it is suitable for every human virtue.

For, as we have said (in the preceding article), virtue ultimately disposes a power for perfect act: but this perfect act is the end to which a power or agent is ordered: hence virtue renders good both the power and the agent, as we have already observed (*ibid.*). Therefore, in the definition of virtue, one element is included which pertains to the perfection of the act, and another which pertains to the perfection of the power or agent.

Now two things are required for the perfection of an act. It is necessary that the act be a good one, and that the habit cannot be the principle of a contrary act. For that which is the principle of both a good and a bad act cannot in itself be the perfect principle of a good act, since a habit is the perfection of a power. Hence it must be the principle of an act which is wholly good and in no way bad. For this reason, the Philosopher says in the *Ethics*, that opinion, which can be true or false, is not a virtue; but science, which is had only of truth, is a virtue. The first requirement is indicated in the words: "by which we live righteously"; the second, by the phrase: "of which no one can make bad use."

With regard to the fact that virtue makes its subject good, three things must be considered. The first is the sub-

ject itself, and this is determined by the word "mind"; for
a human virtue can reside only in that part of man by which
he is truly human. Secondly, the perfection of the intellect,
which is designated by the word "good"; for goodness be-
speaks an order to an end. Thirdly, the manner in which the
virtue inheres in its subject is shown by the word "quality";
for virtue does not inhere as a passion, but as a habit, as
was said above (preceding Article).

All of this belongs to both moral and intellectual virtue,
to theological, to acquired, and to infused virtue. The phrase
which Augustine adds: "which God works in us, without
us," applies only to infused virtue.

Reply to objections:

1. Just as accidents are called beings, not because they
subsist, but because there is some being in them; so virtue
is said to be good, not as though it were itself (its own)
good, but as that by which something is good. Hence it
is not necessary that virtue be good thanks to the goodness
of another, as though it were informed by the goodness of
something else.

2. The good which is convertible with being is not that
which is here placed in the definition of virtue; rather it is
that goodness which is ordered to a moral act.

3. Acts are distinguished according to the diverse forms
of their agents, as heating and freezing. Now good and evil
are, as it were, the form and object of the will—since an
agent always impresses its own form on a patient and a mover
does the same on the object being moved. Hence moral acts,
the principle of which is the will, are specifically diversified
according to good and evil. However, the principle of natural
acts is not the end, but some form. Therefore, in natural
things, species of acts are not distinguished according to good
and evil, as are moral acts.

4. Moral goodness is not included in the notion of quality;
hence the objection proves nothing.

5. Evil constitutes a species, not insofar as it is a privation, but by reason of the subject of the privation, when that subject is lacking in some good. This is how evil constitutes a species.

6. This objection relates to natural, not moral good; it is the latter which is placed in the definition of virtue.

7. Goodness implies no good other than virtue itself, as is clear from what has been said. For virtue is essentially a quality; hence it is manifest that "good" and "quality" do not bespeak diverse acts, but one and the same act.

8. This objection errs with respect to the transcendentals, which embrace all being. For essence is being, and goodness is good, and unity is one; whereas whiteness cannot be called white. The reason is that whatever is grasped by the intellect must fall under the notion of being and, consequently, of goodness and of oneness. Thus essence and goodness and unity cannot be understood save under the aspect of good, one, and being. This is why goodness can be called good, and unity, one.

Is the Will the Subject of Virtue?

It would seem that it is.

Objections:

1. A greater perfection is required in one who commands, that he may do so rightly, than in one who obeys, that he may rightly fulfill a command. The reason for this is that the one who carries out a command is ordered by the one who commands. But the will is related to a virtuous act as

Disputed Question on the Virtues in General, 5. Trans. Reid, *The Virtues (in General)*, pp. 34-39.

commanding it, whereas the irascible and concupiscible powers are the faculties which obey its command and perform the act. Since there is virtue in the irascible and concupiscible powers, as in a subject, it would seem that, a fortiori, there should be virtue in the will.

2. It might be objected that the natural inclination of the will to good suffices for its rectitude. We naturally desire the end; hence there is no need of our being rectified by an added virtuous habit. On the contrary, the will is concerned, not only with the ultimate end, but with other ends as well. As regards these other ends, the will can desire them either rightly or wrongly: Good men present good ends to themselves; bad men seek evil ends. Thus we read in the *Ethics:* "Such as each man is, so does the end seem to him." Therefore, for the rectitude and perfection of the will, a virtuous habit is required.

3. Further, in the cognitive part of the soul there is natural knowledge, namely, of principles; and with respect to this knowledge there is in us the intellectual virtue of understanding, which is the habit of first principles. Consequently, there should be some virtue in the will with respect to that to which it is naturally inclined.

4. Further, just as there is moral virtue to regulate the passions, as temperance and fortitude; so also there is virtue with regard to operations, namely, justice. Now the will acts without any passion, while the irascible and concupiscible powers operate from passion. Therefore, just as there is moral virtue in the irascible and concupiscible appetites, so also in the will.

5. Further, in the *Ethics,* the Philosopher says that love or friendship arises from a passion. But friendship is the result of choice, and the love which is without passion is an act of the will. Since, therefore, friendship may be either with or without passion, according to the *Ethics,* it would seem that there is virtue in the will, as in a subject.

6. Further, charity is the most excellent [*potissima*] of the virtues, as the Apostle declares, in I Cor. 13:13. But only

the will can be the subject of charity, for the lower concupiscible appetite, which extends only to sensible goods,
cannot be its subject. Therefore, the will is the subject of
virtue.

7. Further, according to Augustine, we are immediately
united to God especially by our will. But that which unites
us to God is virtue. Therefore, it would seem that there is
virtue in the will as in a subject.

8. Further, happiness is in the will, according to Hugh of
St. Victor. Now virtues are certain dispositions to happiness.
But since a disposition to and the perfection of anything
reside in the same subject, it would seem that virtue resides
in the will as in a subject.

9. Further, according to Augustine, it is the will by which
we sin or live righteously. But a righteous life derives from
virtue. Hence Augustine remarks in *Contra Iulianum,* that
virtue is a good quality of the mind, by which we live
righteously. Therefore, there is virtue in the will.

10. Further, contraries refer naturally to the same subject. Now the contrary of virtue is sin. Therefore, since every
sin lies in the will, as Augustine says, it would seem that
virtue is in the same faculty.

11. Further, human virtue should be assigned to that part
of the soul which is proper to man. But the will is proper to
man, as also the reason, as being closer to reason than are
the irascible and concupiscible powers. But since the irascible
and concupiscible powers are the subjects of virtue, it would
seem that, a fortiori, so is the will.

On the contrary:

1. Every virtue is either intellectual or moral, as we learn
from the Philosopher, at the end of *I Ethics.* Moral virtue has
for its subject that which is rational, not by its essence, but
by participation; whereas intellectual virtue has for its subject what is rational in its essence. Since the will falls under
neither type of subject: because it is neither a cognitive

power, which is rational in its essence, nor does it belong in the irrational part of the soul, which is rational only by participation; it would seem that the will can in no way be the subject of virtue.

2. Further, there should not be many virtues ordered to the same act. But this would be the case, if the will were the subject of virtue; because it has been shown (in the preceding Article) that there are some virtues in the irascible and concupiscible powers; and, since in some sense the will is concerned with the acts of these powers, it would have to follow that there were certain virtues in the will which ordered these same acts. Therefore, it must be admitted that the will is not the subject of virtue.

I reply:

By a virtuous habit the power which possesses it acquires the perfection of its act. Hence no virtuous habit is necessary for an act to which a power is inclined by its very nature. For virtue ordains powers to good; it is virtue which makes one who possesses it good and renders his operation good.

Now what virtue effects in other powers, the will enjoys by its very nature: for its object is the good. The will tends towards good in the same manner as the concupiscible appetite tends towards what is pleasurable, and as hearing is keyed to sound. Hence the will does not need any virtuous habit, inclining it to the good which is proportionate to it, because it tends towards this by its very nature as a power. However, it does need a virtuous habit to pursue the good which exceeds its proportions as a power.

Since the appetite of every subject tends to the good proper to that subject, a good can exceed the proportion of the will in two ways: first, by reason of the species, secondly, by reason of the individual.

A good may exceed the proportion of the will to its object by reason of the species of man, so that the will must be elevated to tend to this good, which exceeds the limits of human good: and by human I mean what man is capable of by his own natural powers. Now the Divine good is above human good, and to this Divine good the will of man is elevated by charity and by hope.

A good may also exceed a man's natural capacity by reason of the man as an individual, in this sense, that he seeks that which is good for another man, although his will is not carried beyond the limits of human good. Thus justice and all the virtues which regard a man's dealings with others, as liberality and the rest, perfect the will. For justice is "another's good," as the Philosopher says in the *Ethics*.

Consequently, there are two virtues which have the will as their subject, and these are charity and justice. A sign of this is that, although these virtues pertain to the appetite, still they do not regard the passions, as do temperance and fortitude, from which it is clear that they do not reside in the sense appetite, where the passions are found, but in the rational appetite, which is the will, and in which there are no passions. For every passion is in the sensitive part of the soul, as is proved in the *Physics*. For the same reason, those virtues which control the passions, as fortitude with respect to fear and daring, and temperance as regards the concupiscible pleasures, must be in the sensitive appetite. Nor is it necessary that there be any virtue in the will as regards those passions, because the good in them is what is according to reason. Now the will is naturally ordained to this good, by its very constitution as a power, since the good of reason is the proper object of the will.

Reply to objections:

1. The judgment of reason is sufficient for the will's commands; for the will naturally desires what is good according to reason, as the concupiscible appetite desires sensible pleasure.

2. The natural inclination of the will tends not only

towards the ultimate end, but also to good presented to it by
reason. For the object of the will is understood good, to
which this faculty is naturally ordered, as any power is to
its object, which is the good proper to it, as was said above
(in the body of the Article). Yet a man may sin as regards
this very object, insofar as the judgment of reason is clouded
by passion.

3. Knowledge is had through an intentional species. The
intellectual power is not sufficient by itself for knowing, but
must receive a species from a sensible object. Consequently,
we need a habit even for those things which we know
naturally, a habit which in some way begins in the senses, as
it says at the end of *II Posterior Analytics*. But the will is
unlike the intellect in this respect, because it does not need
any species in order to will.

4. The virtues which regulate the passions are in the lower
appetite. No virtue is required in the higher appetite for
these passions, for the reason already stated (in the body
of the Article).

5. Friendship is not properly a virtue, but consequent
upon virtue. From the fact that a man is virtuous, it follows
that he loves those like himself. But it is otherwise with
charity, which is a certain friendship with God, elevating
man to what surpasses his natural good. Hence charity is
in the will, as we have said (in the body of the Article).

From what has been said, the answer to the sixth and
seventh objections is evident, for the virtue which unites
the will to God is charity.

8. Certain things are required as dispositions for happiness,
such as acts of the moral virtues, by which impediments to
happiness are removed: impediments such as mental dis-
quietude, resulting from the passions and from external
disturbances.

Complete beatitude consists essentially in an act of the
reason or intellect. For the happiness of contemplation is
nothing other than the perfect contemplation of supreme
Truth; whereas the happiness of the active life is an act of

prudence by which a man governs himself and those around him.

In beatitude there is an added perfection, namely delight, which perfects happiness as beauty graces youth, as we are told in the *Ethics*. This added perfection pertains to the will. If we are speaking of heavenly beatitude, which is promised to the saints, it is charity which perfects the will and orders it to the perfection of happiness.

But if we are speaking of the happiness of contemplation, which the philosophers have treated, the will is ordered to this sort of delight by natural desire. Thus it is evident that all the virtues need not reside in the will.

9. It is by the will, which commands all our acts, both virtuous and vicious, that we both live righteously and sin; but not as though it were the will which elicited all of these acts. Hence it is not necessary that the will be the proximate subject of every virtue.

10. Every sin is traceable to the will as to its cause insofar as every sin is committed with the will's consent. But it need not follow that every sin be in the will as in its subject, for gluttony and lust are in the concupiscible appetite, while pride is in the irascible.

11. From the propinquity of the will to reason, it happens that the will is in harmony with reason by its very nature as a power. Hence it does not need an added virtue for this, as do the inferior powers, namely, the irascible and concupiscible.

In reply to the first objection raised *On the contrary*, it must be said that charity and hope, which are in the will, are not included in this division of the Philosopher's; for they are of another class of virtues, called the theological virtues. But justice is one of the moral virtues; for the will, like other appetites, participates in reason insofar as it is directed by reason. Although the will belongs to the same nature as the intellective part, still, it does not pertain to the power of reason itself.

To the second objection *On the contrary*, it must be replied that there need be no virtue in the will as regards those acts for which there is virtue in the irascible and concupiscible parts, for the reason given above (in the body of the Article).

The Evil of Lying

That which is evil generically can in no way be good and licit, because in order that something be good it is required that all its aspects concur in a right way; "for the good arises from an integral cause, while evil results from defective individual aspects," as Dionysius says (*On the Divine Names*, 4, 30). But lying is evil generically. It is an act that falls upon improper matter; since words are naturally the signs of what is understood, it is unnatural and unfitting for a person to signify by word what he does not have in his mind.

Thus, the Philosopher says in the *Ethics* (IV, 7, 1127a28), "a lie is of itself mean and something to be avoided, while the truth is good and praiseworthy." Hence, "every lie is a sin," as Augustine says in his book *Against Lying* (c. 1).

In answer to the fourth objection, it should be stated that a lie has the character of a sin not only because of the damage that is done to a neighbor but from its own disorder, as we have said. Now, it is not permitted to use an illicit disorder with the purpose of preventing injuries or losses to other persons; in the same way, it is illicit to steal in order that a man may give alms, unless perhaps in case of necessity, when all things become common. So, it is not licit to tell a lie in order to free a person from some other danger. However, it is permitted to conceal the truth prudently by means of an evasion, as Augustine says in the book *Against Lying* (c. 10).

Summa of Theology, II-II, 110, 3, c, reply to Obj. 4. Trans. V.J.B.

A Moral Consideration of Fornication

Hence appears the folly of those who say that simple fornication is not a sin. For they say: Given a woman free from a husband, and under no control of father or any other person, if any one approaches her with her consent, he does her no wrong, because she is pleased so to act, and has the disposal of her own person: nor does he do any wrong to another, for she is under no one's control: therefore there appears no sin. Nor does it seem to be a sufficient answer to say that she wrongs God, for God is not offended by us except by what we do against our own good: but it does not appear that this conduct is against man's good: hence no wrong seems to be done to God thereby. In like manner also it does not appear a sufficient answer, that wrong is thereby done to one's neighbor, who is scandalised: for sometimes a neighbor is scandalised by what of itself is not a sin, in which case the sin is only incidental: but the question is not whether fornication is a sin incidentally, but whether it is a sin ordinarily and in itself.

We must seek a solution from what has been said before: for it has been seen that God has care of everything according to that which is good for it. Now it is good for everything to gain its end, and evil for it to be diverted from its due end. But as in the whole so also in the parts, our study should be that every part of man and every act of his may attain its due end. Now though the semen is superfluous for the preservation of the individual, yet it is necessary to him for the propagation of the species: while other excretions, such as excrement, urine, sweat, and the like, are needful for no further purpose: hence the only good that comes to man of them is by their removal from the body. But that is not the object in the emission of the semen, but rather the

Summa Against the Gentiles, III, 122. Trans. J. Rickaby, On God and His Creatures, pp. 183-185.

profit of generation, to which the union of the sexes is directed. But in vain would be the generation of man unless due nurture followed, without which the offspring generated could not endure. The emission of the semen then ought to be so directed as that both the proper generation may ensue and the education of the offspring be secured.

Hence it is clear that every emission of the semen is contrary to the good of man, which takes place in a way whereby generation is impossible; and if this is done on purpose, it must be a sin. I mean a way in which generation is impossible *in itself*, as is the case in every emission of the semen without the natural union of male and female: wherefore such sins are called "sins against nature." But if it is *by accident* that generation cannot follow from the emission of the semen, the act is not against nature on that account, nor is it sinful; the case of the woman being barren would be a case in point.

Likewise it must be against the good of man for the semen to be emitted under conditions which, allowing generation to ensue, nevertheless bar the due education of the offspring. We observe that in those animals, dogs for instance, in which the female by herself suffices for the rearing of the offspring, the male and female stay no time together after the performance of the sexual act. But with all animals in which the female by herself does not suffice for the rearing of the offspring, male and female dwell together after the sexual act so long as is necessary for the rearing and training of the offspring. This appears in birds, whose young are incapable of finding their own food immediately they are hatched: for since the bird does not suckle her young with milk, according to the provision made by nature in quadrupeds, but has to seek food abroad for her young, and therefore keep them warm in the period of feeding, the female could not do this duty all alone by herself: hence divine providence has put in the male a natural instinct of standing by the female for the rearing of the brood. Now in the human species the female is clearly insufficient of herself for the rearing of the offspring, since the need of human life makes many demands, which cannot be met by one parent alone. Hence the fitness of human life requires man to stand by woman after the sexual act is done, and not to go off at once and form connexions with any one he meets, as is the way with fornicators. Nor is this reasoning traversed by the fact of some particular woman having wealth and power enough to nourish her offspring all by herself: for in human acts the line of natural rectitude is not drawn to suit the accidental variety of the individual, but the properties common to the whole species.

A further consideration is, that in the human species the young need not only bodily nutrition, as animals do, but also the training of the soul. Other animals have their natural instincts to provide for themselves: but man lives by reason, which takes the experience of a long time to arrive at discretion. Hence children need instruction by the confirmed experience of their parents: nor are they capable of such instruction as soon as they are born, but after a long time, the time in fact taken to arrive at the years of discretion. For this instruction again a long time is needed; and then moreover, because of the assaults of passion, whereby the judgment of prudence is thwarted, there is need not of instruction only, but also of repression. For this purpose the woman by herself is not competent, but at this point especially there is requisite the concurrence of the man, in whom there is at once reason more perfect to instruct, and force more potent to chastise. Therefore in the human race the advancement of the young in good must last, not for a short time, as in birds, but for a long period of life. Hence, whereas it is necessary in all animals for the male to stand by the female for such time as the father's concurrence is requisite for bringing up of the progeny, it is natural for man to be tied to the society of one fixed woman for a long period, not a short one. This social tie we call marriage. Marriage then is natural to man, and an irregular connexion outside of marriage is contrary to the good of man; and therefore fornication must be sinful.

Nor yet should it be counted a slight sin for one to procure the emission of the semen irrespective of the due purpose of generation and rearing of issue, on the pretense that it is a slight sin, or no sin at all, to apply any part of one's body to another use than that to which it is naturally ordained, as if, for example, one were to walk on his hands, or to do with his feet something that ought to be done with his hands. The answer is that by such inordinate applications as those mentioned the good of man is not greatly injured: but the inordinate emission of the semen is repugnant to the good of nature, which is the conservation of the species. Hence, after the sin of murder, whereby a human nature already in actual existence is destroyed, this sort of sin seems to hold the second place, whereby the generation of human nature is precluded.

The Possession and Use of Material Things

Two items are appropriate to man in reference to external realities. One of these is the power to obtain and dispose of them. In regard to this, it is licit for a man to possess things of his own. Indeed, it is even necessary for human life, for three reasons.

The first reason is because a person is more zealous in caring for something that belongs to him alone than for something that is common to all or to a group, because every person avoids work and leaves to the other fellow whatever belongs to the community, as happens where there is a plurality of officials.

The second reason is that human possessions are handled in a more orderly way, if it is incumbent on each person to provide his own things for himself; there would be confusion if each person were to take care of everything without any distinction of work.

The third reason is because this system preserves the condition of mankind in a more peaceful way, provided that each person is satisfied with his own possessions. Consequently, we observe that among those who possess something in common and without any distinction of interest, quarrels frequently arise.

Now, the other thing that is appropriate to man in regard to external things is the use of them. Concerning this, a man should not hold external things as his own but as common; that is, in such a way that one will share them with others in cases of need. Hence, the Apostle says (I Tim. 6:17): *Charge the rich of this world to give readily, sharing with others.*

A Letter on Credit Sales and Usury

To his very dear brother in Christ, James of Viterbo, Lector at Florence, from Brother Thomas of Aquin: Greetings.

I received your letter containing some cases concerning which you requested the opinion of the Archbishop Elect of Capua and myself. After a discussion thereon with the aforesaid Archbishop Elect and afterwards with Cardinal Hugh, I decided that the following reply should be made to the first case.

Assuming that the custom of deferring payment for three months, as is set forth in the case, has been introduced for the common good of merchants, that is, for facilitating commerce, and not for fraudulent usury: then a distinction must be made. For the vendor, while granting credit for the aforesaid interval, sells his goods either (1) for an amount exceeding the just price on account of his waiting for payment, or (2) for an amount equal to the just price.

In the first alternative there is no doubt that contract is usurious, inasmuch as the waiting for a certain time is included in the price. And this is not excused by the fact that the second vendor may be employed by the first, since for no

On Buying and Selling. Trans. A. O'Rahilly, "Notes on St. Thomas on Credit," *Irish Ecclesiastical Record*, XXXI, 1928, 164-165.

cause whatever may the price be increased on account of the
interval for which payment is deferred.

In the second alternative, there is no usury. Nor does the
fact that he would sell for less were payment made immediately make any difference. This can be seen by comparison
with other debts. If an amount due to a person is payable
after a certain date, even though he might remit a portion
of the debt if it were paid him sooner, still in this case it is
clear that the creditor is entirely immune from usury. For
though it smacks of usury to take more than is due on account
of delay in payment, to take less that one may be paid sooner
does not smack of usury, especially on the part of him who
gets less, though on the part of him who gives less on paying
sooner, there seems to be some kind of usury since he sells an
interval of time. Hence also in the case proposed there is
more fear of usury in connection with the buyer who, when
he pays before three months, buys the cloth for less than
the just value, than in connection with the seller who takes
less that he may be sooner paid.

From this it is also clear what should be said concerning
the second case. For if the merchants of Tuscany, bringing
cloth from the Fair of Lagny, to wait for it [payment?] until
Easter, sell the cloth for more than it is worth in the general
market, there is no doubt that this is usury. But if they sell
it, not at more than its worth but at its worth, yet at more
than they would take for it if payment were made immediately
to them, there is no usury.

In the third case a similar reply should be made. For if
those who accept money with usury wish to recover that usury
by selling the cloth at more than its worth on account of the
aforesaid delay, there is no doubt that this is usury since
time is clearly sold. Nor are they excused by the fact that
they wish to indemnify themselves, for no one should indemnify himself by committing mortal sin. And although they can
in selling the cloth lawfully recover other expenses lawfully
contracted, for example, the cost of transporting the cloth,
still they cannot recover the usury they paid, for this was an
unjust payment; especially since by paying usury they sinned

as giving the usurers an occasion for sinning, since the necessity which is urged—namely that they may live more respectably and do a bigger trade—is not such a necessity as suffices to excuse the aforesaid sin. This is clear by comparison; for a man could not in selling cloth recover expenses which he might have incurred carelessly and imprudently.

From what has been said the query in the fourth case is also clear. For if he who owes money payable on a certain date pays before this date that a portion of the debt may be remitted to him, he seems to commit usury, inasmuch as he sells time for paying the money. Hence he is bound to restitution. Nor is he excused by the fact that he is inconvenienced by paying before the date or that he is induced to do this by someone, for all usurers could be excused on the same ground.

This is the firm and definite decision of myself and the aforesaid, namely, the Archbishop Elect of Capua and Cardinal Hugh, concerning the aforesaid cases. Farewell.

RECOMMENDED READINGS

BOURKE, V. J. *Ethics.* New York: Macmillan, 1951.

——. *St. Thomas and the Greek Moralists.* Milwaukee: Marquette University Press, 1947.

DAVITT, T. *The Nature of Law.* St. Louis: Herder, 1951.

ESCHMANN, I. T. "St. Thomas's Approach to Moral Philosophy," *Proceedings of the American Catholic Philosophical Association,* XXXI (1957), 25-36.

GILSON, E. *Moral Values and the Moral Life.* Translated by L. Ward. St. Louis: Herder, 1941.

KLUBERTANZ, G. P. "The Empiricism of Thomistic Ethics," *Proceedings of the American Catholic Philosophical Association,* XXXI (1957), 1-24.

KOSSEL, C. G. "Aquinas, Moral Views of," *Encyclopedia of Morals,* ed. V. Ferm. New York: Philosophical Library, 1956, 11-22.

NOONAN, J. T. *The Scholastic Analysis of Usury*. Cambridge, Mass.: Harvard University Press, 1957.

OESTERLE, J. A. *Ethics*. Englewood Cliffs, N.J.: Prentice-Hall, 1957.

O'NEIL, C. J. *Imprudence in St. Thomas Aquinas*. Milwaukee: Marquette University Press, 1955.

——. "Prudence the Incommunicable Wisdom," *Essays in Thomism*. New York: Sheed and Ward, 1942, 187-204.

RENARD, H. *The Philosophy of Morality*. Milwaukee: Bruce, 1953.

RICKABY, J. *Aquinas Ethicus*. London: Burns, Oates, 1892.

VI. Society and Political Philosophy

Foreword

AQUINAS' APPROACH TO SOCIAL AND POLITICAL PROBLEMS is doubtless somewhat theoretical: he had no political or administrative experience. However, he was the son of a public official, his brothers were active in the political affairs of southern Italy, and Thomas himself was a well-traveled, alert observer of his contemporary situation. While he refused to take on administrative duties (he was offered a bishopric and possibly other situations of preferment), Aquinas was an active participant in many commissions and general meetings of the Order of Preachers. We should not forget that the Dominicans of the thirteenth century adopted many democratic practices within their Order. They used a system of representative government and voted freely on important issues. St. Thomas' shorter works show that he was often consulted by administrative and public officials during his later years.

Two short works are of special importance in this chapter. The treatise *On Kingship* is well known in the history of medieval political theory. This work, addressed to the King of Cyprus, is represented by several extracts in this chapter. It has occasioned much critical discussion both because of the problem of establishing an authentic text and because of the nature of its contents. That the text was added to, or modified, is now rather clear. Several works under the title *On the Governance of Princes* were produced by other writers in the late thirteenth and early fourteenth centuries; they have been confused with the *De Regno* in the early text tradition. Eschmann's Introduction to the English version throws much light on this textual problem. On the other hand, the thoughts expressed by Aquinas in this treatise are perhaps disappointing on first reading. There may be something almost naïve in his instructions to the king on the founding of a new city. But what is important here is the emphasis on the limitation of the power of the chief of state. There is no doubt that Aquinas thought that one man ought to be responsible for the conduct of the affairs of state; there is also no question that he is not a supporter of absolute monarchy. He stresses the role of the people in the selection and criticism of their rulers. There are interesting approaches to democratic thinking in what he says about "polity" as the mixed form of government best calculated to provide good political life.

The second *opusculum* important in political philosophy is the *Letter to the Duchess of Brabant*. This work is sometimes entitled *On the Governance of the Jews*, because the first four questions asked by the Duchess deal with problems presented by Jewish moneylenders in her province. The work is not confined to this topic, as the extract in this chapter shows. Aquinas' advice to the Duchess has occasioned some misunderstanding. Some readers have taken his position to be anti-Semitic. This is not so. His views must be understood in the larger context of his strict position on usury. Aquinas was convinced (as were most Christians in his period) that it was sinful to collect interest for the use of a loan, if the lender charged for the time of the loan. This medieval disapproval of usury has been fully studied by Noonan in the book listed among the readings for Chapter V. Whatever firmness Aquinas recommends in regard to Jewish moneylenders is not a mark of ethnic bias but of his strong opposition to usury. He is equally emphatic in condemning the moneyhandling practices of the non-Jewish bankers of Cahors. A better notion of Thomas' respect for Jewish culture is to be found in his discussion of the laws and customs of the Jews in the *Summa of Theology* (I-II, qq. 98-107).

Of an entirely different character is the *Exposition* of Aristotle's *Politics*. Here Aquinas comments on the well-known political theories of the Stagirite and approves of much of this classic position. The fundamental notion that man has a natural need and bent for social and political life is diametrically opposed to the extreme contract theories of early modern political thought. The family, the village or neighborhood group, and the state, are regarded as natural, not artificially contrived institutions. There is a distinct emphasis on the continuity between good morals and good politics. The common good of a group of human beings is always considered more important than the individual good of a single man, *provided that these goods are on the same level*. But the personal good of ultimate happiness, or eternal life, outranks all temporal common goods. Hence, the individual man is usually obliged to sacrifice his own temporal interests where this is required for the public welfare (on this basis Thomists have always recognized the validity of military-service requirements and of other onerous public duties), but a person is never required to subordinate his own moral welfare, or his right to work for eventual salvation, to the interests of the state. There is no element of totalitarianism in Aquinas' politics.

It is from the foregoing premise that Aquinas' views on the church-state issue emerge. Ecclesiastical and civil societies have different ends and different manners of operating. Aquinas never confuses the laws of his Church with the laws of his State. The purpose of the church is the eternal good of mankind; that of the state is a purely temporal common good. The fact that church-state conflicts arise at times indicates that they are two different types of society and should not be identified. One line of development of Thomistic thinking (in John of Paris) led to fourteenth-century theories of a complete separation of church and state. It is impossible to state with precision what would have been Aquinas' personal attitude toward these later theories, which hinged on a new spirit of nationalism and a laicization of social institutions. It can certainly be said that he was not opposed to the long-established Christian view which distinguished the things of Caesar from those of God.

Social and political problems are also treated at many

points in the two *Summas* and in the other theological writings
of Aquinas. Indeed, these are the best sources of information
on detailed questions. A sampling of such passages is provided
in this chapter. Two extracts are included to illustrate the
general character of his legal thinking. These will indicate
why he is an important figure in the history of jurisprudence.

Political Philosophy as a Practical Science

Now, since human reason has control not only of things that
are available for men's use but also over men themselves who
are ruled by reason, in both cases it moves from simple things
to the complex. This is exemplified in things that are useful
to man, where reason fashions a ship from pieces of wood and
a house from wood and stones; and again in the case of men,
it orders many men into one definite community.

And since there are different degrees and levels of such
communities, the ultimate one is the community of the state
which is organized for the complete fulfillment within itself
[*ad per se sufficientia*] of human life. Hence, this is the most
perfect of all human communities. Moreover, since things
available for the use of man are related to man as to their
end, and since man is more important than these means, therefore this whole that is the state must be more important than
all other wholes that can be known and produced by human
reason.

We can accept four of the political teachings which Aristotle offers in this book.

The first has to do with the necessity of this science. In
fact, of all the things that can be known by reason, some
teaching must be handed on in order to perfect the human
wisdom that is called philosophy. So, because this whole
which is the state is the subject matter for rational judgment,
it was necessary for the full development of philosophy to

Exposition of Aristotle's Politics, I, Lect. 1. Trans. V.J.B.

offer a teaching concerning the state, which is called politics, that is, civil science.

Secondly, we can learn the genus of this science. Now, practical sciences are distinguished from the speculative ones by the fact that the speculative are directed simply to the knowing of the truth, whereas the practical ones are for the sake of some work. Hence, this science must be included under practical philosophy, for a state is a certain whole, which human reason not only can know but also can produce. Again, since reason does some things by way of making, through a transitive action on external matter, and this pertains to the mechanical arts such as the building of houses or ships and the like, while in other cases it works by way of an action which is completed within the agent, as in the case of counseling, choosing, wishing, and other such actions which belong to moral science, it is obvious that political science, being concerned with the direction of men, is not included under the productive sciences, the mechanical arts, but under the active ones which are moral sciences.

Thirdly, we may grasp the importance and the relation of the political to all the other practical sciences. Indeed, the state is the most important thing that can be established by human reason, for all human communities are related to it. Again, all wholes that are fashioned by the mechanical arts from things available for the use of men are related to men, as to their end. So, if the more important science is the one concerned with the more noble and perfect, then, of all the practical sciences the political must be more important and architectonic than all the rest by virtue of its consideration of the ultimate and perfect good in human affairs. This is why the Philosopher says, at the end of the tenth book of the *Ethics*, that philosophy reaches perfection in politics, and it is concerned with human affairs.

Fourthly, from what has been said we may gather the method and order proper to this kind of science. The speculative sciences which consider a whole, by a consideration of its parts and principles, perfect the knowledge of the whole through an explanation of the things which the whole suffers and does. So, too, this science which considers the principles and parts of the state hands on a knowledge of itself by making clear its parts and the things which it suffers and does. And because it is practical, it explains above all how individual actions can be brought to completion—and this is necessary in every practical science.

Man's Dependence on Society

It should be noted that because man is naturally a social animal (in the sense that he needs many things for his life which he, as a solitary individual, cannot provide for himself), it follows that man is naturally a member of some group, through which help in living well is made available to him.

Now, he needs such help for two reasons. First, it is needed for the necessities of life, without which it would be impossible for the present life to be maintained. To this end, man is assisted by the *domestic group* of which he is a member. In fact, every man owes his coming into being, his nourishment, and his training to his parents. Likewise, the individual members of a domestic family assist each other in regard to the necessities of life.

In a second way, man is helped by the group of which he is a member in regard to complete sufficiency; that is to say, so that a man may not merely live but also live well, having all the things that provide for sufficiency in his life. In this way, man is assisted by the *civic group* of which he is a member, not only in regard to bodily things like the many artifacts found in a civil community which a single household could not provide, but also in regard to moral matters. Thus, for instance, juvenile delinquents whom paternal advice is not strong enough to correct may be controlled by public power.

Exposition of Aristotle's Ethics, I, Lect. 1, n. 4. Trans. V.J.B.

Different Kinds of Human Societies

A society is a union of men for the purpose of accomplishing some one objective. Therefore, societies must be distinguished and judgment passed on them, in accord with the diverse objectives that a society may be directed to accomplish; for, judgment about anything whatever is mainly derived from its end. That is why the Philosopher, in the *Ethics* (VIII, 9, 1159b25), distinguishes various associations (which are nothing but societies) according to the different functions in which men associate with each other. He distinguishes friendships according to such associations: of those who are brought up together, for instance, or who do business together, or carry on any other sort of affairs together.

From this, too, comes that distinction of societies that divides them into public and private. That society is called public in which men associate with each other to set up one republic; for instance, all the men of one city, or of one kingdom, are associated in one republic. But a society is private when there is a union to accomplish some private business, as when two or three men enter into a society with the purpose of doing business together.

Now, both these kinds of societies are divisible into perpetual and temporary ones. Sometimes, that for which a group, or even two or three persons, bind themselves together is perpetual. For instance, those who become citizens of a state enter into a perpetual society, because living in a state is the choice of a man's lifetime. This is an example of a political society. Similarly, that private society that obtains between a husband and his wife, or a master and a bond servant, continues perpetually because of the perpetuity of the bond by which they are gathered together. This is an example of a domestic society.

However, when the business for which a group is assembled is chosen to be carried on for a time, the society is not per-

Against the Attackers of the Religious Life, 3. Trans. V.J.B.

petual but temporary. For instance, when many merchants gather at a fair, they are not going to stay there in perpetuity but until their business is finished. This is an example of a society that is public but temporary. Likewise, when two companions engage the same room at an inn, they form not a perpetual but a temporary society. This is an example of a society that is private and temporary.

So, one has to judge these societies in different ways, and he who uses the name society, or association, without distinction simply shows his own ignorance.

All Men Are Naturally Equal in Liberty

Nature has made all men equal in liberty but not in their natural perfections. The free man is he who is his own master, according to the Philosopher (*Metaphysics*, I, 2, 982b26). In fact, one man is not as a result of his nature ordered to another man as to an end. So, the second kind of political authority was not permitted [in a state of integral nature]; for it took away the liberty of the subjects. But the first kind could have been, because it offered nothing prejudicial to liberty, provided the subjects were not subordinated to the good of the sovereign but, on the contrary, the rule of the sovereign were for the good of the subjects whose servants the sovereigns may call themselves, and not inappropriately.

On the Sentences, II, 44, 1, 3, reply to Obj. 1. Trans. V.J.B.

Despotism and the Government of Free Men

That regime is called despotic in which someone rules slaves who possess no ability to resist the command of the ruler, because they have no power of their own. On the other hand, a regime is called politic and regal when someone rules free men who, though subject to the regulation of the sovereign, have nevertheless some power of their own whereby they may oppose the command of the one who gives the orders.

Summa of Theology, I, 81, 3, reply to Obj. 2. Trans. V.J.B.

Polity: The Best Government

We should pay attention to two points concerning the orderly arrangement of the leading men in a state or people. One point is that all should have some part in leadership; in this way the peace of the people is preserved and all men love and protect such an arrangement, as is said in the *Politics*. The other point is that attention be directed to the kind of government, or the system of rule.

There are different kinds of government, as the Philosopher teaches in the *Politics*, yet the chief ones are: kingship, in which one person rules in accord with virtue; and aristocracy, that is, the power of the best men, in which a few men rule in accord with virtue. Hence, the best system of leaders is found in a state or kingdom in which one person is set up to preside over all in accord with virtue. Then, under him are others ruling in accord with virtue. Yet, such a government belongs to all, both because they can be elected out of all, and because they are also elected by all men.

Indeed, such is the best polity, formed by a good mixture of *kingship*, in the sense that one person is the chief, and *aristocracy*, in the sense that many men rule according to virtue, and *democracy* (that is, the power of the people), in the sense that leaders can be elected from among the populace, and further, that the choice of the ruler belongs to the people.

Summa of Theology, I-II, 105, 1, c. Trans. V.J.B.

The Function of a Ruler

[2] The first step in our undertaking must be to set forth what is to be understood by the term *king*.

[3] In all things that are ordered towards an end wherein

On Kingship, I, Ch. 1. Trans. Phelan and Eschmann, *On Kingship,* pp. 3-7.

this or that course may be adopted, some directive principle is needed through which the due end may be reached by the most direct route. A ship, for example, which moves in different directions according to the impulse of the changing winds, would never reach its destination were it not brought to port by the skill of the pilot. Now, man has an end to which his whole life and all his actions are ordered; for man is an intelligent agent, and it is clearly the part of an intelligent agent to act in view of an end. Men also adopt different methods in proceeding towards their proposed end, as the diversity of men's pursuits and actions clearly indicates. Consequently man needs some directive principle to guide him towards his end.

[4] To be sure, the light of reason is placed by nature in every man, to guide him in his acts towards his end. Wherefore, if man were intended to live alone, as many animals do, he would require no other guide to his end. Each man would be a king unto himself, under God, the highest King, inasmuch as he would direct himself in his acts by the light of reason given him from on high. Yet it is natural for man, more than for any other animal, to be a social and political animal, to live in a group.

[5] This is clearly a necessity of man's nature. For all other animals, nature has prepared food, hair as a covering, teeth, horns, claws as means of defence or at least speed in flight, while man alone was made without any natural provisions for these things. Instead of all these, man was endowed with reason, by the use of which he could procure all these things for himself by the work of his hands. Now, one man alone is not able to procure them all for himself, for one man could not sufficiently provide for life, unassisted. It is therefore natural that man should live in the society of many. . . .

[8] If, then, it is natural for man to live in the society of many, it is necessary that there exist among men some means by which the group may be governed. For where there are many men together and each one is looking after his own

interest, the multitude would be broken up and scattered unless there were also an agency to take care of what appertains to the commonweal. In like manner, the body of a man or any other animal would disintegrate unless there were a general ruling force within the body which watches over the common good of all members.—With this in mind, Solomon says: "Where there is no governor, the people shall fall." . . .

[10] Now it happens in certain things which are ordained towards an end that one may proceed in a right way and also in a wrong way. So, too, in the government of a multitude there is a distinction between right and wrong. A thing is rightly directed when it is led towards a befitting end; wrongly when it is led towards an unbefitting end. Now the end which befits a multitude of free men is different from that which befits a multitude of slaves, for the free man is one who exists for his own sake, while the slave, as such, exists for the sake of another. If, therefore, a multitude of free men is ordered by the ruler towards the common good of the multitude, that rulership will be right and just, as is suitable to free men. If, on the other hand, a rulership aims, not at the common good of the multitude, but at the private good of the ruler, it will be an unjust and perverted rulership. The Lord, therefore, threatens such rulers, saying by the mouth of Ezechiel: "Woe to the shepherds that feed themselves [seeking, that is, their own interest]: should not the flocks be fed by the shepherd?" Shepherds indeed should seek the good of their flocks, and every ruler, the good of the multitude subject to him. . . .

[14] Now since man must live in a group, because he is not sufficient unto himself to procure the necessities of life were he to remain solitary, it follows that a society will be the more perfect the more it is sufficient unto itself to procure the necessities of life. There is, to some extent, sufficiency for life in one *family of one household*, namely, insofar as pertains to the natural acts of nourishment and the begetting

of offspring and other things of this kind. Self-sufficiency
exists, furthermore, in one *street* with regard to those things
which belong to the trade of one guild. In a *city*, which is
the perfect community, it exists with regard to all the necessities of life. Still more self-sufficiency is found in a *province*
because of the need of fighting together and of mutual help
against enemies. Hence the man ruling a perfect community,
i.e. a city or a province, is antonomastically called *the* king.
The ruler of a household is called father, not king, although he
bears a certain resemblance to the king, for which reason
kings are sometimes called the fathers of their peoples.

[15] It is plain, therefore, from what has been said, that
a king is one who rules the people of one city or province,
and rules them for the common good. Wherefore Solomon
says: "The king ruleth over all the land subject to him."

One Man Is Preferable as Chief of State

[36] When a choice is to be made between two things, from
both of which danger impends, surely that one should be
chosen from which the lesser evil follows. Now, lesser evil
follows from the corruption of a monarchy (which is tyranny)
than from the corruption of an aristocracy.

[37] Group government [polyarchy] most frequently breeds
dissension. This dissension runs counter to the good of peace
which is the principal social good. A tyrant, on the other
hand, does not destroy this good, rather he obstructs one or
the other individual interests of his subjects—unless, of course,
there be an excess of tyranny and the tyrant rages against
the whole community. Monarchy is therefore to be preferred
to polyarchy, although either form of government might
become dangerous. . . .

On Kingship, I, Ch. 5. Trans. Phelan and Eschmann, *On Kingship*, pp. 21,
23-24, 27.

[40] The strongest objection why monarchy, although it is "the best form of government," is not agreeable to the people is that, in fact, it may deviate into tyranny. Yet tyranny is wont to occur not less but more frequently on the basis of a polyarchy than on the basis of a monarchy. It follows that it is, in any case, more expedient to live under one king than under the rule of several men.

[41] Therefore, since the rule of one man, which is the best, is to be preferred, and since it may happen that it be changed into a tyranny, which is the worst (all this is clear from what has been said), a scheme should be carefully worked out which would prevent the multitude ruled by a king from falling into the hands of a tyrant.

[42] First, it is necessary that the man who is raised up to be king by those whom it concerns should be of such condition that it is improbable that he should become a tyrant. Wherefore Daniel, commending the providence of God with respect to the institution of the king says: "The Lord hath sought him a man according to his own heart, and the Lord hath appointed him to be prince over his people." Then, once the king is established, the government of the kingdom must be so arranged that opportunity to tyrannize is removed. At the same time his power should be so tempered that he cannot easily fall into tyranny. . . .

[49] If to provide itself with a king belongs to the right of a given multitude, it is not unjust that the king be deposed or have his power restricted by that same multitude if, becoming a tyrant, he abuses the royal power. It must not be thought that such a multitude is acting unfaithfully in deposing the tyrant, even though it had previously subjected itself to him in perpetuity, because he himself has deserved that the covenant with his subjects should not be kept, since in ruling the multitude, he did not act faithfully as the office of a king demands. . . .

The Reward of a Good Ruler

[63] It is implanted in the minds of all who have the use of reason that the reward of virtue is happiness. The virtue of anything whatsoever is explained to be that which makes its possessor good and renders his deed good. Moreover, everyone strives by working well to attain that which is most deeply implanted in desire, namely, to be happy. This, no one is able not to wish. It is therefore fitting to expect as a reward for virtue that which makes man happy. Now, if to work well is a virtuous deed, and the king's work is to rule his people well, then that which makes him happy will be the king's reward. What this is has now to be considered. Happiness, we say, is the ultimate end of our desires. Now the movement of desire does not go on to infinity else natural desire would be vain, for infinity cannot be traversed. Since, then, the desire of an intellectual nature is for universal good, that good alone can make it truly happy which, when attained, leaves no further good to be desired. Whence happiness is called the perfect good inasmuch as it comprises in itself all things desirable. But no earthly good is such a good. They who have riches desire to have more, they who enjoy pleasure desire to enjoy more, and the like is clear for the rest: and if they do not seek more, they at least desire that those they have should abide or that others should follow in their stead. For nothing permanent is found in earthly things. Consequently there is nothing earthly which can calm desire. Thus, nothing earthly can make man happy, so that it may be a fitting reward for a king.

[64] Again, the last perfection and perfect good of anything one chooses depends upon something higher, for even bodily things are made better by the addition of better things and worse by being mixed with baser things. If gold is mingled with silver, the silver is made better, while by an admix-

ture of lead it is rendered impure. Now it is manifest that all
earthly things are beneath the human mind. But happiness
is the last perfection and the perfect good of man, which all
men desire to reach. Therefore there is no earthly thing
which could make man happy, nor is any earthly thing a sufficient reward for a king. For, as Augustine says, "We do not
call Christian princes happy merely because they have reigned
a long time, or because after a peaceful death they have left
their sons to rule, or because they subdued the enemies of
the state, or because they were able to guard against or to
suppress citizens who rose up against them. Rather do we
call them happy if they rule justly, if they prefer to rule
their passions rather than nations, and if they do all things
not for the love of vainglory but for the love of eternal happiness. Such Christian emperors we say are happy, now in hope,
afterwards in very fact when that which we await shall come
to pass." But neither is there any other created thing which
would make a man happy and which could be set up as the
reward for a king. For the desire of each thing tends towards
its source, whence is the cause of its being. But the cause of
the human soul is none other than God Who made it to His
own image. Therefore it is God alone Who can still the
desires of man and make him happy and be the fitting reward
for a king.

Dictatorship Is Usually Short-lived

[80] The government of tyrants, on the other hand, cannot
last long because it is hateful to the multitude, and what is
against the wishes of the multitude cannot be long preserved.
For a man can hardly pass through this present life without
suffering some adversities, and in the time of his adversity
occasion cannot be lacking to rise against the tyrant; and
when there is an opportunity there will not be lacking at
least one of the multitude to use it. Then the people will

On Kingship, I, Ch. 10. Trans. Phelan and Eschmann, *On Kingship*, pp. 46-47.

fervently favour the insurgent, and what is attempted with the sympathy of the multitude will not easily fail of its effects. It can thus scarcely come to pass that the government of a tyrant will endure for a long time.

[81] This is very clear, too, if we consider the means by which a tyrannical government is upheld. It is not upheld by love, since there is little or no bond of friendship between the subject multitude and the tyrant, as is evident from what we have said. On the other hand, tyrants cannot rely on the loyalty of their subjects, for such a degree of virtue is not found among the generality of men, that they should be restrained by the virtue of fidelity from throwing off the yoke of unmerited servitude, if they are able to do so. Nor would it perhaps be a violation of fidelity at all, according to the opinion of many, to frustrate the wickedness of tyrants by any means whatsoever. It remains, then, that the government of a tyrant is maintained by fear alone and consequently they strive with all their might to be feared by their subjects. Fear, however, is a weak support. Those who are kept down by fear will rise against their rulers if the opportunity ever occurs when they can hope to do it with impunity, and they will rebel against their rulers all the more furiously the more they have been kept in subjection against their will by fear alone, just as water confined under pressure flows with greater impetus when it finds an outlet. That very fear itself is not without danger, because many become desperate from excessive fear, and despair of safety impels a man boldly to dare anything. Therefore the government of a tyrant cannot be of long duration.

The Characteristics of a Good Ruler

[93] The next point to be considered is what the kingly office is and what qualities the king should have. Since things

On Kingship, II, Ch. 1-4. Trans. Phelan and Eschmann, On Kingship, pp. 53-54, 65-67.

which are in accordance with art are an imitation of the things which are in accordance with nature (from which we accept the rules to act according to reason), it seems best that we learn about the kingly office from the pattern of the regime of nature.

[94] In things of nature there is both a universal and a particular government. The former is God's government Whose rule embraces all things and Whose providence governs them all. The latter is found in man and it is much like the divine government. Hence man is called a *microcosmos*. Indeed there is a similitude between both governments in regard to their form; for just as the universe of corporeal creatures and all spiritual powers comes under the divine government, in like manner the members of the human body and all the powers of the soul are governed by reason. Thus, in a proportionate manner, reason is to man what God is to the world. Since, however, man is by nature a social animal living in a multitude, as we have pointed out above, the analogy with the divine government is found in him not only in this way that one man governs himself by reason, but also in that the multitude of men is governed by the reason of one man. This is what first of all constitutes the office of a king. True, among certain animals that live socially there is a likeness to the king's rulership; so we say that there are kings among bees. Yet animals exercise rulership not through reason but through their natural instinct which is implanted in them by the Great Ruler, the Author of nature.

[95] Therefore let the king recognize that such is the office which he undertakes, namely, that he is to be in the kingdom what the soul is in the body, and what God is in the world. If he reflect seriously upon this, a zeal for justice will be enkindled in him when he contemplates that he has been appointed to this position in place of God, to exercise judgment in his kingdom; further, he will acquire the gentleness of clemency and mildness when he considers as his own members those individuals who are subject to his rule. . . .

[116] Thus the king, taught the law of God, should have for his principal concern the means by which the multitude subject to him may live well.

[117] This concern is threefold: first of all, to establish a virtuous life in the multitude subject to him; second, to preserve it once established; and third, having preserved it, to promote its greater perfection.

[118] For an individual man to lead a good life two things are required. The first and most important is to act in a virtuous manner (for virtue is that by which one lives well); the second, which is secondary and instrumental, is a sufficiency of those bodily goods whose use is necessary for virtuous life. Yet the unity of man is brought about by nature, while the unity of multitude, which we call peace, must be procured through the efforts of the ruler. Therefore, to establish virtuous living in a multitude three things are necessary. First of all, that the multitude be established in the unity of peace. Second, that the multitude thus united in the bond of peace, be directed to acting well. For just as a man can do nothing well unless unity within his members be presupposed, so a multitude of men lacking the unity of peace will be hindered from virtuous action by the fact that it is fighting against itself. In the third place, it is necessary that there be at hand a sufficient supply of the things required for proper living, procured by the ruler's efforts.

[119] When virtuous living is set up in the multitude by the efforts of the king, it then remains for him to look to its conservation. Now there are three things which prevent the permanence of the public good. One of these arises from nature. The good of the multitude should not be established for one time only; it should be in a sense perpetual. Men, on the other hand, cannot abide forever, because they are mortal. Even while they are alive they do not always preserve the same vigour, for the life of man is subject to many changes, and thus a man is not equally suited to the performance of the same duties throughout the whole span of his life. A second impediment to the preservation of the public good, which comes from within, consists in the perversity of the

wills of men, inasmuch as they are either too lazy to perform what the commonweal demands, or, still further, they are harmful to the peace of the multitude because, by transgressing justice, they disturb the peace of others. The third hindrance to the preservation of the commonweal comes from without, namely, when peace is destroyed through the attacks of enemies and, as it sometimes happens, the kingdom or city is completely blotted out.

[120] In regard to these three dangers, a triple charge is laid upon the king. First of all, he must take care of the appointment of men to succeed or replace others in charge of the various offices. Just as in regard to corruptible things (which cannot remain the same forever) the government of God made provision that through generation one would take the place of another in order that, in this way, the integrity of the universe might be maintained, so too the good of the multitude subject to the king will be preserved through his care when he sets himself to attend to the appointment of new men to fill the place of those who drop out. In the second place, by his laws and orders, punishments and rewards, he should restrain the men subject to him from wickedness and induce them to virtuous deeds, following the example of God, Who gave His law to man and requites those who observe it with rewards, and those who transgress it with punishments. The king's third charge is to keep the multitude entrusted to him safe from the enemy, for it would be useless to prevent internal dangers if the multitude could not be defended against external dangers.

[121] Finally, for the proper direction of the multitude there remains the third duty of the kingly office, namely, that he be solicitous for its improvement. He performs this duty when, in each of the things we have mentioned, he corrects what is out of order and supplies what is lacking, and if any of them can be done better he tries to do so. This is why the Apostle exhorts the faithful to be "zealous for the better gifts."

[122] These then are the duties of the kingly office, each of which must now be treated in greater detail.

How a Ruler Should Govern

[102] Just as the founding of a city or kingdom may suitably be learned from the way in which the world was created, so too the way to govern may be learned from the divine government of the world.

[103] Before going into that, however, we should consider that to govern is to lead the thing governed in a suitable way towards its proper end. Thus a ship is said to be governed when, through the skill of the pilot, it is brought unharmed and by a direct route to harbour. Consequently, if a thing be directed to an end outside itself (as a ship to the harbour), it is the governor's duty, not only to preserve the thing unharmed, but further to guide it towards this end. If, on the contrary, there be a thing whose end is not outside itself, then the governor's endeavours will merely tend to preserve the thing undamaged in its proper perfection.

[104] Nothing of this kind is to be found in reality, except God Himself, Who is the end of all. However, as concerns the thing which is directed to an end outside itself, care is exercised by different providers in different ways. One might have the task of preserving a thing in its being, another of bringing it to a further perfection. Such is clearly the case in the example of the ship (the first meaning of the word *gubernator* [governor] is *pilot*). It is the carpenter's business to repair anything which might be broken, while the pilot bears the responsibility of bringing the ship to port. It is the same with man. The doctor sees to it that a man's life is preserved; the tradesman supplies the necessities of life; the teacher takes care that man may learn the truth; and the tutor sees that he lives according to reason.

[105] Now if man were not ordained to another end outside himself, the above-mentioned cares would be sufficient for him. But as long as man's mortal life endures there is

On Kingship, II, Ch. 3. Trans. Phelan and Eschmann, *On Kingship*, pp. 58-61.

an extrinsic good for him, namely, final beatitude which is
looked for after death in the enjoyment of God, for as the
Apostle says: "As long as we are in the body we are far from
the Lord." Consequently the Christian man, for whom that
beatitude has been purchased by the blood of Christ, and
who, in order to attain it, has received the earnest of the Holy
Ghost, needs another and spiritual care to direct him to the
harbour of eternal salvation, and this care is provided for
the faithful by the ministers of the church of Christ.

[106] Now the same judgment is to be formed about the
end of society as a whole as about the end of one man. If,
therefore, the ultimate end of man were some good that
existed in himself, then the ultimate end of the multitude to
be governed would likewise be for the multitude to acquire
such good, and persevere in its possession. If such an ultimate
end either of an individual man or a multitude were a corporeal one, namely, life and health of body, to govern would
then be a physician's charge. If that ultimate end were an
abundance of wealth, then knowledge of economics would
have the last word in the community's government. If the
good of the knowledge of truth were of such a kind that the
multitude might attain to it, the king would have to be a
teacher. It is, however, clear that the end of a multitude
gathered together is to live virtuously. For men form a group
for the purpose of *living well* together, a thing which the
individual man living alone could not attain, and *good life*
is virtuous life. Therefore, virtuous life is the end for which
men gather together. The evidence for this lies in the fact
that only those who render mutual assistance to one another
in living well form a genuine part of an assembled multitude.
If men assembled merely to live, then animals and slaves
would form a part of the civil community. Or, if men assembled only to accrue wealth, then all those who traded
together would belong to one city. Yet we see that only such
are regarded as forming one multitude as are directed by the
same laws and the same government to live well.

[107] Yet through virtuous living man is further ordained
to a higher end, which consists in the enjoyment of God, as

we have said above. Consequently, since society must have the same end as the individual man, it is not the ultimate end of an assembled multitude to live virtuously, but through virtuous living to attain to the possession of God.

[108] If this end could be attained by the power of human nature, then the duty of a king would have to include the direction of men to it. We are supposing, of course, that he is called king to whom the supreme power of governing in human affairs is entrusted. Now the higher the end to which a government is ordained, the loftier that government is. Indeed, we always find that the one to whom it pertains to achieve the final end commands those who execute the things that are ordained to that end. For example, the captain, whose business it is to regulate navigation, tells the ship-builder what kind of ship he must construct to be suitable for navigation; and the ruler of a city, who makes use of arms, tells the blacksmith what kind of arms to make. But because a man does not attain his end, which is the possession of God, by human power but by divine—according to the words of the Apostle: "By the grace of God life everlasting"— therefore the task of leading him to that last end does not pertain to human but to divine government.

Public Positions and State Revenues

I have received Your Excellency's letter, from which I have learned in full measure both your pious concern for the regulation of your subjects and the devoted affection that you have for the Brothers of our Order. I give thanks to God Who has inspired your heart with the seeds of so many virtues. However, because you have asked me in this letter to reply to certain questions, it has certainly been a problem for me: both because of my duties which the work of a lector impose, and also because it would have pleased me had you sought on these points the advice of others more experienced

Letter to the Duchess of Brabant. Trans. V.J.B.

in such matters. In truth, because I deem it unfitting to be found a negligent assistant to your concern, or an ungrateful recipient of your affection, I have taken care to answer here the questions that you have proposed, without prejudice to a better judgment. . . .

Your fifth question asks, concerning your bailiffs and public officials, whether it might be permissible to sell them their offices, or to accept a certain amount from them as a loan until they could collect that amount from their official activities.

The answer to this is that the question seems to present two problems, of which the first is concerned with the selling of such positions. In this connection, it seems necessary to consider what the Apostle says: that many things are permitted that are not, however, advisable. Of course, since you turn over to your bailiffs and officials nothing but a position of temporal power, I do not see why it is not permissible for you to sell these offices to them, provided that it could be presumed that the sales be made to people of the type that would be fitted to carry out such duties, and provided that the offices are not sold for such a large price that it would be impossible for them to indemnify themselves without serious inconveniences to your subjects.

However, such selling does not seem advisable. The first reason is that frequently those who are best suited for carrying out such duties are poor men, so that they would not be able to buy them. Even if there are some rich ones, the better among them will not aspire to such positions, nor will they crave the wealth to be acquired from public service. So, the consequence would be that in most cases the people who would accept these offices in your country would be of the worst type, strivers for public positions and money-lovers. These are also the kind who would probably oppress your subjects and be unfaithful in promoting your interests. Hence, it seems more advisable for you to choose good and suitable men to take on public positions and, if they are reluctant, you may even require them to accept, if that becomes necessary. The reason is that greater advantages will accrue to you and your subjects by virtue of their goodness and industry than from the aforesaid practice of selling offices to those able to buy them.

The second problem in this question could arise from the loan. It seems that the answer to this is that if they give this agreed loan in order to get the position, then without doubt the contract is usury, because they receive the powers of office on the basis of a loan, and so you give them the occasion for sinning. They, in turn, are then obliged to resign from an office obtained in such a way. However, if you were to give them the position freely and later to accept a loan from them which they might recover from their office, it is possible that this might be done without any sin.

Your sixth question is whether you are permitted to make levies on your Christian subjects. On this point, you should bear in mind that earthly rulers are established by God not so that they may seek to obtain wealth for themselves but in order that they may promote the common welfare of their people. . . . Hence, land revenues were established for rulers so that by living on them they might refrain from exploiting their subjects. . . .

It may happen, however, that rulers will not have revenues sufficient for the management of their country, or for other reasonably necessary expenses of government. In such a case, it is right for the subjects to provide that whereby their common welfare may be secured. That is why, by ancient custom, in some territories the lords impose definite taxes on their subjects. If these are not excessive, they can be collected without sin, for according to the Apostle (I Cor. 9:7), no man serves in the army at his own expense.

Hence, the ruler who serves the common welfare may live on the common funds and may promote community business, either by means of revenues that are regularly collected, or, if these are lacking or insufficient, by means of collections made from individual citizens. And the reasoning seems to be the same if some special emergency arises in which great expenditures are required for the common welfare; or if the maintenance of the proper estate of the ruler requires it, when his own revenues are inadequate; or if the usual taxes are insufficient, for instance, when an enemy has invaded the territory or some similar emergency arises. In that case, rulers may licitly require from their subjects something over and above the ordinary taxes, for the sake of the public welfare. However, if they crave to collect in excess of what is customary simply because of a lust for possession, or because of excessive and immoderate expenditures, this is not at all licit. Indeed, rulers' revenues are like wages; they ought to be satisfied with them and not demand more, except for the reason that was mentioned and provided that the advantage be to the community. . . .

These are, O illustrious and pious lady, the answers that come to mind now to your questions. On these points, I am not forcing my judgment on you; rather, I should urge that the judgment of more experienced men be followed.

May your reign last for a still longer period.

Why the Jewish People Have Special Laws

The Old Law manifested the precepts of the law of nature and it added some precepts of its own. So, in regard to those rules that the Old Law included from the law of nature, all men were obliged to observe the Old Law, not because they belonged to the Old Law but because they belonged to the law of nature. But in regard to those rules that the Old Law added, men were not required to obey the Old Law, with the sole exception of the Jewish people.

The reason for this is that the Old Law, as we have said, was given to the Jewish people so that they might acquire a special character of holiness, out of reverence for Christ Who was to be born from this people. Certain rules that are enacted for the special sanctification of certain men are binding on them only; thus, because they are devoted to the divine ministry, clerics are obligated to certain actions which

Summa of Theology, I-II, 98, 5, c. Trans. V.J.B.

lay persons are not obligated to; similarly, members of a religious order are obligated to certain works of perfection as a result of their vows, and the secular clergy are not subject to these obligations. Likewise, this [Jewish] people was subjected to special obligations which did not apply to other peoples.

May Nonbelievers Exercise Political Authority?

Nonbelief considered in itself is not repugnant to political dominion, because dominion stems from the law of peoples which is human law; whereas, the distinction between believers and nonbelievers is based on divine law, which does not remove human law. However, a person who sins by infidelity can lose the right to govern as a result of court judgment, as sometimes occurs in the case of other guilty acts. It is not the function of the Church to punish infidelity in those who have never received the faith, according to the text of the Apostle (I Cor. 5:12): *For what have I to do with judging those outside?* But it can punish judicially the infidelity of those who have received the faith.

Summa of Theology, II-II, 12, 2, c. Trans. V.J.B.

Children and Parental Rights

The custom of the Church has the greatest authority and it is always to be emulated in all matters. Now, since the very teaching of Catholic Doctors receives its authority from the Church, one should rely on the authority of the Church rather than on the authority of Augustine, or Jerome, or any Doctor.

Now, the practice of the Church never held that the chil

Summa of Theology, II-II, 10, 12, c. Trans. V.J.B.

dren of Jews should be baptized against the will of their parents, although in times past there were many powerful Catholic leaders, like Constantine and Theodosius, with whom very holy bishops were friendly (as Sylvester with Constantine and Ambrose with Theodosius) and who would in no way have refused their requests, if they were consonant with reason. Therefore, it seems dangerous to bring forward this new view, that contrary to the previously established custom of the Church, the children of Jews should be baptized against the will of their parents.

There are two reasons for this position. One stems from danger to faith. For, if children without the use of reason were to receive baptism, then after reaching maturity they could easily be persuaded by their parents to relinquish what they had received in ignorance. This would tend to do harm to the faith.

The second reason is that it is opposed to natural justice. Indeed, a son is naturally something belonging to the father. First, because he is not distinct in his body from his parents, as long as he is contained within his mother's womb. Later, after proceeding from the womb and before he has the use of free choice, he is contained under parental care as if within a spiritual womb. In fact, as long as the boy is without the use of reason, he does not differ from an irrational animal. Hence, just as an ox or a horse belongs to some owner to be used at will as a proper instrument, according to civil law, so is it a matter of natural right that a son, before he has the use of reason, is under the care of his father. Hence, it would be against natural justice for the boy, before he has the use of reason, to be removed from the care of his parents, or for anything to be arranged for him against the will of his parents. Now, after he begins to have the use of free choice, he then begins to be in charge of himself and, as far as things that come under divine or natural law are concerned, he is able to manage these for himself. And at that time, he is to be brought to the faith not by force but by persuasion. He can, then, even consent to the faith and be baptized against the will of his parents; but not before he has the use of reason.

An Analysis and Definition of Law

Law [*lex*] is any rule and measure of actions whereby one is impelled toward, or restrained from, acting. The word for law comes from the verb *ligare* (to bind), because it obligates in regard to action. Now, the rule and measure of human actions is reason, for it is the primary principle of human actions. Indeed, it is the function of reason to order toward an end, and according to the Philosopher (*Physics*, II, 9, 200a22; *Ethics*, VII, 8, 1151a16), the end is the first principle in the field of actions. Now, in each genus that which is the principle is the standard and rule of that genus; thus are unity in the genus of numbers and the primary motion in the general class of motions. The conclusion, then, is that law is something that belongs to reason.

Replying to the second objection: just as we have to think in the sphere of overt actions of both the operation and the thing produced by the operation (for example, the action of building and the edifice that is built), so, too, among the works of reason we have to think of the action of reason itself (which is understanding and reasoning) and of something that is produced by an action of this type. Now, in speculative reasoning what is produced, first, is the definition, secondly, the proposition, and thirdly, the syllogism or argumentation. And since practical reasoning also employs some sort of syllogistic reasoning in regard to operative matters . . . we should discover something in practical reasoning that stands in relation to actions in the way that the proposition does to the conclusions of speculative reasoning. Now, these universal propositions of practical reasoning that are ordered to actions have the essential character of a law. Sometimes, such propositions are actually being thought,

Summa of Theology, I-II, 90, 1-4. Trans. V.J.B.

but at other times, they are kept in a habitual state by the power of reason.

Replying to the third objection: we should say that reason gets its moving force from the will; for, due to the fact that a person desires an end, his reason commands the means related to this end. But in regard to the things that are commanded, the will must be regulated by some reasoning, so that it may have the essential character of a law. This is the way to understand the statement that the will of the sovereign has the force of law: otherwise, the will of the sovereign would be equivalent to iniquity rather than law.

(*Article 2*) As we have said, law pertains to that which functions as the principle of human actions, due to the fact that it is a rule and standard. Now, just as reason is the principle of human actions, so also is there something within the area of reasoning that is a principle in relation to all the rest. Hence, law must primarily and chiefly pertain to this principle. Now, the first principle in the field of operations, with which practical reasoning deals, is the ultimate end. But the ultimate end of human life is happiness or beatitude, as we have said before. Hence, law must be concerned above all with the ordering that is directed toward happiness. Again, since every part may be ordered to its whole as something imperfect to the perfect, and since man is but a part of a perfect community, in the proper sense law must be concerned with ordering toward community happiness. . . . Now, in every class of things, the chief subject of discussion is the principle of all else and the other matters are talked about in relation to it. . . . Hence, because law is chiefly talked about in reference to the common good, it must be that no rule governing a particular action will have the character of a law unless it be ordered for the common good. Therefore, every law is ordered for the common good.

(*Article 3*) We must say that law, in the proper sense, is primarily and chiefly concerned with an ordering for the common good. Now, the function of ordering anything to the common good belongs either to the whole group or to some person acting as representative of the whole group. Hence, to establish a law is the prerogative of either the whole group or of a public person who has charge of the whole group, because the ordering of all other things to their end belongs to him to whom that end more especially pertains.

(*Article 4*) As we have said, law is imposed on others in the manner of a rule and standard. Now, the imposition of a rule and standard requires that it be applied to the subjects that are regulated and measured. So, in order that law may achieve the obligatory force proper to it, it must be applied to the men who are to be ruled in accord with it.

Such application is accomplished through its being brought to their attention by the act of promulgation. Hence, this promulgation is necessary in order that law may have its force.

And so, we may gather a definition of law from the four points in our explanation: Law is simply any reasonable ordinance that is promulgated for the common good by the one who has charge of a community.

Are Human Laws Morally Obligatory?

Laws that are humanly imposed are either just or unjust. Now, if they are just, they have the power of binding in conscience as a result of the eternal law from which they are derived, according to the text of Prov. 8:15: *By Me kings reign and lawmakers decree just things.* Laws are said to be just: (1) from their ends, when they are ordered for the common good; (2) from their author, when the law as passed does not exceed the power of its maker; and (3) from their form, when their burdens are imposed on the subjects according to a proportional equality in relation to the common good.

Summa of Theology, I-II, 96, 4, c. Trans. V.J.B.

Since an individual man is a part of a group, each man belongs to the group in his existence and possessions, just as every part owes its actual being to the whole. That is why any nature will permit the harming of one of its parts in order to save the whole. On this basis, those laws that impose burdens in a proportionate manner are just; and they bind in conscience and are legitimate laws.

However, laws may be unjust in two senses. One involves being in opposition to human welfare, contrary to the above-mentioned conditions: either (1) from their end, as when a sovereign imposes on his subjects onerous laws that are not directed to the common welfare but instead to his own cupidity or advancement; or (2) from their author, as when someone passes a law beyond the power committed to him; or also (3) from their form, for instance when burdens are assigned unequally within a group, even if they be ordered to the common good. Now, these are instruments of violence rather than laws; as Augustine says *On Free Choice* (I, 5): "That which is not just is evidently no law." Such laws are not binding in the forum of conscience, unless perhaps for the purpose of avoiding scandal or public disturbance, which are reasons why a man should give up his right, according to Matt. 5:40-42: *And whoever forces thee to go for one mile, go with him two; and if he take away thy tunic, give him thy cloak as well.*

The second way that laws can be unjust is by contrariety to the divine good, as are the laws of tyrants who lead people into idolatry or anything else that is against divine law. Such laws may not be observed at all, because of what is said in Acts 5:29: *We must obey God rather than men.*

Patriotism as a Type of Piety

A man becomes the debtor of others according to their different excellences and the diverse benefits received from

Summa of Theology, II-II, 91, 1, c. Trans. V.J.B.

them. Now, on both counts God holds the highest place: He is most excellent and He is the first principle of our existence and our governance.

Secondarily, however, the sources of our being and governance are our parents and our country; from whom, and in which, we are born and raised. And so, after God, man is most indebted to his parents and country. Hence, just as the act of showing reverence to God belongs to religion, so on a secondary level the showing of reverence to parents and country belongs to piety. Under the reverence of parents is included the respect for all blood relatives, because they are called such by virtue of their descent from the same parents, as is evident from the Philosopher in the *Ethics* (VIII, 12, 1161b29). Under the reverence of country is understood respect for all fellow citizens and for all the friends of one's country.

The Community of All Men Under God

That a person loves another as he does himself is due to the fact that they have some communion with each other. For, to the extent that any two items are in simultaneous agreement, they are considered as one; thus, one of them is related to the other as to itself.

Now, it is possible for two persons to agree in many ways. Some may agree by a natural agreement based on fleshly generation, as in the case of those who stem from the same parents. Others agree on the basis of civil agreement; for instance, those who are citizens of the same state are under the same sovereign and are governed by the same laws. Also, some agreement or community is found in every kind of work or business. Take, for example, those who are associates in doing business, or in soldiering, or in the handling or manufacture of cloth, or in anything else like that.

Of course, the affections of close associates like that can

On the Perfection of the Spiritual Life, Ch. 13. Trans. V.J.B.

be upright and just, but they are not by this fact called holy; rather, this would be due only to the fact that the love of one's neighbor is related to God. Just as men who are associates in a state agree on this point, that they are the subjects of one prince by whose laws they are governed, so, too, do all men, to the extent that they naturally tend toward beatitude, have a certain general agreement in relation to God, as to the highest Prince of all, the Source of beatitude and the Legislator of the whole of justice. Now, it should be borne in mind that the common good is, according to right reason, to be preferred to one's proper good. As a result, each member of the body is directed to the good of the whole by a natural instinct. An indication of this is that a person uses his hand to block a blow, in order to protect his heart or his head, on which his whole life may depend. In the aforementioned community in which all men agree as to the end that is beatitude, each man is considered as a part, while the common good of the whole is God Himself, in Whom the beatitude of all men lies. And so, according to right reason and the instinct of nature, each person orders himself toward God as a part is ordered to the good of the whole. This is brought to perfection through charity, whereby man loves himself for the sake of God. So, when a person also loves his neighbor for the sake of God, he loves his neighbor as he does himself; and in this way love becomes holy.

RECOMMENDED READINGS

Bigongiari, D. (ed.). *The Political Ideas of St. Thomas Aquinas.* New York: Hafner, 1953.

D'Entreves, A. P., and Dawson, J. G. *Aquinas, Selected Political Writings.* Oxford: Clarendon Press, 1948.

Eschmann, I. T. "Introduction" to St. Thomas, *On Kingship.* Toronto: Pontifical Institute of Mediaeval Studies, 1949.

———. "Thomistic Social Philosophy and the Theology of Original Sin," *Mediaeval Studies,* IX (1947), 19-55.

GILBY, T. *The Political Thought of Thomas Aquinas*. Chicago: University of Chicago Press, 1958.

GRIESBACH, M. "John of Paris as a Representative of Thomistic Political Philosophy," *An Etienne Gilson Tribute*. Milwaukee: Marquette University Press, 1959, 33–50.

HUTCHINS, R. M. *St. Thomas and the World State*. Milwaukee: Marquette University Press, 1949.

MARITAIN, J. *Man and the State*. Chicago: University of Chicago Press, 1951.

———. *The Person and the Common Good*. New York: Scribner's, 1947.

MURRAY, J. C. "Contemporary Orientations of Catholic Thought on Church and State," *Theological Studies*, X (1949), 177 ff.

ROMMEN, H. *The State in Catholic Thought*. St. Louis: Herder, 1945.

SIMON, Y. *The Nature and Functions of Authority*. Milwaukee: Marquette University Press, 1940.

VII. Beauty and Art

Foreword

THE ESTHETIC THINKING OF AQUINAS is somewhat fragmentary; yet he has made a valid contribution to this field of study. Best known is his definition of the beautiful as "that which pleases when it is perceived." It will be noted that this description of the concretely beautiful is neither wholly objective nor wholly subjective. That there are certain extramental features of a thing that entitle it to be regarded as esthetically appealing is taken as a fact of experience by Aquinas. Such objective factors as *integrity* (perfection and completeness of the parts of a thing), *proportion* (harmonious balance of these parts), and *clarity* (a special quality of brilliant appeal) are frequently stressed. But he is also aware of the element of personal response in the esthetic experience; there is a pleasure felt within the beholder who appreciates a well-formed artifact or natural object.

Another area of beauty lies in the spiritual order. The attractiveness of a well-ordered moral character is frequently discussed. Indeed, Aquinas had a special motive for investigating this immaterial dimension of the beautiful. He knew that beauty is one of the attributes traditionally associated with the divinity. A portion of his commentary on that strange treatise *On the Divine Names,* by Dionysius the Pseudo-Areopagite, deals with this question of God's beauty. Part of it is translated below. This extract also illustrates something of the influence of Neoplatonic participation theory on Aquinas' esthetic speculations. In reading it, it will be helpful to bear in mind the distinction made between "the beautiful" (*pulchrum*) and "beauty-in-itself" (*pulchritu-do*). The former names a limited, finite instance of beauty; while the latter designates not an abstraction but the most real and highest instance of beauty. Obviously, in such a view, it is the perfect being, God, Who is Beauty.

Aquinas' views on art and the work of the artist are strongly influenced by the classic Greek tradition, and by the early Christian meditations on God as the Architect of the universe. Both lines of thought converge in St. Thomas, leading him to see art as a special habit or skill in the mind of the artist. He usually defines art, with Aristotle, as *recta ratio factibilium*, right reasoning applied to the making of things. Like some of the painters of the Renaissance, he lays little stress on manual techniques but puts much emphasis on creative intelligence. He clearly distinguishes artistic from moral excellence. There is no confusion of art with prudence.

Several of the modern studies listed at the end of this chapter (notably those of Maritain, Gilson, and Noon) go well beyond the fragmentary esthetic speculations of Aquinas. However, these contemporary writings illustrate very well the possibilities latent in Thomistic esthetics.

That Which Pleases in Its Very Apprehension Is Beautiful

The beautiful and the good are the same in the concrete existent [*in subjecto*], for they are based on the same thing, namely, on the form. For this reason, the good is approvingly called the beautiful. Yet, they differ in their intelligibility [*ratione*]. For the good appeals to appetite: indeed, the good is what all desire. So, it has the intelligible character of an end, for appetite is a sort of motion toward a thing. On the other hand, the beautiful appeals to the cognitive power:

Summa of Theology, I, 5, 4, reply to Obj. 1; I-II, 27, 1, reply to Obj. 3. Trans. V.J.B.

for things that give pleasure when they are perceived [*quae visa placent*] are called beautiful.

Hence, the beautiful consists in a due proportion, since the sense power takes pleasure in things that are duly proportioned, as in things like itself, for sense is also a sort of ratio, as is every knowing power. Since knowledge is produced by assimilation, and since similitude is a formal relation, the beautiful properly belongs to the intelligible character [*ratio*] of the formal cause. . . .

The beautiful is the same as the good, differing only in intelligibility [*sola ratione*]. For, since the good is what all desire, it pertains to the intelligible meaning of the good that appetite find its rest in it; but it pertains to the intelligibility of the beautiful that in looking upon or knowing it, the appetite finds its rest. Hence, those sense powers that are most cognitive, namely, sight and hearing, which are the servants of reason, are chiefly concerned with the beautiful. In fact, we speak of visible things and beautiful sounds as beautiful. We do not use the name "beauty" in regard to the objects of the other senses; we do not speak of beautiful tastes or odors. Thus, it is apparent that the beautiful adds to the meaning of the good a relation to the cognitive power. So, the good simply means what satisfies appetite, but the beautiful means that whose very apprehension gives pleasure.

Integrity, Proportion, and Brilliance

Three items are required for beauty: first, *integrity* or *perfection* [*integritas sive perfectio*], for things that are lessened are ugly by this very fact; second, *due proportion* or *harmony* [*debita proportio sive consonantia*]; and third, *brilliance* [*claritas*]—thus, things that have a bright color are said to be beautiful.

Summa of Theology, I, 39, 8, c; II-II, 145, 2, c; II-II, 180, 2, reply to Obj. 3. Trans. V.J.B.

As can be gathered from the words of Dionysius, in the fourth chapter, *On the Divine Names,* both brilliance [*claritas*] and due proportion coalesce in the intelligible meaning of the beautiful. He says that God is called beautiful as the Cause of the harmony and brilliance of all things. Hence, bodily beauty consists in the fact that a man has the members of his body well proportioned, along with a due brilliance of coloration. Similarly, spiritual beauty consists in the fact that a man's behavior, or his activity, is well proportioned according to a spiritual meaning of brilliance.

Now, this pertains to the meaning of the morally decorous [*honestum*], which we have stated to be the same as virtue, for it moderates all human affairs according to reason. So, the decent [*honestum*] is the same as the spiritually decorous. Hence, Augustine says, in the book *On Eighty-Three Questions:* "I call the decent [*honestum*] intelligible beauty, what we properly speak of as spiritual." Later, he adds that there are many things beautiful to sight that are less properly called decent.

The object that moves the appetite is an apprehended good. That it appears decorous in the act of being apprehended is taken as fitting and good; so Dionysius says, in the fourth chapter, *On the Divine Names,* that the beautiful and good is lovable to all. Consequently, the decent itself, as possessed of spiritual decorousness, becomes an object of appetite.

Beauty, as we said above, consists in a certain brilliance and due proportion. Both characteristics are found, basically, in reason, to which it is appropriate to give light and to regulate due proportion in other things.

So, in the contemplative life, which consists in the act of reason, beauty is found *per se* and essentially. Hence, the book of *Wisd.* 8:2, says: *I became a lover of her beauty.*

However, beauty is found by participation in the moral virtues, namely, inasmuch as they participate in the order of reason; this is especially so of temperance, which represses the movements of concupiscence that are most obfuscating to the light of reason. That is why the virtue of chastity makes a man well disposed for contemplation, inasmuch as sexual pleasures most especially turn the mind down to sensible matters, as Augustine says in the *Soliloquies*.

Various Pleasures and Their Effects

In fact, we see that in any field of rational activity, those who enjoy their work are better able to judge detailed matters, and to make a precise investigation into those things that are accomplished with pleasure. Thus, geometers, who take pleasure in the considerations proper to geometry, are better able to understand the detailed points in this kind of thinking because the mind is more attentive to that in which pleasure is found. And the same argument goes for all the others; for instance, for those who like musical performances and take pleasure in them, and for those who enjoy the art of building, and for all others—because, by the fact that they take pleasure in such work, they make a great contribution to their kind of work. So, it is clear that pleasures increase activities.

Now, it is apparent that items which cause increase are proper to the things that are increased. So, different items must increase different things. Therefore, if the kinds of work that are increased by pleasures are of different species, as has been shown, it follows that these pleasures that cause the increase are different in species.

However, it is quite apparent that pleasures are of different kinds, in view of the discovery that an appropriate pleasure increases activity while a foreign one impedes it. Indeed, we see that lovers of organ music cannot pay attention to the sermons addressed to them when they are listening to organ-playing, for the very reason that they take more pleasure in the working of the art of the pipes than in the present work, that is, in the hearing of the words spoken to them. So, it is evident that the pleasure that accompanies the working of the art of organ-playing is destructive of the speech activities.

Exposition of Aristotle's Ethics, X, 5, Lect. 7, nn. 2043-2047. Trans. V.J.B.

And we see the same thing occurring in other instances; it happens in any case where two activities are going on at once.

For, it is obvious that the more enjoyable activity excludes the other, to the extent that if there be a great difference in the amount of pleasure, a man may entirely give up doing the work that brings him less pleasure. That is why we can do nothing else when we keenly enjoy any one thing. On the other hand, when some things give us moderate pleasure, that is, mild or small, we can also do other things. This is evident in the case of people who enjoy shows and games. In fact, those who take little enjoyment in what they see there can turn their attention to munching corn—which is not very enjoyable. This is specially true of men watching performers who fail to put on a good show, with the result that the watching of this kind of performance is not enjoyable to them.

Therefore, since the appropriate pleasure strengthens the activities with which it is associated, so that a man attends to them more forcefully, and works at them for longer periods, and does them better (that is, they attain their end more perfectly), and since pleasures that are distracting, which accompany some other activities, get in the way and are hindrances, it clearly follows that pleasures differ greatly from each other, because what one pleasure helps, another hinders.

Harmony, Brilliance, and Due Size

According to Dionysius (*On the Divine Names*, c. 4), two aspects concur in the intelligible meaning of beauty, namely, harmony [*consonantia*] and brilliance [*claritas*]. Indeed, he says that God is the cause of all beauty because He is the Cause of harmony and brilliance. Thus, we call men beauti-

---

On the Sentences, I, 31, 2, 1, Response, reply to Obj. 4; *and Exposition of Aristotle's Ethics*, IV, Lect. 8, n. 738. Trans. V.J.B.

ful who have well-proportioned members and brilliant color. The Philosopher adds a third aspect to these (*Ethics* IV, 6) when he says that beauty is only present in a large body—hence small men may be called well-proportioned and pretty [*formosi*] but not beautiful.

Beauty does not have the rational character [*ratio*] of an object of appetite unless to the extent that it takes on the character of the good; for, in that way, even the true is an object of appetite. By its own rational character [beauty] has clarity and the other aspects that were mentioned. . . .

Beauty is found in a large body. Hence, those who are small may be called pretty [*formosi*] because of an appropriateness of color and a due proportion of members, but they cannot be called beautiful because of a lack of magnitude.

Beauty and Moral Properties

He [Aristotle] shows that activities in accord with virtue are not only pleasurable but also beautiful and good. They are pleasurable in relation to the agent to whom they are agreeable by virtue of a proper habit. They are beautiful because of a due order of circumstances, as of certain parts. For, beauty consists in a due commensuration of parts. They are good because of an order to the end. . . .

There are certain aspects of external goods which produce a sort of beauty of happiness, inasmuch as they make a man pleasing in the eyes of others; and this pertains to the meaning of beauty. To this point he adds that to be deprived of certain external goods defiles happiness, in that it renders a man somewhat contemptible in the eyes of others, as appears in the case of him who lacks nobility, or good offspring, or even bodily beauty. For, he is not wholly happy who presents an ugly appearance, since by this fact he is made contemptible and despicable in the eyes of others.

Exposition of Aristotle's Ethics, I, Lect. 13, nn. 159, 163. Trans. V.J.B.

Beauty and Ugliness in the Spiritual Life

Shame is always concerned with the ugly; and the ugly
the opposite of the beautiful. Hence, we should understan
the distinguishing characteristic of ugliness and shame o
the basis of the specific character of the beautiful. In fac
there are two kinds of beauty. One is spiritual and
consists in a due ordering and abundance of spiritual good
Hence, everything that proceeds from a lack of spiritu
good, or that manifests internal disorder, is ugly. Anothe
kind is external beauty, which consists in a due ordering o
the body and an abundance of external things that a
related to the body. Conversely, disorder of the body, or
lack of temporal things, is ugly.

Now, just as both kinds of beauty delight and arous
desire, so does ugliness give rise to shame in both cases. Fo
a person is ashamed of the fact that he is a pauper, or that h
has a deformed body, or that he is ignorant, or that he pe
forms disorderly actions. Therefore, since interior ugline
must always be held in contempt, everything that involve
shame arising from this kind of ugliness must be disapprove
The confession of sins is not an instance of this, becaus
the penitent is not ashamed of the act of confessing but o
the sin which confession reveals.

Now, a lack, or ugliness, of external things is contemne
by holy men, yet sometimes, with a view to perfection, it
assumed by them for the sake of Christ. So, he who
ashamed of this ugliness is not always to be disapprove
rather, he may sometimes be greatly praised, when he adopt
it because of humility. Now, to beg has a certain shame a
sociated with it on the basis of this second kind of ugliness
for every beggar shows himself as a pauper and sometime
he lowers himself to the man from whom he begs and th
pertains to external deficiency. Hence, mendicancy adopte
for Christ's sake is not only not to be disapproved, it shoul
be praised greatly.

Against the Attackers of the Religious Life, Ch. 7, reply to Obj. 9. Tran
V.J.B.

Beautiful Things Participate in Divine Beauty

He [Dionysius] shows how they are attributed to creatures. He says that the beautiful and beauty are distinguished in existing things according to the participant and the participated. Thus, the beautiful is called that which participates in beauty; beauty is the participation of the first cause which makes all things beautiful. Indeed, the beauty of a creature is nothing but the likeness of divine beauty participated in things.

Next, when he says, "The supersubstantial beautiful is called beauty because what is beautiful in each thing has been handed down from It to all existing things," he shows how the aforesaid items are attributed to God. First, how the beautiful is attributed to Him, in the text: "Now the beautiful is at once the most beautiful and the superbeautiful." Therefore, he says first that God, Who is the supersubstantially beautiful, is called Beauty, "because of the fact that He gives beauty to all created beings in accord with the limitations of each."

For, there is one kind of beauty of the spirit and another of the body and another of this and that body. And he shows in what the meaning of beauty consists, when he adds that God so hands down beauty that He is "the cause of harmony and brilliance" in all. Thus, we call a man beautiful because of a fitting proportion of members in size and position, and because of the fact that he possesses a brilliant and bright color. Hence, it should be taken proportionally in the case of others that each thing is called beautiful because it has the brilliance of its genus, either spiritual or corporeal, and because it is established in due proportion.

He shows how God is the Cause of brilliance, when he adds that God with a flash sends down to all creatures a

Exposition of Dionysius on the Divine Names, Ch. 4, Lect. 5-6. Trans. V.J.B.

share of His luminous ray, and it is the source of all light. These glittering communications of the divine ray should be understood according to the participation of likeness. And these communications are "pulchrifying," that is, producing beauty in things.

There is a twofold harmony in things. The first is according to the relation of creatures to God. He touches on this when he says that God is the cause of harmony, "as calling all things to Himself," in that He turns all toward Himself as to an end, as was said above. For this reason beauty is named *kalos* in Greek, which is derived from the verb "to call." The second kind of harmony is present in things by virtue of their ordering among themselves. He touches this point when he adds that He gathers all things to the same in all. And this can be understood according to the Platonic view that the higher things are present to the lower by participation, while the lower things are in the higher by eminence, and thus all things are in all. Finally, from the fact that all things are found in all by some order it follows that all things are ordered to the same ultimate thing.

Next, when he says, "The beautiful is at once the most beautiful and the superbeautiful and the superexistent according to the same," he shows how the beautiful is predicated of God. First, he shows that it is predicated by way of excess; second, that it is predicated by way of cause, in this text: "It is from the beautiful in itself that individually beautiful things exist according to a character of their own." He makes two remarks on the first point. In the first place, he advances the notion of *excess;* next, he explains it, in this statement: "and the superexistent according to the same." Now, excess is twofold: one sort is within a genus and it is signified by the comparative or superlative; another kind is beyond the genus and it is signified by the addition of the preposition *super*. For example, if we wish to say that fire is in excess, by virtue of an excess within the genus, we say that it is most hot—but the sun exceeds by an excess that goes beyond the genus, so we do not say that it is most hot but superhot, for its heat is not in it in the same way but more eminently. Now, though these two meanings of excess do not combine into identity in the case of caused things, yet, in the case of God, we say that He is most beautiful and superbeautiful, not in the sense that He is in a genus but that all that belong to any genus whatever are attributed to Him.

Then, when he says, "and the superexistent," he explains what he had said. First, he explains why God is called most beautiful; second, why He is called superbeautiful, in this text: "and like the One Who already possesses the source-beauty of every beautiful thing within Himself." Indeed, just as something is called white though it is mixed with black, so also is a thing called more beautiful by virtue of a removal of a deficiency of beauty. Now, there are two deficiencies of beauty in creatures. One occurs because certain things possess a variable beauty, as is evident in corruptible things. He first excludes this kind of deficiency from God, saying that God is always beautiful in the same sense and the same way. Thus, the alteration of beauty is excluded. Moreover, there is in Him neither generation nor corruption of beauty, nor again increase or decrease of it, such as we find in bodily things. The second defect of beauty is the fact that all creatures have some sort of particular beauty, as they also have a particular nature. He excludes this deficiency from God on the basis of every kind of particularity and he says that God is not beautiful in one part and ugly in another, as sometimes happens in particular things. Nor is He so in one time and not so in another, as happens in those things whose beauty falls within time. Nor, again, is He beautiful in regard to one aspect and not in another, as happens in all things directed to one definite use or end (if they are employed for something else, their harmony will not be maintained, nor will their beauty). Nor even is He beautiful in one place and not beautiful in another, which in fact happens in some things because they seem beautiful to some people and not so to others. Instead, God is beautiful in the view of all and without qualification.

He gives the reason for all the foregoing when he adds

that He is beautiful "according to Himself." By this phrase, these exclusions are made: He is not beautiful in one part only, nor in a certain time only, nor in a certain place only. In fact, that which belongs to a subject, in himself and primarily, belongs to Him as a whole, and always, and everywhere. Again, God is beautiful in Himself and not in relation to some limited terminus; thus, it cannot be said that for one He is beautiful and to another not beautiful; nor is He beautiful to some people and not so to others. Again, He is uniformly beautiful and by this is excluded the first deficiency of beauty, namely, variability.

Next, when he adds, "and like the One Who already possesses the source-beauty by way of excess within Himself," he shows for what reason God may be called superbeautiful, inasmuch as He possesses eminently in Himself, and before all others, the source of beauty in its entirety. In that simple and supernatural nature of all beautiful things that are derived from it, every beauty and every beautiful thing pre-exist, not, of course, in a divided way but uniformly, in the manner whereby multiple effects pre-exist in their cause.

Then, when he says, "It is from this beautiful thing that individually beautiful things exist according to a character of their own," he shows how beautiful is predicated of God causally. He first asserts the causality of the beautiful, then he explains it in this phrase: "And He is the Beginning [*principium*] of all beautiful things." Therefore, he says, first, that being comes to all existents from this Beautiful. Now, brilliance pertains to the consideration of beauty, as has been said. Every form, by which a thing has being [*esse*], is a participation in the divine brilliance. This is why he adds that "individual things" are "beautiful according to a character of their own," that is, in accord with a proper form. Hence, it is clear that the being [*esse*] of all things is derived from the divine Beauty. Likewise, it was also said that harmony belongs to the intelligibility of beauty; hence, all things that pertain in any manner to harmony proceed from the divine Beauty. This is why he adds that for the sake of the divine good all things that pertain to rational creatures are "concordant" in regard to understanding (for those beings are concordant who agree to the same judgment), "and friendships" in regard to the effect, "and communions" in regard to the act, or toward any extrinsic thing whatever; and universally all creatures have, from the power of the beautiful, however much unification they may possess.

Next, when he says, "and He is the Beginning of all beautiful things," he explains what he had said on the causality of the beautiful: first, in regard to the meaning of causation; second, in regard to the diversity of effects, in this text: "This one good and beautiful being is in a singular manner the cause of all the many beautiful and good things." He makes two remarks on the first. One, he indicates according to what rational principle the beautiful may be called a cause; two, he infers a sort of corollary from the statement, in this phrase: "Because of this the beautiful is the same as the good."

First of all, he says, then, that "the beautiful is indeed the Beginning of all things, as an efficient cause," giving being, and like a "moving" cause, and like a "containing" cause, that is, conserving all things. But an agent cause acts by virtue of a desire of the end, because it is an imperfect agent not yet possessing what it desires. However, it pertains to a perfect agent to act by virtue of love for what it possesses, and for this reason he adds that the beautiful that is God is the efficient, moving, and containing cause, "by a love of His own Beauty." Since He has His own Beauty, he wishes to multiply it as far as possible, that is to say, by the communication of His likeness.

In the second place, he states that the beautiful that is God is "the end of all, like a final cause" of all things. Indeed, all things are made in order to imitate divine beauty in some fashion. Thirdly, He is the exemplary cause, for all things are distinguished in accord with the divinely beautiful, and the mark of this is that no one cares to make an image or a representation, except for the sake of the beautiful.

Next, when he says, "For this reason the beautiful is the same as the good," he infers a sort of corollary from the statement, saying that since the beautiful is the cause of all in so many ways, as a consequence the good and the beautiful are the same, for all things desire the beautiful and the good, as cause, in all ways. And since there is nothing that does not participate in the beautiful and good, and each thing is beautiful and good according to its own form, we might daringly say even this: "that the nonexistent," that is, prime matter, "participates in the beautiful and the good." For the first nonexistent being has a likeness to the divine beautiful and good, because the beautiful and good in God are praised by the removal of all. However, removal is considered in prime matter as a defect, while in God it is by way of excess, in that He supersubstantially exists. Now, although the beautiful and the good are the same in the concrete subject, since both brilliance and harmony are contained under the meaning of the good, nevertheless they are different in their rational intelligibility, for the beautiful adds to the good a directed relation to the power that knows an object of this kind.

"This one, good and beautiful, is in a unique manner the cause of all the many and good things." After Dionysius has explained by what characteristic the beautiful is a cause, he here shows of what things it is the cause. On this point he makes two observations. First, he offers a general statement; second, he continues by distinguishing them in detail, in this text: "From this are the substantial essences of all existents."

So, he says first of all that "the good and beautiful," though one in being, is nevertheless "the cause of all good and beautiful things"—and they are many.

Next, when he says, "From this are the substantial essences of all existents," he continues in detail concerning those things of which the beautiful is the cause: first, in regard to being itself; secondly, in regard to the one, in the text: "unions and distinctions"; thirdly, in regard to their order, in the text: "the providences of higher things"; and fourthly, in regard to rest and movement, in the text: "all resting places and movements." Therefore, he says that all the substantial essences of beings are caused out of the beautiful. For, every essence is either a simple form or gets its perfection through form. Now, form is a certain irradiation coming forth from the first brilliance. Of course, brilliance belongs to the rational character of beauty, as we have said.

Then, when he adds, "unions and distinctions," he states the items that belong to the meaning of the one. On this we should observe that "one" adds indivision to the meaning of being. For, one being is undivided; hence, distinction or discreteness is the opposite to unity. So, he first states that the "unions and distinctions" of things are caused by divine Beauty. Now, a unit in substance produces the same, while a distinction in substance produces diversity; hence, he adds: "othernesses and diversities."

From a unit in quality a like thing is caused, while from a discrete distinction an unlike product results. So, he speaks next of "dissimilitudes." Similarly, a unit in quantity causes equality, and a discrete distinction inequality; but he does not speak of these because they belong to the commensuration of things, which he will treat later.

This may be noticed in things: that even the unlike items in something are in agreement, as, for instance, the contraries in a genus and in matter, and they are unified on some basis, but they remain distinct as parts within the whole. So, he adds, "the communions of contraries," in regard to the first point, and the "nonmixtures of unified items," in regard to the second. Now, all these points are reduced to the causality of the beautiful, since they pertain to harmony, and it is one of the rational characteristics of beauty, as was said.

Next he speaks of "the providences of higher things," and he names the items pertaining to the ordering of things. First, in regard to action, insofar as higher beings exercise providence over the lower ones, and he touches on this when he says, "the opposed relations of mutually ordered things," that is, of equals; again, insofar as lower things are turned to receive perfection and regulation from the higher ones, and this is where he speaks of "conversions of the less well-endowed." Second, he touches on those items that pertain to the existence of things in themselves, and this is where he adds that from the beautiful are "the dwelling places that preserve the same things," that is, of any things in themselves. For, something is preserved by the fact that it remains within the limits of its nature, for if it flows entirely beyond itself, it perishes. Yet, he adds, "and the not unlike collocations," that is, the foundations. For, just as something is preserved because it remains within itself, so something is not capable of passing away because it has something solid within itself on which it is based. Third, he states those items that pertain to the dwelling of one thing in another.

Consequently, we should note that when something requires to be constituted out of others, it is first of all necessary for the parts to be in agreement. For example, as the many stones from which a house is constructed must fit each other, likewise all the parts of the universe must agree in the principle of their existence. And so he says that not only are the dwelling places of things in themselves derived from the beautiful, but also "the communions of all things in all things in accord with what is proper to each." For all things are not in all in merely one way; instead, the higher things are in the lower ones by participation, while the lower are in the higher by eminence. Yet, all have something in common with all.

Secondly, it is a requirement of parts that in their very diversification they can be mutually adapted to each other. For a house is not made from cement and stone unless they be made suitable to each other. Likewise, the parts of the whole of things are mutually adapted, so that they can fall under one ordering—and this is where he speaks of "adaptations."

Thirdly, it is required that one part be helped by another, as the wall and the roof are supported by the foundation, and the roof covers the wall and foundation. Likewise, in the whole of things the higher ones give perfection to the lower ones, and the strength of the higher is manifested in the lower ones. This is where he says, "and the unconfused friendships," because mutual assistance is without prejudice to the distinction of things.

Fourthly, there is required a due proportion among the parts, for instance, that the foundation be such as to fit the other parts. This is where he says, "and the harmony of the thing in the whole," that is, of all parts of the universe. For harmony is caused in the members as a result of a due proportion of numbers. With the parts so arranged, their composition into a whole follows. In this way, one universe of things is constituted out of all the parts of the whole. This is where he adds, "in everything," that is, in the whole, are "concretions." This concretion of parts in the whole is observed in two ways. First, by way of local containment, as the higher things are in beings in some way in the place of lower things (and this may be so either of spiritual or corporeal being). This is where he speaks of "unbreakable containers of existents," in the sense that the higher things contain the lower in an unbreakable order. Second, it pertains to temporal succession (but in this case only in things subject to generation and corruption, in which things the later ones come after the earlier ones). Here, he speaks of "the unfailing successions of things that are made." Now, they are called the unfailing successions of things, not in the sense that there are everlasting genera but that without any gap some members follow after others as long as the course of this world lasts. Now, all these features are caused by the beautiful, he says, because they belong to the meaning of harmony which is essential to beauty.

Then, when he speaks of "all the resting places and the movements," he continues in regard to rest and motion. These, too, belong to the meaning of harmony and beauty, in that they imply a relationship of one item to another. On this he makes three points. First, he states the causality of the beautiful in relation to rest and motion; second, he explains certain motions that seemed to be unmoved, in the phrase: "and indeed divine minds are said to be moved"; third, he offers a conclusion in the text: "therefore, the beautiful and good is the cause, the container, and the end, of three motions in these sensible things in this whole, and much more primarily of the dwelling places and resting places and collocations of each and every thing."

So, he asserts first of all the divine causation of "all resting places," that is, states of rest, "and motions," whether "of minds" or "of bodies." This he says, because that greatest part which is above all rest and motion is the cause of all things both at rest and in motion, in the sense that it gathers into place each thing in its proper essential character, in which the thing has its resting place, and in the sense that it moves all things toward the divine motion. For the motions of all things are ordered to the motion whereby they may be moved in God, in the same way that the motions toward secondary ends are related to the motion toward the ultimate end. Now, the form, on which the proper essence of the thing depends, pertains to brilliance; while the ordering to the end pertains to harmony. Thus, motion and rest are brought back to the causality of the beautiful.

Art as a Personal Skill

Art is nothing but right reasoning concerning works that are to be made. However, the good of these things does not lie in the fact that they are related to the human appetite in some way but in the fact that the product that is made is good in itself. For, it does not pertain to the praise of the artist, as an artist, that he works with a certain disposition of will but, rather, what is the kind of work that he produces. So, art is strictly speaking an operative habit.

Yet, in some fashion it resembles speculative habits, since it is also important to these speculative habits how the thing that they consider is in itself, but not how the human appetite stands in regard to them.

Provided a geometer makes a true demonstration, it is of no importance how he stands in regard to his appetitive part,

Summa of Theology, I-II, 57, 3, c, replies to Obj. 1-3. Trans. V.J.B.

whether he be joyful or angry; nor has this any importance in the artist, as we have said. So, art has the rational character of a virtue in the same way that a speculative habit does. That is to say, neither art nor a speculative habit makes a work good in regard to use, and this latter is what is proper to a virtue perfecting appetite, but it does so only in regard to the ability to act well.

1. When a possessor of an art produces a bad artifact, this is not a work of art, rather it is contrary to art, just as when a knower lies about a truth, what he says is not in accord with knowledge but contrary to knowledge. Hence, just as knowledge is always related to the good, as has been said, so also is art; and in this sense it is called a virtue. Yet, it is deficient in regard to the perfect character of virtue, because it does not make the use itself good, but, for this, something else is required, even though use cannot be good without art.

2. In order that a man may make good use of the art that he possesses, good will is needed and it is perfected by moral virtue. So, the Philosopher says that art is a virtue, namely, a moral one, in that some moral virtue is required for its good use. It is obvious that an artist is inclined to make a faithful work by means of justice, which rectifies the will.

3. Even in the case of speculative matters there is something after the fashion of a work; for example, the construction of a syllogism, or of an agreeable speech, or the work of numbering or measuring. So, whatever speculative habits are directed to rational works of this kind are called arts, that is, liberal ones, by virtue of a resemblance. This is to distinguish them from the arts that are directed to works performed by the body, which are somewhat servile, because the body is subject to the soul in a servile manner, but man is free in regard to his soul. Of course, sciences that are directed toward no work of this sort are simply called sciences and not arts. The fact that the liberal arts are more noble is not the reason why the essential character of art is applicable to them.

How Art Differs from Prudence

Now, art simply provides the faculty for good work, since it is not concerned with appetite. Prudence, however, not only provides the faculty for good work, but also the use, for it is concerned with appetite, as presupposing rectitude of appetite.

The principle of this difference is that art is right reason of things to be made, while prudence is right reason of actions to be done. To make and to act differ because, as is said in the *Metaphysics* (VIII, 8, 1050a30), making is an act passing into external matter, such as building, cutting, and the like; acting, however, is an act remaining within the agent, such as seeing, willing, and the like. And so, prudence is related to this kind of human acts, that are uses of the powers and habits, in the way that art stands toward external actions of making; for each is a perfected reason in regard to the objects to which they are related.

Now, the perfection and rightness of reason in speculative matters depend on the principles from which reason syllogizes; as has been said, scientific knowledge depends on understanding, which is the habit of principles, and is based on it. "In human acts, ends stand in the same position as principles do in the area of speculative acts," as is said in the *Ethics* (VIII, 4, 1151a16). So, for prudence, which is right reason in regard to actions that may be done, it is required that man be well disposed in regard to ends, and this is through right appetite. So, moral virtue is needed for prudence, whereby the appetite is rectified.

But the good of art products is not the good of human appetite but the good of the art works themselves. So, art does not presuppose right appetite. Hence, the artist is more highly regarded who makes a mistake willingly than he who does so unwillingly. On the other hand, it is more contrary to prudence for a person to be at fault willingly than unwill-

Summa of Theology, I-II, 57, 4, c. Trans. V.J.B.

ingly, because rightness of will is of the rational essence of prudence but is not essential to art. And so, it is evident that prudence is a virtue distinct from art.

How Art Imitates Nature

Art imitates nature, as the Philosopher teaches in the second book of the *Physics*. Now, the reason for this is that operations and effects are related to each other in the same proportionate way that their principles are. The principle of artifacts is the human intellect, which is derived by some sort of likeness from the divine intellect, and this latter is the principle of all natural things. Hence, not only must artistic operations imitate nature but also art products must imitate things that exist in nature.

So, if a master artist were to produce a work of art, it would behoove the learner desiring to acquire the art from him to pay attention to his art work, so that he might work in the same way. That is why the human intellect, which depends on the divine intellect for its intelligible light, must be informed concerning the things it makes by observation of things that are naturally produced, so that it may work in like manner.

Hence, the Philosopher remarks that if art were to make the things which exist in nature, it would work in the same way that nature does; and conversely, if nature made artifacts, it would make them just as art does. But, of course, nature does not completely produce artifacts; it merely provides certain principles and offers some sort of working model. In fact, art can observe things in nature and use them to complete its own work; of course, it cannot completely produce these natural things.

It is clear from this that human reason is merely cognitive in regard to things that exist in nature, but in regard to those which are artifacts it is both cognitive and productive. Hence, human sciences which deal with natural things must be

Exposition of Aristotle's Politics, I, Lect. 1. Trans. V.J.B.

speculative, while those which deal with things produced by man must be practical or operative according to the imitation of nature.

In its work, nature proceeds from simple things to complex ones; so, in the case of things made by the working of nature, that which is most complex is perfect and whole and the end of the others, as is clear in the relation of all whole things to their parts. So, too, human reason as operative proceeds from simple things to complex, going as it were from the imperfect to the perfect.

RECOMMENDED READINGS

CALLAHAN, L. *A Theory of Esthetic according to the Principles of St. Thomas Aquinas.* Washington: Catholic University Press, 1927.

DUFFY, J. *A Philosophy of Poetry: Based on Thomistic Principles.* Washington: Catholic University Press, 1945.

GILBY, T. *Poetic Experience: An Introduction to Thomist Aesthetic.* London: Sheed and Ward, 1934.

GILSON, E. "The Forgotten Transcendental: *Pulchrum,*" *Elements of Christian Philosophy.* New York: Doubleday, 1960, 159-163.

——. *Painting and Reality* (Mellon Lectures). New York: Pantheon Books, 1957.

MARITAIN, J. *Art and Scholasticism.* New York: Scribner's, 1930.

——. *Creative Intuition in Art and Poetry* (Mellon Lectures). New York: Pantheon Books, 1953.

NOON, W. T. *Joyce and Aquinas.* New Haven: Yale University Press, 1957.

PHELAN, G. B. "The Concept of Beauty in St. Thomas," *Aspects of the New Scholastic Philosophy.* New York: Benziger, 1932, 121-145.

VIII. Revelation and Theology

Foreword

IT IS AS A THEOLOGIAN that St. Thomas best displays his gifts and clarity of understanding. The extracts that make up this chapter in no way represent the whole scope of Thomistic theology. They are but brief samplings on a few key topics, from his many theological writings. His views are well developed in his famous *Summa of Theology*, of course, but it is clear from its opening articles (printed below) that Aquinas regarded this vast treatise as but a sketch of his thought on this subject.

The textbook of theology that was used by his early followers is his *Commentary on Peter Lombard's Four Books of Sentences*. This work probably contains the elements of some of his first teaching at the University of Paris. It has not, as yet, been translated into English. However, for the topics that they cover, the *Disputed Questions* offer the most thorough and complete presentation of Aquinas' religious thought. His expositions of several books of both the Old and the New Testaments show that he by no means neglected the study of the Bible. However, these Scripture commentaries have not yet been critically edited; the Latin printings that we have are textually somewhat defective. Most of Aquinas' shorter works are theological in character. Of these, the most interesting is the *Compendium of Theology*, a work in which Christian teaching is arranged under the three theological virtues. It was left incomplete by its author. As far as the method of sacred theology and its relations to other disciplines are concerned, the *Exposition of Boethius on the Trinity* is a precious source of information.

It is well to note briefly certain precisions made by Aquinas in the extracts that open this chapter. Faith is not theology. Faith is a habit or quality of understanding given to man by God, so that he may assent to certain divine truths on divine authority but without fully understanding them. In this sense, faith is needed by all men, if they are to achieve everlasting life with God. Such faith requires no study; it is a gift of God. As Aquinas said in his famous *Sermon on the Creed* (introductory section): "No philosopher before the coming of Christ could, with all his striving, know as much about God and the things required for eternal life as an old woman could through faith, after Christ's coming." Fortunately, one does not have to be a theologian, much less a philosopher, to get to Heaven.

Theology, as Aquinas sees it, is a demonstrative science beginning with the data of faith and using information and techniques from the other areas of human knowledge to achieve an expert understanding of what can be known about divinity in this life. Since it rises above metaphysics to a special view of the highest causes of being, sacred theology is also a wisdom. Aquinas' theology comes as a climax to a long effort of early Christianity to understand its heritage. It is one of the great advances in the program launched by John Damascene and Augustine, and continued by Anselm, under the slogan of medieval intellectualism: "faith seeking understanding."

Faith Is Not Demonstrative Knowledge

That the world did not always exist is held by faith alone and it cannot be proved demonstratively, just as we said above of the mystery of the Trinity. The reason for this is that the

Summa of Theology, I, 46, 2, c. Trans. V.J.B.

beginning [*novitas*] of the world cannot receive a demonstration from the side of the world itself. Indeed, the starting point of a generation is that which is. But each thing in its specific intelligibility abstracts from the here and now. This is why it is said that "universals are everywhere and forever." Hence, it cannot be demonstrated that man, or the heavens, or a stone did not always exist.

Likewise, it cannot be demonstrated from the side of the agent-cause that acts by means of will. For, the will of God cannot be investigated rationally, except for those items that it is absolutely necessary for God to will. Now, such items are not what He wills in regard to creatures, as we have said.

Of course, it is possible for the divine will to be manifested through revelation, on which faith rests. Hence, that the world had a beginning is a matter of belief [*credibile*] but not of demonstration or of science.

And this is a useful thing to consider, lest someone who perhaps presumes to demonstrate what is of faith brings forward arguments lacking in necessity; for, these would provide unbelievers with matter for ridicule and they would think that we believe items pertaining to the faith because of arguments of this kind.

Why One Should Believe

Someone may say: "Isn't it stupid to believe what is not seen; shouldn't we refuse to believe things that are not seen?"

In answering this, I say first of all that the imperfection of our understanding takes away the force of this difficulty. As a matter of fact, if man could know perfectly all things visible and invisible, it would be stupid to believe what we do not see. However, our knowledge is so imperfect that no philosopher has ever been able to make a perfect investigation

Sermon on the Creed, Prologue. Trans. V.J.B.

of the nature of one fly. We read that a certain philosopher spent thirty years in solitude, so that he might study the nature of a bee. If our intellect is so feeble, then, isn't it stupid to refuse to believe anything about God, other than what man can know by himself? And so, against this objection it is stated in Job 36:26: *Behold God is great, exceeding our knowledge.*

In the second place, it can be replied that if some master teacher said something within the area of his own science and if some unlearned person said that this master's teaching was not so because he did not understand it, one might grant that this person would be considered rather stupid. Now, it is obvious that an angel's understanding surpasses the intellect of the greatest philosopher far more than does the intellect of the great philosopher in relation to that of the unlearned man. So, the reason of the philosopher is unwise if he refuses to believe what the angels say, and much more so if he refuses credence to what God says. Again, against this objection stands the statement in Ecclus. 3:25: *For many things are shown to thee above the understanding of men.*

Thirdly, it can be answered that if man refused to believe anything unless he knew it himself, then it would be quite impossible to live in this world. How could a person live, if he did not believe someone? How could he even accept the fact that a certain man is his father? Indeed, a man has to believe someone in regard to those things that he cannot know by himself. But no one is as worthy of belief as God is. Hence, those who do not believe the statements of the faith are not wise; rather, they are foolish and proud; as the Apostle says (I Tim. 6:4): *He is proud, knowing nothing.* For this reason he also said (II Tim. 1:12): *I know whom I have believed, and I am certain;* and Ecclus. 2:8 reads: *Ye that fear the Lord, believe Him.*

In the fourth place, one may also reply that God proves that the teachings of the faith are true. Suppose a king sent a letter stamped with his own seal, no one would dare deny that this letter had been sent with the king's approval. Now, it is clear that all the things that the saints believed concerning the faith of Christ, which they have handed down to us, are marked with God's seal. This seal is manifested by those works which no mere creature can perform. These are the miracles whereby Christ confirmed the statements of the Apostles and the saints.

If you object that no one has seen miracles occurring, I can give an answer to that. It is well known, in fact, that the whole world used to worship idols and to persecute Christ's faith. To this even the histories written by pagans give testimony. Today, however, all are converted to Christ—the wise men, the nobles, the rich, the powerful, and the great—all are converted to the preaching of those who are simple and poor, of those few men who preach Christ. Now, this was either accomplished miraculously, or it was not. If done miraculously, the point is proved. If not, then I say that there could be no greater miracle than this fact, that the whole world was converted without miracles. So, we need not look for anything else. Hence, no one should doubt concerning the faith; rather, he ought to believe things pertinent to faith more than what he sees; for man's sight can be deceived but God's knowledge is never mistaken.

Why Faith Is Necessary for Mankind

Faith has something in common with opinion and something with science and understanding; for which reason it is placed between science and opinion by Hugh of St. Victor. With science and understanding, indeed, it shares a sure and solid assent, differing on this basis from opinion, which accepts one contrary but with some hesitation about the other; and differing from doubt, which fluctuates between two contraries. However, it shares with opinion the fact that it is concerned with things that are not clear to the understanding, and

Exposition of Boethius on the Trinity, III, 1, c. Trans. V.J.B.

on this basis it is different from science and understanding.

Now, when something is not evident to human cognition, there are two possible explanations, as is said in the *Metaphysics* (II, 1, 993b7); that is, because of a defect in the knowable things themselves, or because of a defect in our intellect. It may be due to a defect in the things, as in the case of singular and contingent things that are far removed from our senses; for instance, men's deeds, statements, and thoughts, which are such that they can be known by one person and yet ignored by others. Now, since it is necessary in the common intercourse of men that one person make use of another in regard to those items which he cannot provide for himself, he has to stand by the things that another man knows and which he does not know, just as one adheres to what he knows on his own part. As a result, faith is necessary in the intercourse of men, that trust whereby one man believes what another man says. This is the foundation of justice, as Cicero says in his *Offices* (I, 7, 23). That is why there is no lie that is without wrong, for this faith that is so necessary is injured by every instance of lying.

It is due to a defect on our part that divine and necessary things are not apparent, for they are most knowable in their own nature. Thus, we are not immediately equipped at the start to investigate such things, because it is incumbent on us to proceed from things that are in their own nature less knowable, and rather secondary, to the things that are in their nature more knowable and primary. Yet, since the things that we know at the beginning are known through the force of the things that we learn later, it is also necessary for us to have some acquaintance with those things that are most knowable in themselves: this cannot be done without believing.

And this is even evident in the ordering of the sciences, because the science that deals with the highest causes, namely metaphysics, comes last in man's process of learning; yet, in the preliminary sciences, certain points have to be presupposed that are only fully known in metaphysics. As a result, each science has its suppositions to which the learner gives credence. So, since the end of human life is beatitude, which lies in the full knowledge of divine matters, it is necessary for the direction of human life toward beatitude to have immediately at the beginning a faith in divine things, whose full knowledge is looked forward to, in the final perfection of man.

For some such things, full knowledge is possible to man as an achievement of reason, even in the present state of life. Yet, in regard to such things, although knowledge is possible and is achieved by some people, it is still necessary to have faith, for the five reasons that are stated by Rabbi Moses [Maimonides]. First, there is the profundity and subtlety of their matter, whereby divine things are hidden from the intellect of men. Consequently, lest man be without any knowledge whatever of these things, provision was made that he might know divine matters at least by faith: Eccles. 7:25: *A great depth, who shall find it out?* Second, there is the weakness of the human intellect from the beginning. Indeed, its full development does not come to it until toward the end. So, in order that no part of its time should be devoid of divine knowledge, it needs faith whereby it may accept divine things from the very start. Third, there is the need for many items of preliminary knowledge that are required in order to achieve a knowledge of God by way of reasoning. In fact, the knowledge of nearly all the sciences is required for this, since the end of all is the knowledge of divine things. Yet, very few men attain even these preliminaries. Hence, so that the majority of men would not remain devoid of divine knowledge, the way of faith was divinely provided for man. Fourth, since many men are not disposed by their natural endowments to attain perfection of understanding by way of reasoning, as a consequence the way of faith was provided, so that even these men should not be without divine knowledge. Fifth, there are the manifold occupations at which men must busy themselves, as a result of which it is impossible for all men to attain by way of reasoning what is necessary for knowledge about God. So, for this reason, the way of faith has been made available and this applies to those items that are known by some people but are presented as articles of faith to others.

Then, there are other divine matters for the full knowledge of which human reason in no way suffices. Instead, the full knowledge of these things is awaited in the future life, when beatitude will be complete: for instance, the unity and trinity of the one God. Man will be advanced to this knowledge not by what is owed to his nature but by divine grace alone. Hence, even for this perfect knowledge, certain bases are offered at the beginning to man as items of belief. Direction is received from these toward the full knowledge of those things that he has believed from the start. This is the same as what occurs in the other sciences, as we have stated. Hence, it is said in Isa. 7:9: *Unless you have believed, you will not understand.* And these basic articles are those that are items of belief in all cases, being known or understood by no man in this life.

Theology Goes Beyond Philosophy

Now, the points that have been discussed above concerning God have been subtly considered by many of the pagan philosophers, although some of them have made mistakes on these points. Moreover, those who have stated the truth on these matters have scarcely been able to reach it after a long and laborious search. But there are other truths handed down to us in the teaching of Christian religion that they were unable to attain; regarding these truths that transcend human perception, we are instructed according to the Christian faith. The point is this: although God is One and Simple, as has been shown, He is nevertheless God the Father, and God the Son, and God the Holy Spirit—yet these three are not three Gods but one God. This is what we propose to consider, to the extent that we are able.

Compendium of Theology, I, c. 36. Trans. V.J.B.

St. John's Contemplation

John's contemplation, then, was ample, exalted, and perfect.
Observe, however, that the various sciences share these three
modes of contemplation in different ways. Moral science
possesses the perfection of contemplation, for it is concerned
with the ultimate end. Natural science has ampleness, for it
considers things proceeding from God. And among the
physical [philosophical?] sciences, metaphysics has exaltation
of contemplation. But the Gospel of John contains together
and at once what these sciences have in fragments—and so it
is most perfect.

Exposition of St. John's Gospel, Prologue. Trans. V.J.B.

The Divine Trinity Is Believed, Not Demonstrated

That God is threefold and one is solely an item of belief and
it can in no way be demonstrated, although some arguments
can be given that are not necessarily convincing, or even very
probable, except for a believer. This is evident from the fact
that we know God in this life only from His effects, as is
clear from our preceding explanations. So, we are able, by
natural reasoning, to know about God only what is perceived
of Him from the relation of His effects to Him: for instance,
those items that indicate His causality and eminence over
caused things, and those which remove from Him the imperfect conditions of His effects. Now, the Trinity of Persons cannot be grasped from this divine causality because the causality
belongs in common to the whole Trinity. Nor can it be ex-

Exposition of Boethius on the Trinity, I, 4, c. Trans. V.J.B.

pressed according to the method of removal. Hence, there can be no demonstrative proof that God is threefold and one.

Procedural Distinction Between Philosophy and Theology

Just as the beginning of natural knowledge consists in a knowing about creatures as a result of sense perception, so the beginning of the knowledge that is given from above consists in the knowing of the first truth by means of infused faith. As a consequence, the process from such beginnings follows different orders. The philosophers, who follow the order of natural cognition, place the scientific knowledge of creatures before the divine science; that is, the philosophy of nature comes before metaphysics. On the other hand, the contrary procedure is followed among the theologians, so that the consideration of the Creator precedes the consideration of creatures.

Exposition of Boethius on the Trinity, Prologue. Trans. V.J.B.

On the Use of Philosophy by the Theologian

As sacred doctrine is based on the light of faith, so is philosophy founded on the natural light of reason. Hence, it is impossible for items that belong to philosophy to be contrary to those that pertain to faith; but the former may be defective in comparison with the latter. Yet, they contain some like-

Exposition of Boethius on the Trinity, II, 3, c. Trans. V.J.B.

nesses and some prolegomena to the latter, just as nature is a preamble to grace. If any point among the statements of the philosophers is found contrary to faith, this is not philosophy but rather an abuse of philosophy, resulting from a defect in reasoning. So, it is possible, from the principles of philosophy, to refute an error of this kind, either by showing that it is an impossibility, or by showing that it is not a necessary conclusion. Just as items of faith cannot be proved demonstratively, so items that are contrary to them cannot demonstratively be shown to be false; yet, it is possible to show that they are not necessarily convincing.

And so, we can use philosophy in sacred doctrine in three ways: (1) to demonstrate items that are preambles to faith, such as those things that are proved about God by natural processes of reasoning: that God exists, that God is one, and similar points about God or creatures that are proved in philosophy and which faith takes as established; (2) to make known those items that belong to the faith by means of certain similitudes; thus, Augustine (in his book *On Order*, 9-12) uses many likenesses taken from philosophical teachings to show something about the Trinity; and (3) to oppose statements against the faith, either by showing that they are false, or by showing that they are not necessarily true.

All Things Are Created by God

The Ancients made progress in considering the natures of things by following the order of human knowledge. Since human knowledge reaches understanding by taking its start in sensation, the earlier philosophers concentrated on sense things and little by little moved from these toward intelligible objects. Moreover, since accidental forms are capable of being sensed in themselves, while substantial forms are not, the

Disputed Questions on the Power of God, III, 5, c. Trans. V.J.B.

first philosophers said that all forms are accidents and that
matter alone is substance. Then, because substance is adequate
as a cause of accidents which are produced out of the principles of substance, the consequence is that the first philosophers
asserted that there is no other cause than matter. They claimed
that all things observed as developing in the area of sense
objects are caused by it. Thus, they were forced to conclude
that there is no cause of matter and to deny the efficient
cause entirely.

Then, subsequent philosophers began to give some thought
to substantial forms; not that they achieved a knowledge of
universals, for their whole attention was directed toward
special forms. So, some of them postulated certain agent
causes, not those that give the act of being [esse] to all
things universally but those that transmute matter into this
or that form; for example, intelligence, friendship, and strife.
They assigned the activity of these to the processes of re-
pulsion and attraction. Thus, even in their view, not all beings
proceeded from an efficient cause, for matter was presupposed
as a basis for the action of the agent cause.

Still later philosophers, like Plato, Aristotle, and their
schools, did reach the point of thinking about the universal
act of being. So, they alone claimed that there is a universal
cause of real things by which all other things are brought
forth into actual being, as is evident from Augustine (City of
God, VIII, 4).

Now, the Catholic faith agrees with this view. It can be
demonstrated by three arguments, of which this is the first.
If some one item is found in common in many things, it must
be caused in them by some one cause. Indeed, it is impossible
for what is common to two things to be proper to both of them,
because to the extent that one thing is itself, it is different
from another thing. Different causes produce diverse effects.
Therefore, since the act of being is found in common in all
things (which, because of the fact that they exist, are mutually distinct), the act of being must necessarily be assigned
to them, not as arising from themselves but from some one

real cause. This is seen to be Plato's argument, for he stressed the point that prior to every plurality there is a unity, not merely numerical but even in the natures of things.

The second argument is this. When anything is found to be shared in different ways by many things, it must be attributed to all those subjects in which it is found imperfectly by that subject in which it exists most perfectly. For, things that admit of positive degrees of more or less owe this fact to their approaching more closely or more remotely to some one item. Indeed, if this item belonged to each of them because of each thing itself, there would be no reason why it would be found more perfectly in one than in another. Thus, we see that fire, which is the ultimate in the order of heat, is the principle of heat in all hot bodies. So, we should grant one being that is most perfectly and truly a being. This is proved from the fact that there is some mover that is completely immobile and most perfect, as is demonstrated by the philosophers. Therefore, all other things, being less perfect, must receive actual being from it. This is the Philosopher's proof (Aristotle, *Metaphysics*, II, 1).

The third argument is this. Whatever exists by virtue of another being may be traced back to a cause that exists by virtue of itself. Hence, if there were a heat that existed by virtue of itself, it would have to be the cause of all hot things that possess heat by way of participation. Now, we have to admit a being that is itself its own act of being. This is proved by the fact that there must be some first being which is pure act and in which there is no composition. Hence, from that one being all others must be, whatsoever things that are not their own act of being but possess being by means of participation. This is Avicenna's argument (*Metaphysics*, VIII, 7; IX, 4).

And so, that all things are created by God is demonstrated by reason and held by faith.

On Sacred Doctrine

Prologue

Since the teacher of Catholic truth not only ought to instruct advanced scholars but also has as his function to teach beginners, in accord with the Apostle's text (I Cor. 3:1), *as to little ones in Christ, I fed you with milk, not with solid food,* what we propose to do in this work is to treat those items that are pertinent to the Christian religion in a manner that is adapted to the teaching of beginners.

As a matter of fact, we have thought that new students of this doctrine are held back by several features of the writings produced by different authors: partly by the multiplication of useless questions, articles, and arguments; partly, too, because the things that such students must know are not treated according to the order of learning but according to the order that the development of textbooks has required, or according to whatever order the occurrence of a disputation has dictated; and partly because frequent repetition of the same points has generated both boredom and confusion in the minds of their listeners.

So, in the effort to avoid these and other impediments, we shall try, with trust in divine assistance, to go through the pertinent points in sacred doctrine briefly and clearly, to the extent that the subject matter permits.

Question 1: On Sacred Doctrine: What Kind It Is and What It Covers

Now, in order that our plan be kept within definite limits, it is first necessary to study something about sacred doctrine, what kind it is, and what it covers. On this, ten questions are to be asked.

Summa of Theology, I, Prologue and Quest. 1. Trans. V.J.B.

1. On the necessity of this doctrine.
2. Whether it is a science.
3. Whether it is one or many.
4. Whether it is speculative or practical.
5. On the relation between it and other sciences.
6. Whether it is a wisdom.
7. What its subject is.
8. Whether it uses argumentation.
9. Whether it should use metaphorical or symbolic terminology.
10. Whether the Sacred Scriptures of this doctrine should be expounded according to different meanings.

Article 1: Whether Besides the Philosophical Disciplines It Is Necessary to Have Another Doctrine

As for this first problem, it appears that it is not necessary to have a doctrine other than the philosophical disciplines.

1. Man should not crave for information that is above reason, according to Ecclus. 3:22: *Seek not the things that are too high for thee.* But those matters that are subject to reason are adequately treated in philosophical studies. So, it seems superfluous for any teaching to be entertained apart from the philosophical disciplines.

2. Doctrine can deal with being only, for nothing is known unless it be true and the true is convertible with being. But a treatment of all beings, even of God, is offered in the philosophical studies; thus, one part of philosophy is called theology, or divine science, as is evident from the Philosopher in the *Metaphysics* (V, 1, 1026a19). So, it was unnecessary to have any doctrine apart from the philosophical studies.

To the contrary is the statement in II Tim. 3:16: *All scripture, inspired of God, is profitable to teach, to reprove, to correct, to instruct in justice.* Now, divinely inspired Scripture does not belong in the philosophical disciplines, for they are discovered by human reason. So, it is of utility that there be another divinely inspired science, apart from the philosophical studies.

In reply, I say that it was necessary for man's salvation that there be a doctrine in accord with divine revelation, besides the philosophical studies. First, because man is ordered toward God as an end which surpasses the grasp of reason, according to the text of Isa. 64:4: *Eye hath not seen, O God, besides thee, what things thou hast prepared for them that wait for thee*. Now, the end should be known in advance by men who ought to order their intentions and actions toward the end. Hence, it was necessary to the salvation of man that some things be made known to him through divine revelation, things that exceed human reason.

It was also necessary for man to be instructed by divine revelation concerning those things pertaining to God that can be investigated by human reason. For, the truth about God as investigated by reason could come to but few men, and after a long time, and with the admixture of many errors. Yet, on the knowledge of this truth the whole salvation of man depends, for salvation lies in God. Therefore, in order that salvation might come to men, both more fittingly and more certainly, it was necessary that they be instructed concerning divine matters through divine revelation.

So, it was necessary to have, apart from the philosophical disciplines which make their investigation through reason, a sacred doctrine through revelation.

Answers to objections:

1. Although those things that are higher than man's knowledge are not to be sought after by man using his reason, they are nevertheless to be accepted on faith when they are revealed by God. Thus, in the same text it is added (Ecclus. 3:25): *For many things are shown to thee above the understanding of men*. And sacred doctrine consists in things of this kind.

2. A different cognitive principle [*ratio cognoscibilis*] produces a differentiation in the sciences. For, the astronomer and the natural philosopher may demonstrate the same con-

clusion: for instance, that the earth is spherical. But the astronomer does it by a mathematical method, by one that abstracts from matter, while the natural philosopher does it by means of a consideration based on matter. Hence, nothing prevents treatment of the same things by philosophy, according as they are knowable by the light of natural reason, and by another science, inasmuch as they are known by the light of divine revelation. Hence, the theology that belongs under sacred doctrine differs generically from that theology which is offered as a part of philosophy.

Article 2: Whether Sacred Doctrine Is a Science

As for the second problem, it appears that sacred doctrine is not a science.

1. Indeed, every science proceeds from self-known principles. But sacred doctrine proceeds from articles of faith which are not self-known, since they are not accepted by all men; *for all men have not faith*, as is said in II Thess. 3:2. Therefore, sacred doctrine is not a science.

2. A science does not treat individuals. But sacred doctrine treats individuals, for instance, the deeds of Abraham, Isaac, and Jacob, and the like. So sacred doctrine is not a science.

To the contrary is the statement of Augustine, in *De Trinitate*, XIV, c. 7: "To this science is attributed only that whereby faith most safely develops, is nourished, is defended, and is strengthened." Now, this pertains to no other science than sacred doctrine. So, sacred doctrine is a science.

In reply, I say that sacred doctrine is a science. However, it should be understood that there are two kinds of sciences. There are some that proceed from principles known by the natural light of the intellect, such as arithmetic, geometry, and the like. Then, there are others that proceed from principles known by the light of a higher science, as optics proceeds from principles known through geometry, and music from principles known through arithmetic. Now, sacred doctrine is a science in this latter way, for it proceeds from principles known by the light of a higher science, namely, the knowledge proper to God and the blessed. Hence, just as music takes on faith the principles handed over to it by the arithmetical expert, so does sacred doctrine believe the principles revealed to it by God.

Answers to objections:

1. The principles of each science are either self-evident or they are grounded in the knowledge of a higher science. Such are the principles of sacred doctrine, as has been said.

2. Individuals are treated in sacred doctrine not as the chief objects studied but sometimes as illustrations of life (as in the moral sciences), sometimes to establish the authority of the men through whom divine revelation has come to us, on which Sacred Scripture or doctrine is based.

Article 3: Whether Sacred Doctrine Is One Science

As for the third problem, it appears that sacred doctrine is not one science.

1. Because, according to the Philosopher in the first book of the *Posterior Analytics* (28, 87a38): "A science is one when it has one kind of subject matter." Now, the Creator and creatures, both of which are treated in sacred doctrine, are not contained within one genus of subject matter. So, sacred doctrine is not one science.

2. In sacred doctrine a treatment is given of angels, bodily creatures, and the customs of mankind. Now, the foregoing belong to different philosophical sciences. Therefore, sacred doctrine is not one science.

To the contrary is the fact that Sacred Scripture speaks of it as one science; for, it is said in Wisd. 10:10: *She gave him the science of the holy things.*

In reply, I say that sacred doctrine is one science. In fact, the unity of a power and a habit must be considered according to the object not taken materially but according to the formal intelligibility of the object. Thus, man, donkey, and stone agree in one formal character—they are all colored and this is the object of sight. So, because Sacred Scripture considers certain items inasmuch as they are divinely revealed (as we have said), all things whatsoever that are divinely revealed share in the one formal intelligibility of the object of this science. So, they are included under sacred doctrine as under one science.

Answers to objections:

1. Sacred doctrine does not provide information about God and about creatures in equal fashion, but about God principally and about creatures as they are related to God as to a source or an end. Hence, the unity of the science is not hindered.

2. Nothing prevents lower powers or habits from being diversified in relation to the subject matters that fall under one higher power or habit, for the higher power or habit looks to the object under a more universal formal character. For example, the object of the general power of sense perception [*sensus communis*] is the sensible, yet it includes both the visible and the audible; consequently, the general power of sense, since it is but one potency, extends to all the objects of the five external senses. Likewise, sacred doctrine, while remaining one, can consider the things that are treated in various philosophical sciences under one intelligibility, that is, insofar as they are divinely revealable. Thus, sacred doctrine is somewhat like an imprint from the divine knowledge which is one and simple for all things.

Article 4: Whether Sacred Doctrine Is a Practical Science

As to the fourth problem: it appears that sacred doctrine is a practical science.

1. "The end of practical knowledge is action," according to the Philosopher in the *Metaphysics* (II, 4, 993b21). Now,

sacred doctrine is directed toward action, according to Jas. 1:22: *Be ye doers of the word and not hearers only*. Therefore, sacred doctrine is a practical science.

2. Sacred doctrine is divided by the Old Law and the New. Now, law belongs to moral science, which is a practical science. Therefore, sacred doctrine is a practical science.

To the contrary, every practical science deals with things that can be done by man, as moral science does with human acts and the knowledge of how to build with buildings. Now, sacred science is chiefly concerned with God, Whose works men are. So, it is not a practical science but rather a speculative one.

In reply, I say that sacred doctrine being one, as we have said, covers the matters that pertain to the various philosophical sciences by virtue of the formal intelligibility which it considers in these different fields, namely, the fact that they are knowable by means of the divine light. Hence, although there is a difference between the speculative and the practical in the philosophical sciences, yet sacred doctrine comprehends both within itself, just as God knows Himself and what He has made, through the same knowledge.

However, it is more speculative than it is practical, for it treats divine matters more especially than it does human acts, and it treats the latter inasmuch as man is directed, through these acts, to the perfect knowing of God, in which eternal beatitude lies.

And the reply to the objections is clear from this answer.

Article 5: Whether Sacred Doctrine Is of Greater Worth than the Other Sciences

As for the fifth problem, it seems that sacred doctrine has not greater worth than the other sciences.

1. Certitude is pertinent to the worth of a science. But the other sciences, whose principles cannot be doubted, appear to be more certain than sacred doctrine, for its principles,

the articles of faith, are subject to doubt. Therefore, the other sciences seem of greater worth than this one.

2. It is appropriate to a lower science for it to take something from a higher one, as the musician does from the mathematician. But sacred doctrine takes something from the philosophical studies. Indeed, Jerome says in a letter *To Magnus* (Epist. LXX, PL 22, 668): "The ancient doctors filled their books with the teachings and views of the philosophers, so that you would not know what you should admire first in them, their secular learning or their knowledge of the Scriptures." So, sacred doctrine is lower than the other sciences.

To the contrary is the fact that the other sciences are called its handmaiden: Prov. 9:3: *She hath sent her maids to invite to the tower.*

In reply, I say that this science is speculative in regard to one area and practical in regard to another, but it transcends the others both speculative and practical. One speculative science is said to be of greater worth than another, at times because of its certitude, at other times because of the value of its subject matter. Now, this science surpasses the other speculative sciences in both respects. As far as certitude is concerned, the other sciences get their certitude from the natural light of human reason, while this one receives its certitude from the light of divine knowledge, which cannot be deceived. And as far as the value of the subject matter goes, this science deals principally with those matters that exceed the limits of human reason, while the others deal only with items subject to reason.

Now, among practical sciences that one is more worthy which orders to a more ultimate end; for instance, politics is above the military, since the good of an army is subordinated to that of the state. But the end of this doctrine, considered as practical, is eternal beatitude, and all the other ends of the practical sciences are ordered to it as to a last end. So, it is plain that from every point of view, it is of greater worth than the others.

Answers to objections:

1. Nothing prevents what is more certain in its own nature from being less certain on our part, because of the weakness of our intellect, which "is related to the most evident things in nature as the owl's eye is to the light of the sun," according to the statement in the *Metaphysics* (II, 1, 993b9). Hence, the doubt which occurs in some cases concerning articles of faith is not due to a lack of certitude in the reality but rather to the weakness of the human intellect. And yet, the very little knowledge that can be attained concerning the highest things is more desirable than the most certain knowledge that can be gained about things of slight importance, as is said in the treatise *On the Parts of Animals* (I, 5, 644b31).

2. This science can take something from the philosophical disciplines, not because it necessarily requires such borrowings but for greater clarity in the explanation of what is treated in this science. Actually, it does not take its principles from the other sciences but directly from God through revelation. So, it does not borrow from the other sciences as superiors but uses them as inferiors and servants, as architecture uses the services of subordinated skills, and as politics uses the military. Moreover, this fact, that it uses them in this way, is not due to its imperfection or inadequacy but to the deficiency of our intellect, which is more easily led up to the things that are above reason, and are treated in this science, by starting from the things known by natural reason, from which the other sciences also proceed.

Article 6: Whether This Doctrine Is a Wisdom

As to the sixth problem, it appears that this doctrine is not a wisdom.

1. In fact, no doctrine that bases its principles on some other source is worthy of the name wisdom; for, "it is proper to the wise man to order and not be ordered" (*Metaphysics,* I, 2, 982a18). But this doctrine does base its principles on another source, as is clear from what has been said. So, this doctrine is not a wisdom.

2. It belongs to wisdom to prove the principles of the other sciences; hence, it is called the "head" of the sciences, in the *Ethics* (VII, 3, 1141a20). But this doctrine does not prove the principles of the other sciences. So, it is not a wisdom.

3. This doctrine is learned by study. Now, wisdom is possessed as a result of infusion; consequently, it is numbered among the seven Gifts of the Holy Spirit, as is clear from Isa. 11:2. Therefore, this doctrine is not a wisdom.

To the contrary is the text in Deut. 4:6 on the beginning of the Law: *For this is your wisdom and understanding in the sight of nations.*

In reply, I say that this doctrine is, in the greatest way, the wisdom above all human wisdoms, not merely in some one genus but without limitation. Since it is the function of the wise man to order and to judge, and since judgment of inferiors is made by means of a higher cause, he who considers the highest cause in a given generic field is called wise in that field. Thus, in the generic field of building, the architect who decides on the form of the house is deemed wise, and so is the contractor in relation to the lower workmen who cut the lumber or prepare the stones. Hence, it is stated in I Cor. 3:10: *As a wise architect, I have laid the foundation.*

Again, in the field of human life as a whole, the prudent man is called wise because he orders human actions to their proper end. Hence, it is said in Prov. 10:23: *Wisdom is prudence to a man.* So, he who considers without restriction the highest cause of the whole universe, which is God, is deemed wise in the greatest way. As a further consequence, wisdom is said to be the knowledge of divine things, as is clear in Augustine, *On the Trinity* (XII, 14). Now, sacred doctrine, in a most special way, treats of God as the highest cause: for, it does so not only by virtue of the fact that He is knowable through creatures (which is known to the philosophers, as is said in Rom. 1:19: *That which is known of God is manifest in them*) but also on the basis of what is known to Himself alone about Himself, and to others through

shared revelation. Hence, sacred doctrine is especially called
a wisdom.

Answers to objections:

1. Sacred doctrine does not base its principles on a human
science but on divine knowledge, whereby all our knowledge
is ordered as by a highest wisdom.

2. The principles of the other sciences are either self-
evident and cannot be proved, or they are proved by some
natural reasoning in another science. Now, the knowledge
proper to this science is that which comes through revelation,
not that which is achieved by natural reasoning. So, its function is not to prove the principles of the other sciences but
simply to judge them; whatever in these other sciences is
found repugnant to the truth of this science is wholly condemned as false. Hence, it is said, II Cor. 10:4-5: *destroying
counsels, and every height that exalteth itself against the
knowledge of God.*

3. Since judgment belongs to the wise man, wisdom is
understood as twofold according to the two ways of judging.
A person may judge in one fashion, *by way of inclination;* for
instance, the man possessed of a habit of virtue judges rightly of the things that are to be done virtuously, because he is
inclined toward them. Thus, it is said in the *Ethics* (X, 5,
1176a17) that the virtuous man is the measure and rule of
human actions. The second kind of judgment is *by way of
knowledge;* for example, a person learned in moral science
might judge concerning virtuous actions, even though he
possessed no virtue. So, the first way of judging about divine
matters belongs to the wisdom that is placed among the
Gifts of the Holy Spirit, according to I Cor. 2:15: *For the
spiritual man judgeth all things;* and Dionysius says, *On
the Divine Names* (c. 2): "Hierotheus was learned not only
in regard to teaching divine matters but also in experiencing
them." Now, the second way of judging belongs to this doctrine, according as it may be achieved by study, even though
its principles are received from revelation.

Article 7: Whether God Is the Subject of This Science

As for the seventh problem, it appears that God is not the subject of this science.

1. In every science, it is necessary to posit what the subject is, according to the Philosopher in the *Posterior Analytics* (I, 4, 71a13). But this science does not posit what God is; indeed, Damascene says (*On the Orthodox Faith*, I, 4): "In regard to God, it is impossible to say what He is." Therefore, God is not the subject of this science.

2. All things that are treated in a science are included within the subject of that science. But many things other than God are treated in Sacred Scripture; for example, creatures and the customs of men. So, God is not the subject of this science.

To the contrary, the subject of a science is what is talked about in it. But in this science, one does talk about God; indeed, it is called theology, which means talking about God. So, God is the subject of this science.

In reply, I say that God is the subject of this science. In fact, the subject is related to the science as the object is to a potency or habit. Now, something is properly assigned as the object of a potency or habit when all the items that are related to the potency or habit are included under its intelligibility. Thus, man and stone are referred to the power of sight because they are colored; hence, the colored is the proper object of sight. Now, all things are treated in sacred doctrine under the intelligibility of God, either because they are God Himself, or because they have some relation to God, either as source or as end. Hence, it follows that God is truly the subject of this science.

This is also evident from the principles of this science, for they are articles of faith and it is concerned with God. Now, the subject of the principles is the same as that of the entire science, since the whole science is virtually contained in the principles.

Of course, some thinkers who look to the things treated

in this science and not to the intelligibility under which they are considered have assigned some other subject to the science: either reality and its signs, or the works of redemption, or the whole Christ as Head and members. Indeed, a treatment of all of these is offered in this science but according to their relationship to God.

Answers to objections:

1. Although we cannot know what God is, nevertheless we make use in this doctrine of His effects, either those of nature or of grace, in place of a definition, for the sake of those matters that are considered in this doctrine. Similarly, in some of the philosophical sciences, we demonstrate something about a cause by means of the effects, taking the effect in place of a definition of the cause.

2. All other things that are treated in sacred doctrine are comprehended under God, not as parts, or species, or accidents, but as ordered in some fashion to Him.

Article 8: Whether This Doctrine Uses Argumentation

As for the eighth problem, it appears that this doctrine does not use arguments.

1. Ambrose says, *On the Catholic Faith* (I, c. 13): "Take away the arguments when it becomes a question of the faith." But in this doctrine the question is chiefly concerned with faith; thus, it is said in John 20:31: *These things are written that you may believe.* Therefore, sacred doctrine does not use arguments.

2. If it were argumentative, it would either argue from authority or from reason. If it be from authority, then this does not seem to suit its dignity because an argument from authority is very weak, according to Boethius (*On Cicero's Topics*, I, PL 64, 1166). Even if it be from reason, this is not appropriate to its end, because, according to Gregory,

Homilies on the Gospels (II, 26): "Faith has no merit when human reason provides its experiential basis." So, sacred doctrine does not use arguments.

To the contrary is the text of Titus 1:9 concerning the bishop: *Embracing that faithful word which is according to doctrine, that he may be able to exhort in sound doctrine and to argue against the gainsayers.*

In reply, I say that arguments are not used in the other sciences to prove their principles; instead, arguments are made from principles to show other things in these sciences. So, too, this doctrine does not use arguments to prove its principles, which are articles of faith, but it proceeds to show something from them. Thus, the Apostle, I Cor. 15:12, uses an argument from the resurrection of Christ to prove the general resurrection.

However, we should keep in mind that in the area of the philosophical sciences, the lower sciences neither prove their principles nor do they dispute against a person who denies the principles; rather, they leave this to the higher science. Of course, the highest among them, metaphysics, does dispute against the person who denies the principles, provided the adversary makes any concession; however, if he concedes nothing, it is impossible to dispute with him, but one can show the defects of his reasonings. Hence, Sacred Scripture, because it has no superior study, does dispute with one who denies its principles, even using arguments if the adversary concedes something of the content of divine revelation. Thus, we dispute against heretics, using the texts of sacred doctrine, and use one article of faith against those who deny another. However, if an adversary believes nothing that has been divinely revealed, no further way remains of proving the articles of faith by reasoning, but one can criticize his reasonings against the faith, provided he advances any. Indeed, if the faith is based on infallible truth and it is impossible for what is contrary to the true to be demonstrated, then it is clear that arguments advanced against the faith are not demonstrative and can be disproved.

Answers to objections:

1. Though arguments using human reasoning have no place in proving what pertains to faith, still this doctrine does use arguments from the articles of the faith to other conclusions, as was said.

2. To argue from authority is most appropriate to this doctrine, because the principles of this doctrine are attained through revelation, and so credence must be granted to the authority of those by whom revelation is accomplished. Nor does this depreciate the value of this doctrine, for, while the argument from authority that is based on human reasoning is the weakest, on the other hand the argument from authority that is based on divine revelation is most effective.

However, sacred doctrine uses human reasoning, not to prove the faith, for the merit of faith would thereby be removed, but it does so in order to show some other conclusions that are handed down in this doctrine. Indeed, since grace does not take away nature, but perfects it, natural reason must serve under faith, just as a natural inclination of the will must be subject to charity. Hence, the Apostle says, II Cor. 10:5: *bringing into captivity every understanding unto the obedience of Christ.* And as a result, sacred doctrine even uses standard passages from the philosophers wherever they have been able to know the truth through natural reason; thus, Paul (Acts 17:28), cites a text from Aratus, saying: *As some of your own poets said, "For we are also God's offspring."*

Nevertheless, sacred doctrine uses such texts as extrinsic arguments and as probable. Properly it uses the texts of the canonical Scriptures, when arguing from necessity, and it uses the texts of other doctors of the Church, when arguing from its own sources but only in a probable way. In fact, our faith is founded on revelation that was made by the Apostles and Prophets who wrote the canonical Books, but not on revelation, if such there was, accomplished through the other doctors. So, Augustine says in his *Letter to Jerome* (Epist. 82, 1): "I have learned to pay this honor only to the books of Scripture that are called canonical, namely, to believe most firmly that none of their authors has erred in writing them. Now I read other authors with such an attitude that, however great their reputation for sanctity or teaching, I need not regard something as true simply because they have so thought or written."

Article 9: Whether Sacred Scripture Should Use Metaphors

As for the ninth problem, it seems that Sacred Scripture should not use metaphors.

1. Indeed, what is proper to a lowest grade of doctrine does not seem appropriate to this doctrine which holds a supreme place among the other disciplines, as has already been stated. Now, to proceed by means of various likenesses and figures is proper to the poetic art, which is the lowest among all forms of teaching. Therefore, to use similitudes of this kind is not appropriate to this science.

2. This doctrine appears to be directed to the manifestation of truth; hence, a reward is promised to those engaged in its manifestation: Ecclus. 24:31: *They that explain me shall have life everlasting.* But the truth is hidden by such similitudes. So, it does not befit this doctrine to treat divine matters under the likeness of bodily things.

3. The more sublime certain creatures may be, the more do they approach divine likeness. So, if any creatures are to be transferred to the level of discourse about God, then such transference should especially be made from the more sublime creatures and not from the lowest. Yet, this is often found in Scripture.

To the contrary is the statement in Osee 12:10: *I have multiplied visions and I have used similitudes by the ministry of the prophets.* Now, to treat something under a similitude is metaphor. Therefore, to use metaphors pertains to sacred doctrine.

In reply, I say that it is appropriate to Sacred Scripture to treat divine and spiritual matters under the similitude of bodily things. Indeed, God provides for all in accord with what is suitable to their nature. Now, it is natural to man to come to intelligible things through sensible things, since all our knowledge takes its start from sensation. Hence, in Sacred Scripture, spiritual matters are quite appropriately conveyed to us under corporeal metaphors. This is what Dionysius says, *On the Celestial Hierarchy* (1, 2): "It is impossible for the divine ray to enlighten us in any other way than as hidden under a diversity of sacred veils."

It is also appropriate to Sacred Scripture, for it is offered to all men in general, according to the text (Rom. 1:14): *To the wise and to the unwise, I am a debtor.* Thus, spiritual matters are presented under corporeal similitudes so that even the uninstructed, who are not prepared to grasp intelligible things in themselves, may in this way be able to grasp it.

Answers to objections:

1. Poetry uses metaphors for the sake of lively description; such description is naturally appealing to man. But sacred doctrine uses metaphors for the sake of necessity and utility, as we have said.

2. The light ray of divine revelation is not destroyed by the sensible figures under which it is veiled, as Dionysius says, but it endures in its truth so that it may not allow the minds through which revelation is made to remain in similitudes; instead, it elevates them to the knowing of intelligible things, and through those by whom revelation is accomplished, others are also instructed in these matters. As a result, those points that are treated metaphorically in one text of Scripture are explained more plainly in other texts. And even this hiding of the meaning in figures of speech is useful for the exercise of learned minds, and against the ridicule of unbelievers, of whom it is said (Matt. 7:6): *Give not that which is holy to dogs.*

3. As Dionysius teaches, *On the Celestial Hierarchy* (1, 2), it is more appropriate that divine matters in Scripture be

treated under the figures of unworthy bodies than of ones of higher worth. And this is so, for three reasons. First, because in this way the human mind is made freer from error. Indeed, it is quite evident that these things are not predicated of divine things with literal propriety, which would not be so if divine things were described under the figures of nobler bodies, particularly in the case of people unable to think of anything nobler than bodies. Second, because this way is more suited to the knowledge that we have of God in this life. What He is not is more evident to us than what He is; so, the similitudes of things that are more removed from God give us a truer notion that He is above what we are saying or thinking about God. Third, divine teachings are better hidden from unworthy people by expressions of this kind.

Article 10: Whether Sacred Scripture Has Plural Meanings for One Text

As to the tenth problem, it appears that Sacred Scripture does not have plural meanings for one text, namely, the historical or literal, the allegorical, the tropological or moral, and the anagogical.

1. In fact, a multitude of meanings in one text of Scripture produces confusion and deception, and it removes the solid base for arguing. Hence, no argument can proceed from a multitude of propositions; instead, certain fallacies are attributed to this procedure. Now, Sacred Scripture ought to be effective in showing truth without any fallacy. So, plural meanings should not be conveyed under one text in it.

2. Augustine says, *On the Advantage of Believing* (c. 3), that "the Scripture that is called the Old Testament has a fourfold message, namely, historical, etiological, analogical, and allegorical." Now, these four seem to be quite different from the four meanings mentioned earlier. So, it does not seem appropriate for the same text of Sacred Scripture to be expounded according to the four meanings stated earlier.

3. In addition to the aforesaid meanings, there is also the parabolic, which is not included among those four senses.

To the contrary is the statement by Gregory, *Morals* (XX, 1): "Sacred Scripture surpasses all the sciences in its manner of speaking: while it tells about a deed, it conveys a mystery."

In reply, I say that the author of Sacred Scripture is God, within Whose power it is not only to adjust words to their meaning (which even man can do) but also to adjust things themselves. So, since words signify something in all sciences, this science has a special character: the very things that are signified by words are themselves the signs of something. Therefore, this first level of signification, whereby words signify things, belongs to the first meaning, which is the historical or literal sense. Then, that other level of signification, in which things signified by words in turn signify other things, is called the spiritual sense, which is based on the literal and presupposes it.

Now, this spiritual sense is divided in three ways. As the Apostle says, Heb. 7:19, the old law prefigures the new law; and the new law, as Dionysius says, *Ecclesiastical Hierarchy* (5, 2), is a figure of future glory; and further, in the new law the deeds of the Head are signs of the acts that we ought to do. So, according as the things in the old law are signs of what happens under the new law, this is the allegorical sense; and according as the things done in Christ, or in those items that signify Christ, are signs of what we should do, this is the moral sense. While, according as they signify those things that belong in eternal glory, this is the anagogical sense.

Now, since the literal sense is the one that the author intends, and since the author of Sacred Scripture is God, Who comprehends all things at once in His understanding, it is not inappropriate (as Augustine says, *Confessions*, XII, 13) for there to be even several literal meanings in one text of Scripture.

Answers to objections:

1. The multiplicity of these meanings is not productive of equivocation or any kind of duplicity; for, as we have said, these senses are not pluralized in the manner of one word having many meanings, but in that the things signified by the words can be the signs of other things. And so, too, no confusion ensues in Sacred Scripture, since all the senses are based on one, the literal, from which alone an argument can be drawn, and not from the things that are said allegorically, as Augustine states in his *Letter Against Vincent* (93, 8). Nor does Sacred Scripture lose anything as a result of this, for there is nothing contained under the spiritual sense that Scripture does not clearly treat elsewhere under the literal sense.

2. These three, the historical, etiological, and analogical, belong to the one literal sense. For it is history, as Augustine himself explains, when something is presented without qualification; it is etiology when a cause is assigned to what is said; for example, when the Lord gave as cause why Moses permitted the freedom of repudiating wives that it was because of the hardness of their hearts (Matt. 19:8). It is analogy when the truth of one passage in Scripture is shown to be not incompatible with the truth of another text. Now, only allegory among these four represents the three spiritual senses; indeed, Hugh of St. Victor includes even the anagogical under the allegorical, putting down in his *Sentences* only three senses, the historical, the allegorical, and the tropological.

3. The parabolical sense is included under the literal; for, one thing may be signified by words properly and another thing figuratively. And the literal sense is not this figure but what is represented by the figure. Indeed, when Scripture speaks of God's arm, the literal sense is not that a bodily member of this sort belongs to God but it is what is signified by this member, namely, the power to do things. On this basis, it is evident that nothing false can be expressed under the literal sense of Sacred Scripture.

On the Interpretation of Scripture

As Augustine says (*Confessions*, XII, 23), there are two ways of looking at this question [when was matter created?]: one looks to the real truth of the matter; the other considers the literal meaning of the explanation that Moses (who was divinely inspired) gave us concerning the beginning of the world.

As to the first way, two things should be avoided: first, we must not make any false assertion on this question, especially any that is opposed to the truth of faith; second, a person should not claim that something that he believes to be true becomes an article of faith as soon as he says it. Indeed, as Augustine states (*Confessions*, XII, 25), if a person thinks that something false—something that he believes and stubbornly dares to assert, on a point of which he is ignorant—belongs formally to the essential doctrine of godliness, then he is an adversary. Now, Augustine says that this man is a hindrance, because the true faith is thus made a laughingstock before nonbelievers when something is set up by an uninstructed believer as a part of the faith, something that the most authoritative documents show to be false; and he says more about this in the first book of the *Literal Commentary on Genesis*.

Concerning the second way of considering this question, there are also two errors to be avoided. The first point is that no one should say that something patently false is to be understood in the texts of Scripture that deal with the creation of things. Indeed, falsity cannot form the basis of divine Scripture which has been handed down by the Holy Spirit; nor can there be falsity in the faith that is taught therein. The other point to be avoided is that no one should try to restrict Scripture to one meaning, to such an extent that other meanings, containing some truth and quite possible in

Disputed Questions on the Power of God, IV, 1, c. Trans. V.J.B.

relation to the context, would be excluded. In fact, it belongs to the dignity of divine Scripture to contain many meanings in one text, so that in this way it may be appropriate to the various understandings of men for each man to marvel at the fact that he can find the truth that he has conceived in his own mind expressed in divine Scripture. Also, this makes it more easily defended against nonbelievers; for, if something that a person wants to understand in Sacred Scripture appears false, then he may be referred to an alternative meaning.

Consequently, it is not unbelievable that Moses and the other writers of Sacred Scripture were divinely inspired so that they would know the different true meanings that men would be able to find, and so that they could express them in one textual form, in such a way that each of them is the author's meaning. Hence, even if some truths that the writer did not have in mind are associated with the text of Sacred Scripture by commentators, there is no doubt that the Holy Spirit understood them, for He is the principal Author of divine Scripture. Thus, every truth that can be fittingly related to divine Scripture, in view of the context, is its meaning.

On the Trinity and the Incarnation

[Chapter 1] Foreword

"Lo, these things are said in part of His ways: and seeing we have heard scarce a little drop of His word, who shall be able to behold the thunder of His greatness?" (Job 26:14)

[1] The human intellect, to which it is connatural to derive its knowledge from sensible things, is not able through itself to reach the vision of the divine substance in itself, which is above all sensible things and, indeed, improportionately

Summa Against the Gentiles, IV, 1, 2, 26, 39-41, 49; Trans. Pegis, Anderson, Bourke, O'Neil, *On the Truth of the Catholic Faith, Book Four*, pp. 35-42, 143-146, 189-197, 208-211.

above all other things. Yet, because man's perfect good is that he somehow know God, lest such a noble creature might seem to be created to no purpose, as being unable to reach its own end, there is given to man a certain way through which he can rise to the knowledge of God: so that, since the perfections of things descend in a certain order from the highest summit of things—God—man may progress in the knowledge of God by beginning with lower things and gradually ascending. Now, even in bodily movements, the way of descending is the same as the way of ascending, distinguished by beginning and end.

[2] There is a twofold account of the descent of perfections from God just mentioned. One account looks to the first origin of things: for divine Wisdom, to put perfection in things, produced them in such order that the universe of creatures should embrace the highest of things and the lowest. The other account comes from the things themselves. For, since causes are more noble than their effects, the very first caused things are lower than the First Cause, which is God, and still stand out above their effects. And so it goes until one arrives at the lowest of things. And because in the highest summit of things, God, one finds the most perfect unity—and because everything, the more it is one, is the more powerful and more worthy—it follows that the farther one gets from the first principle, the greater is the diversity and variation one finds in things. The process of emanation from God must, then, be unified in the principle itself, but multiplied in the lower things which are its terms. In this way, according to the diversity of things, there appears the diversity of the ways, as though these ways began in one principle and terminated in various ends.

[3] Through these ways our intellect can rise to the knowledge of God. But because of the weakness of the intellect we are not able to know perfectly even the ways themselves. For the sense, from which our knowledge begins, is occupied with external accidents, which are the proper sensibles—for example, color, odor, and the like. As a result, through such external accidents the intellect can scarcely reach the perfect

knowledge of a lower nature, even in the case of those natures whose accidents it comprehends perfectly through the sense. Much less will the intellect arrive at comprehending the natures of those things of which we grasp few accidents by sense; and it will do so even less in the case of those things whose accidents cannot be grasped by the senses, though they may be perceived through certain deficient effects. But, even though the natures of things themselves were known to us, we can have only a little knowledge of their order, according as divine Providence disposes them in relation to one another and directs them to the end, since we do not come to know the plan of divine Providence. If, then, we imperfectly know the ways themselves, how shall we be able to arrive at a perfect knowledge of the source of these ways? And because that source transcends the above-mentioned ways beyond proportion, even if we knew the ways themselves perfectly we would yet not have within our grasp a perfect knowledge of the source.

[4] Therefore, since it was a feeble knowledge of God that man could reach in the ways mentioned—by a kind of intellectual glimpse, so to say—out of a superabundant goodness, therefore, so that man might have a firmer knowledge of Him, God revealed certain things about Himself that transcend the human intellect. In this revelation, in harmony with man, a certain order is preserved, so that little by little he comes from the imperfect to the perfect—just as happens in the rest of changeable things. First, therefore, these things are so revealed to man as, for all that, not to be understood, but only to be believed as heard, for the human intellect in this state in which it is connected with things sensible cannot be elevated entirely to gaze upon things which exceed every proportion of sense. But, when it shall have been freed from the connection with sensibles, then it will be elevated to gaze upon the things which are revealed.

[5] There is, then, in man a threefold knowledge of things divine. Of these, the first is that in which man, by the natural light of reason, ascends to a knowledge of God through crea-

tures. The second is that by which the divine truth—exceeding
the human intellect—descends on us in the manner of revelation, not, however, as something made clear to be seen, but as
something spoken in words to be believed. The third is that
by which the human mind will be elevated to gaze perfectly
upon the things revealed.

[6] It is this threefold cognition which Job suggests in the
words set down. The words, "Lo, these things are said in part
of His ways," refer to that knowledge by which our intellect
ascends to a knowledge of God by the ways of creatures. And
because we know these ways imperfectly, he rightly added:
"in part." "For we know in part," as the Apostle says (I Cor.
13:9).

[7] What is added, however, "and seeing we have heard
scarce a little drop of His word," refers to the second knowledge, in that the divine things we are to believe are revealed
to us in speech; "faith then," as Romans (10:17) says,
"cometh by hearing; and hearing by the word of God." Of
this John (17:17) also says: "sanctify them in truth. Thy
word is truth." Thus, then, since the revealed truth is proposed not about divine things to be seen, but to be believed,
Job rightly says: "we have heard." But, since this imperfect
knowledge flows down from that perfect knowledge wherein
the divine Truth is seen in itself, while God reveals it to us
through the ministry of angels who "see the face" of the
Father (Matt. 18:10), Job rightly names it "a drop." Hence,
Joel (3:18) also says: "In that day the mountains shall drop
down sweetness." Since not all the mysteries known in the
vision of the First Truth by the angels and the other blessed,
but a certain few are revealed to us, Job adds significantly:
"a little." For Ecclesiasticus (43:35-36) says: "Who shall
magnify Him as He is from the beginning? There are many
things hidden from us that are greater than these: for we have
seen but a few of His words." And our Lord says to the disciples in John (16:12): "I have yet many things to say to
you: but you cannot hear them now." The few things also
which are revealed to us are set forth in similitudes and the
obscurities of words—as a result, only the studious arrive at

any sort of grasp of them at all. Others, however, venerate them as things hidden, and unbelievers cannot attack them; hence, the Apostle says: "We see now through a glass in a dark manner" (I Cor. 13:12). Significantly, then, does Job add "scarce" to bring out the difficulty.

[8] But this addition, "Who shall be able to behold the thunder of His greatness," refers to the third kind of knowledge, in which the First Truth will be known, not as believed, but as seen; "We shall see Him as He is," we read (I John 3:2). So Job adds: "to behold." Nor will one perceive some measure of the divine mysteries: the divine majesty itself will be seen and all the perfection of goods; hence, the Lord said to Moses: "I will shew thee all good" (Exod. 33:19). Rightly, then, does Job say "greatness." Nor will the truth be set before man hidden under any veils, but will be entirely manifest; hence, our Lord says to His disciples: "The hour cometh when I will no more speak to you in proverbs; but will shew you plainly of the Father" (John 16:25). Significantly, therefore, does Job speak of "the thunder" to suggest the manifestation.

[9] Now, the words set down fit our purpose. In what has preceded we have dealt with divine things according as the natural reason can arrive at the knowledge of divine things through creatures. This way is imperfect, nevertheless, and in keeping with the reason's native capacity. That is why we can say with Job (26:14): "These things are said in part of His ways." We must now deal with those divine things that have been divinely revealed to us to be believed, since they transcend the human intellect.

[10] And the manner of proceeding in such matters the words set down do teach us. For, since we have hardly heard the truth of this kind in Sacred Scripture as a little drop descending upon us, and since one cannot in the state of this life behold the thunder of the greatness, this will be the method to follow: What has been passed on to us in the words of Sacred Scripture may be taken as principles, so to say; thus, the things in those writings passed on to us in a hidden fashion we may endeavor to grasp mentally in some way or

other, defending them from the attacks of the infidels. Nonetheless, that no presumption of knowing perfectly may be present, points of this kind must be proved from Sacred Scripture, but not from natural reason. For all that, one must show that such things are not opposed to natural reason, in order to defend them from infidel attack. This was also the method fixed upon in the beginning of this work.

[11] But, since natural reason ascends to a knowledge of God through creatures and, conversely, the knowledge of faith descends from God to us by a divine revelation—since the way of ascent and descent is still the same—we must proceed in the same way in the things above reason which are believed as we proceeded in the foregoing with the investigation of God by reason. First, to be specific, we must treat of the things about God Himself which surpass reason and are proposed for belief: such is the confession of the Trinity; second, of course, the things which surpass reason that have been done by God, such as the work of the Incarnation and what follows thereon; third, however, the things surpassing reason which are looked for in the ultimate end of man, such as the resurrection and glorification of bodies, the everlasting beatitude of souls, and matters related to these.

[Chapter 2] That There Is Generation, Paternity, and Sonship in the Divinity

[1] Let us take the beginning of our study from the secret of the divine generation, and first set down what one must hold about it according to the testimonies of Sacred Scripture. Then we may set out the arguments against the truth of the faith which unbelief has invented; by achieving the solution of these we will be pursuing the purpose of this study.

[2] Sacred Scripture, then, hands on to us the names of "paternity" and "sonship" in the divinity, insisting that Jesus Christ is the Son of God. One finds this most frequently in the books of the New Testament. Thus, Matthew (11:27): "No one knoweth the Son but the Father: neither doth any one

know the Father but the Son." With this Mark begins his Gospel, saying: "The beginning of the gospel of Jesus Christ, the Son of God." John the Evangelist also frequently points to this, for he says: "The Father loveth the Son and He hath given all things into His hand" (3:35) and "As the Father raiseth up the dead, and giveth life: so the Son also giveth life to whom He will" (5:21). Paul the Apostle also frequently inserts these words, for he calls himself in Romans (1:1-3) "separated unto the gospel of God, which He had promised before by His prophets in the holy scriptures concerning His Son"; and says in Hebrews (1:1): "God, who, at sundry times and in divers manners, spoke in times past to the fathers by the prophets, last of all in these days hath spoken to us by His Son."

[3] This is also given us, although more rarely, in the books of the Old Testament. Thus, Proverbs (30:4) says: "What is His name, and what is the name of His Son, if thou knowest?" One reads it also in the Psalms (2:7; 88:27): "The Lord hath said to me: Thou art My Son"; and again: "He shall cry out to Me: Thou art My Father."

[4] To be sure, some would like to twist these last two sayings into another sense, so as to refer "The Lord hath said to Me: Thou art My Son" to David; and so as to ascribe "He shall cry out to Me: Thou art My Father" to Solomon. Nevertheless, the additions in each instance show that this cannot be quite the case. For David cannot be fitted into this addition: "This day have I begotten Thee" (Ps. 2:7); nor into this one: "I will give Thee the Gentiles for Thy inheritance, and the utmost parts of the earth for Thy possession" (2:8); since David's kingdom was not extended to the utmost parts of the earth, as the history of the Book of Kings shows. No more is the saying: "He shall cry out to Me: Thou art My Father" fitting to Solomon, since there follows: "I will make His rule to endure for evermore: and His throne as the days of heaven" (Ps. 88:30). Hence, one is given to understand that because some of the things joined to the texts mentioned are suitable to David and Solomon, some absolutely unsuit-

able, what is said of David and Solomon in these words is said, as customarily in Scripture, figuratively of that other in whom the whole is fulfilled.

[5] However, since the names of "Father" and "Son" follow on a generation, Scripture has not been silent about the very name of "divine generation." For in the Psalm (2:7), as was said, one reads: "This day have I begotten Thee." And Proverbs (8:24-25): "The depths were not as yet and I was already conceived: before the hills I was brought forth"; or, according to another reading: "Before all the hills did the Lord beget me." And Isaias (66:9, 8) also says: "Shall not I that make others to bring forth . . . Myself bring forth, saith the Lord? Shall I that give generation to others be barren, saith the Lord thy God?" We grant that one can say that this text must be related to the multiplication of the children of Israel returning from captivity into their own country, because earlier this is said: "Sion hath been in labour and hath brought forth her children." But this does not defeat our purpose. For, however the essence of it be adapted, the essence of it which is given from the voice of God remains fixed and stable thus: If He Himself grants generation to others, He is not sterile. Nor would it become Him who makes others generate truly to generate Himself not truly but by a likeness. For a thing must be more nobly in its cause than in that which is caused, as was shown. Again, it says in John (1:14): "We saw His glory, the glory as it were of the only begotten of the Father"; and later: "The only-begotten Son who is in the bosom of the Father, He hath declared Him" (1:18). And Paul says: "And again when He bringeth in the first-begotten into the world He saith: And let all the angels of God adore Him" (Heb. 1:6). . . .

[Chapter 26] *That There Are but Three Persons in Divinity: the Father, the Son, and the Holy Spirit*

[1] From what has been said, then, one must hold that in the divine nature three Persons subsist: the Father, the Son,

and the Holy Spirit; and that these three are one God, distinguished from one another by relations only. For the Father is distinguished from the Son by the relations of paternity and innascibility; the Son from the Father by the relation of sonship; the Father and the Son from the Holy Spirit by spiration, so to say; and the Holy Spirit from the Father and the Son by the procession of love; by this He proceeds from each of Them.

[2] Beside these three Persons, no fourth in the divine nature can be asserted. For the divine Persons, since they agree in essence, cannot be distinguished except by relation of origin, as is clear. These relations of origin one must understand not as a procession which inclines to what is without—for what proceeds thus is not co-essential with its principle —one must understand them as proceeding within. Of course, a thing which proceeds and remains its own principle is found only in the operation of the intellect and will, as was made clear. Hence, the divine Persons cannot be multiplied save by the requirements of the procession of the intellect and will in God. It is, of course, not possible that there be in God more than one proceeding within His understanding, because His act of understanding is one, simple, and perfect, for in understanding Himself He understands all things else. And thus, there can be in God but one proceeding of the Word. In like manner, too, must the proceeding of Love be one only, for the divine will act is one and simple—by loving Himself He loves all things else. Therefore, it is not possible that in God there be more than two Persons proceeding: one by way of intellect, as Word—namely the Son; the other by way of Love, as the Holy Spirit. There is also one Person who does not proceed—namely, the Father. Therefore, in the Trinity there can be only three Persons.

[3] Again, let the divine Persons be distinguished by proceeding. But the mode of a person in proceeding can be but threefold: namely, to be altogether not proceeding, which is the Father's mode; to be proceeding from one who does not proceed, which is the Son's; to be proceeding from one who

proceeds, which is the Holy Spirit's. Therefore, it is impossible to assert more than three Persons.

[4] We grant, of course, that in other living things relations of origin can be multiplied—for example, in human nature there can be many fathers and many sons—but in the divine nature this is altogether impossible. For sonship, since in one nature it is of one species, cannot be multiplied except by matter or by subject; this is also the case with other forms. Hence, since in God there is neither matter nor subject, and since the relations are themselves subsistent (which is clear from what was said above) it is impossible that there be a plurality of sonships of God. The same reasoning holds for the other Persons. Thus, in God there are only three Persons.

[5] Of course, an objector may say that in the Son who is perfect God there is infinite intellective power, and thus He can produce a word; in like fashion, since there is in the Holy Spirit infinite goodness which is the principle of communication, He will be able to communicate the divine nature to another person. But such a one ought to consider that the Son is God, as begotten not as begetting; and so the intellective power is in Him as proceeding in the way of the Word, and not in Him as producing the Word. Similarly, since the Holy Spirit is God as proceeding, there is infinite goodness in Him as the Person receiving, and not in Him as communicating the infinite goodness to another. For the Persons are not distinguished from one another except by relations, as is clear from the things said above. Therefore, all the fullness of divinity is in the Son, numerically identical with that in the Father, but with the relation of birth, as it is in the Father with the relation of active generation. Hence, if the relation of the Father be attributed to the Son, all distinction is removed. And the same reasoning holds for the Holy Spirit.

[6] Now, this divine Trinity has a likeness in the human mind which we can consider. For the mind itself, because it understands itself, conceives within itself a word. And this is nothing but the intelligible intention of the mind, which is called *the mind understood* and exists within the mind. When this mind further loves itself, it produces its very self in the

will as beloved. Of course, it does not proceed further within itself, but the cycle is concluded when by love it returns to the very substance from which the proceeding began by the intention understood. The proceeding extends to external effects when from love of itself it proceeds to make something. Thus, three things are discovered in the mind: the mind itself, the source of the proceeding, existing in its nature; and mind conceived in the intellect; and mind beloved in the will. For all that, these three are not one nature, for the mind's act of understanding is not its being; and its will act is neither its being, nor its act of understanding. For this reason, also, the mind understood and the mind beloved are not persons, since they are not subsisting. Even the mind itself existing in its nature is not a person, for it is not the whole which subsists, but a part of the subsistent; namely, of the man.

[7] Therefore, in our mind one finds a likeness of the divine Trinity in regard to proceeding, "and this multiplies the Trinity." For from the exposition this is clear: there is in the divine nature God unbegotten, who is the source of the whole divine proceeding, namely the Father; there is God begotten by way of a word conceived in the intellect, namely the Son; there is God by way of love proceeding, namely the Holy Spirit. Of course, no further proceeding is discovered within the divine nature, but only a proceeding to exterior effects. In this, of course, the mind fails in representing the divine Trinity: the Father and the Son and the Holy Spirit are one in nature, and in each of these the person is perfect, simply because the act of understanding and the act of will are the divine being itself, as was shown. For this reason one considers the divine likeness in man just as one considers the likeness of Hercules in stone: with regard to the representation of form, not with regard to the agreement of nature. And so one says that in the mind of man there is the "image of God" according to the Word: "Let us make man to our image and likeness" (Gen. 1:26).

[8] One also finds in other things a likeness of the divine Trinity, so far as anything in its substance is one, formed in a kind of species, ordered in some fashion. Just as is clear from

the things said, the conception of the intellect in intelligible being is like the species formation in natural being; love, of course, is like the inclination or order in a thing of nature. And so the species of things in nature from afar represent the Son; their order, of course, the Holy Spirit. Accordingly, by reason of the remote and obscure representation in irrational things, one speaks of the "vestige" of the Trinity in them, not of the "image"; so we read in Job (11:7): "Thou wilt comprehend the steps of God," and so forth.

[9] And this is enough to say about the divine Trinity for the present. . . .

[Chapter 39] What the Catholic Faith Holds About the Incarnation of Christ

[1] From what has been set down above it is clear that according to the tradition of the Catholic faith we must say that in Christ there is a perfect divine nature and a perfect human nature, constituted by a rational soul and human flesh; and that these two natures are united in Christ not by indwelling only, nor in an accidental mode, as a man is united to his garments, nor in a personal relation and property only, but in one hypostasis and one supposit. Only in this way can we save what the Scriptures hand on about the Incarnation. Since, then, Sacred Scripture without distinction attributes the things of God to that man, and the things of that man to God (as is plain from the foregoing), He of whom each class is said must be one and the same.

[2] But opposites cannot be said truly of the same thing in the same way: the divine and human things said of Christ are, of course, in opposition, *suffering* and *incapable of suffering*, for example, or *dead* and *immortal*, and the remainder of this kind; therefore, it is necessarily in different ways that the divine and the human are predicated of Christ. So, then, with respect to the "about which" each class is predicated no distinction must be made, but unity is discovered. But with respect to "what" is predicated, a distinction must be made. Natural properties, of course, are predicated of everything according to

its nature; thus to be borne downward is predicated of this stone consequently on its nature as heavy. Since, then, there are different ways of predicating things human and divine of Christ, one must say there are in Christ two natures neither confused nor mixed. But that about which one predicates natural properties consequently on the proper nature pertaining to the genus of substance is the hypostasis and supposit of that nature. Since, then, that is not distinct and is one about which one predicates things divine and human concerning Christ, one must say that Christ is one hypostasis and one supposit of a human and a divine nature. For thus truly and properly will things divine be predicated of that man in accord with the fact that the man bears the supposit not only of the human but of the divine nature; conversely, one predicates things human of God's Word in that He is the supposit of the human nature.

[3] It is clear also from this that, although the Son is incarnate, neither the Father nor the Holy Spirit, for all that, need be incarnate, since the Incarnation did not take place by a union in the nature in which the three divine Persons are together, but in hypostasis or supposit, wherein the three Persons are distinguished. And thus, as in the Trinity there is a plurality of Persons subsisting in one nature, so in the mystery of the Incarnation there is one Person subsisting in a plurality of natures.

[Chapter 40] Objections Against Faith in the Incarnation

[1] But against this statement of the Catholic faith many difficulties come together, and by reason of these the adversaries of the faith attack the Incarnation. [See below, ch. 49, for the solutions.]

[2] We showed in Book I that God is neither a body nor a power in a body. But, if He assumed flesh, it follows either that He was changed into a body or that He was a power in a body after the Incarnation. It seems, then, impossible that God was incarnate.

[3] Again, whatever acquires a new nature is subject to sub-

stantial change; for in this is a thing generated, that it acquires a nature. Then, if the hypostasis of the Son of God becomes a subsistent anew in human nature, it appears that it was substantially changed.

[4] Furthermore, no hypostasis of a nature extends outside that nature; rather, indeed, the nature is found outside the hypostasis, since there are many hypostases under the nature. If, then, the hypostasis of the Son of God becomes by the Incarnation the hypostasis of a human nature, the Son of God —one must conclude—is not everywhere after the Incarnation, since the human nature is not everywhere.

[5] Once again; one and the same thing has only one *what-it-is*, for by this one means a thing's substance and of one there is but one. But the nature of any thing at all is its *what-it-is*, "for the nature of a thing is what the definition signifies" [Aristotle, *Physics*, II, 1, 193a30]. It seems impossible, then, that one hypostasis subsist in two natures.

[6] Furthermore, in things which are without matter, the quiddity of a thing is not other than the thing, as was shown above. And this is especially the case in God, who is not only His own quiddity, but also His own act of being. But human nature cannot be identified with a divine hypostasis. Therefore, it seems impossible that a divine hypostasis subsist in human nature.

[7] Once again; a nature is more simple and more formal than the hypostasis which subsists therein, for it is by the addition of something material that the common nature is individuated to this hypostasis. If, then, a divine hypostasis subsists in human nature, it seems to follow that human nature is more simple and more formal than a divine hypostasis. And this is altogether impossible.

[8] It is, furthermore, only in matter and form composites that one finds a difference between the singular thing and its quiddity. This is because the singular is individuated by designated matter, and in the quiddity and nature of the species the latter is not included. For, in marking off Socrates, one includes this matter, but one does not in his account of human nature. Therefore, every hypostasis subsisting in human nature

is constituted by signate matter. This cannot be said of the divine hypostasis. So, it does not seem possible that the hypostasis of God's Word subsist in human nature.

[9] Furthermore, the soul and body in Christ were not less in power than in other men. But in other men their union constitutes a supposit, an hypostasis, and a person. Therefore, in Christ the union of soul and body constitutes a supposit, hypostasis, and person of the Word of God; this is eternal. Therefore in Christ there is another supposit, hypostasis, and person beside the supposit, hypostasis, and person of the Word of God. Or so it seems.

[10] There is more. Just as soul and body constitute human nature in common, so this soul and this body constitute *this man,* and this is the hypostasis of a man. But this soul and this body were in Christ. Therefore, their union constitutes an hypostasis, it seems. And we conclude exactly as before.

[11] Again, this man who is Christ, considered as consisting of soul alone and body, is a certain substance; not, of course, a universal one; therefore, a particular one. Therefore, it is an hypostasis.

[12] Moreover, if the supposit of the human and the divine nature in Christ is identified, then in one's understanding of the man who is Christ there ought to be a divine hypostasis. Of course, this is not in one's understanding of other men. Therefore, *man* will be said equivocally of Christ and others. Hence, He will not belong to the same species with us.

[13] In Christ, what is more, one finds three things, as is clear from what was said: a body, a soul, and divinity. The soul, of course, since it is nobler than the body, is not the supposit of the body, but its form. Neither, then, is what is divine the supposit of the human nature; it is, rather, formally related to that nature.

[14] Furthermore, whatever accrues to something after its being is complete accrues to it accidentally. But, since the Word is from eternity, plainly the flesh assumed accrues to Him after His being is complete. Therefore, it accrues to Him accidentally.

[*Chapter 41*] *How One Should Understand the Incarnation of the Son of God*

[1] Now, to get at the solution of these objections, one must begin somewhat more fundamentally. Since Eutyches set it down that the union of God and man took place in nature; Nestorius, that it was neither in nature nor in person; but the Catholic faith holds this: that the union takes place in Person, not in nature—it seems necessary to know first what it is "to be made one in nature," and what it is "to be made one in person."

[2] Grant, then, that *nature* is a word used in many ways: the generation of living things, and the principle of generation and of motion, and the matter and the form are all called nature. Sometimes, also, nature is said of the *what-it-is* of a thing, which includes the things that bear on the integrity of the species; in this way we say that human nature is common to all men, and say the same in all other cases. Those things, therefore, are made one in nature from which the integrity of a species is established; just as the soul and human body are made one to establish the species of the animal, so, universally, whatever the parts of a species are.

[3] Of course, it is impossible that to a species already established in its integrity something extrinsic be united for the unity of its nature without losing the species. For, since species are like numbers, and in these any unity added or subtracted makes the species vary, if to a species already perfected something be added, necessarily it is now another species; thus, if to animate substance one adds only *sensible,* one will have another species, for animal and plant are different species. It does happen, nonetheless, that one finds something which is not integral to the species; in an individual included under that species—white and dressed, for instance, in Socrates or in Plato, or a sixth finger, or something of the sort. Hence, nothing prevents some things being made one in the individual which are not united in one integrity of species; thus, human nature and whiteness and music in Socrates; and things of this kind are united and are called "one by subject." Now, the

individual in the genus of substance is called *hypostasis,* and even in rational substances is called *person;* therefore, all things such as those mentioned are suitably said to be united "in the hypostasis" or even "in the person." Clearly, then, nothing prevents some things not united in nature from being united in hypostasis or person.

[4] But, when the heretics heard that in Christ a union of God and man took place, they approached the exposition of this point in contrary ways, but neglected the way of the truth. For some thought of this union after the mode of things united into one nature: so Arius and Apollinaris, holding that the Word stood to the body of Christ as soul or as mind; and so Eutyches, who held that before the Incarnation there were two natures of God and man, but after the Incarnation only one.

[5] But others, seeing the impossibility of this position, went off on a contrary road. Now, the things which accrue to one having a nature, but do not belong to the integrity of that nature, seem either to be accidents—say, whiteness and music; or to stand in an accidental relation—say, a ring, a garment, a house, and the like. Of course, they weighed this: Since the human nature accrues to the Word of God without belonging to the integrity of His nature, it is necessary (so they thought) that the human nature have an accidental union with the Word. To be sure, it clearly cannot be in the Word as an accident: both because God is not susceptible to an accident (as was previously proved); and because human nature, being in the genus of substance, cannot be the accident of anything. Hence there appeared to be this remaining: Human nature accrues to the Word, not as an accident, but as a thing accidentally related to the Word. Nestorius, then, held that the human nature of Christ stood to the Word as a kind of temple, so that only by indwelling was the union of the Word to the human nature to be understood. And because a temple possesses its individuation apart from him who dwells in the temple, and the individuation suitable to human nature is personality, this was left: that the personality of the human

nature was one, and that of the Word another. Thus, the Word and that man were two persons.

[6] To be sure, others wished to avoid this awkwardness. So, regarding the human nature they introduced a disposition such that personality could not be properly suitable to it. They said that the soul and the body, in which the integrity of human nature consists, were so assumed by the Word that the soul was not united to the body to establish any substance, lest they be forced to say that the substance so established fulfilled the account of person. But they held the union of the Word to soul and body to be like a union to things in an accidental relation, for instance, of the clothed to his clothes. In this they were somehow imitating Nestorius.

[7] Now, with these accounts set aside by the foregoing, it must be laid down that the union of the Word and the man was such that one nature was not breathed together out of two; and that the union of the Word to the human nature was not like that of a substance—a man, say—to those externals which are accidentally related to him, like a house and a garment. But let the Word be set down as subsisting in a human nature as in one made His very own by the Incarnation; and in consequence that body is truly the body of the Word of God, and the soul in like manner, and the Word of God is truly man.

[8] And although to explain this union perfectly is beyond man's strength, nonetheless, in accord with our measure and power, we will try to say something "for the upbuilding of the faith" (cf. Eph. 4:29), so that concerning this mystery the Catholic faith may be defended from the infidels.

[9] Now, in all created things nothing is found so like this union as the union of soul to body. And the likeness would be greater, as Augustine also says, in *Against Felician* [ch. 12], if there were one intellect in all men. So some have held, and according to them one ought to say that the pre-existing intellect is in such wise united anew to a man's conception that from each of these two a new person is made; just as we hold that the pre-existing Word is united to the human nature in a unity of person. Accordingly, and by reason of the likeness

of these two unions, Athanasius says in the Creed: "as the rational soul and flesh are one man, so God and man are one Christ."

[10] However, since the rational soul is united to the body both as to matter and as to an instrument, there cannot be a likeness so far as the first mode of union is concerned, for thus from God and man one nature would be made, since the matter and the form properly establish the nature of a species. Therefore, what is left is to look upon the likeness so far as the soul is united to the body as an instrument. With this, also, there is the concordance of the ancient Doctors, who held that the human nature in Christ was "a kind of organ of the divinity," just as the body is held to be an organ of the soul.

[11] Now, the body and its parts are the organ of the soul in one fashion; external instruments in quite another. For this axe is not the soul's very own instrument, as this hand is, for by an axe many can operate, but this hand is deputy to this soul in its very own operation. For this reason the hand is an instrument of the soul united to it and its very own, but the axe is an instrument both external and common. This is the way, then, in which even the union of God and man can be considered. For all men are related to God as instruments of a sort, and by these He works: "for it is God who worketh in you both to will and to accomplish according to His good will" (Phil. 2:3), as the Apostle says. But other men are related to God as extrinsic and separated instruments, so to say; for God does not move them only to operations which are His very own, but to the operations common to every rational nature, to understand the truth, for example, to love the good, to do what is just. But the human nature in Christ is assumed with the result that instrumentally He performs the things which are the proper operation of God alone: to wash away sins, for example, to enlighten minds by grace, to lead into the perfection of eternal life. The human nature of Christ, then, is compared to God as a proper and conjoined instrument is compared, as the hand is compared to the soul.

[12] Nor is there departure from the course of natural things because one thing is by nature the proper instrument of an-

other, and this other is not its form. For the tongue, so far as
it is the instrument of speech, is the intellect's very own organ;
and the intellect is nevertheless, as the Philosopher proves
[*On the Soul*, III, 4, 429a25], not the act of any part of the
body. In like manner, too, one finds an instrument which
does not pertain to the nature of the species, which is, nevertheless, on the material side fitted to this individual; a sixth
finger, for example, or something of the sort. Therefore, nothing prevents our putting the union of the human nature to the
Word in this way: that the human nature be, so to speak, an
instrument of the Word not a separated, but a conjoined, instrument; and the human nature, nonetheless, does not belong
to the nature of the Word, and the Word is not its form;
nevertheless the human nature belongs to His person.

[13] But the examples mentioned have not been set down
so that one should look in them for an all-round likeness; for
one should understand that the Word of God was able to be
much more sublimely and more intimately united to human
nature than the soul to its very own instrument of whatever
sort, especially since He is said to be united to the entire
human nature with the intellect as medium. And although
the Word of God by His power penetrates all things, conserving all, that is, and supporting all, it is to the intellectual
creatures, who can properly enjoy the Word and share with
Him, that from a kind of kinship of likeness He can be both
more eminently and more ineffably united. . . .

[Chapter 49] Solution of the Arguments Against the Incarnation Given Above

[1] With what has now been said the points made previously against faith in the Incarnation are easily disposed of.

[2] For it has been shown that one must not understand
the Incarnation of the Word thus: that the Word was converted into flesh or that He is united to the body as a form.
Hence, it is not a consequence of the Word's Incarnation that
He who is truly God is a body or a power in a body as the first
argument was trying to proceed.

[3] Neither does it follow that the Word was substantially changed by the fact that He assumed human nature. For no change was made in the Word of God Himself, but only in the human nature which was assumed by the Word, in accord with which it is proper that the Word was both temporally generated and born, but to the Word Himself this was not fitting.

[4] What is proposed in the third argument is also without necessity. For an hypostasis is not extended beyond the limits of that nature from which it has subsistence. The Word of God, of course, has no subsistence from the human nature; rather, He draws the human nature to His subsistence or personality. It is not through, but in, human nature that He subsists. Hence, nothing prevents the Word of God from being everywhere, although the human nature assumed by the Word of God is not everywhere.

[5] Thus, also, the fourth is answered. For in any subsistent thing there must be only one nature by which it has being simply. And so, the Word of God has being simply by the divine nature alone, not, however, by the human nature; by human nature He has being *this*—namely, being a man.

[6] The fifth also is disposed of in the very same way. For it is impossible that the nature by which the Word subsists be other than the very person of the Word. Of course, He subsists by the divine nature and not by the human nature, but He draws the latter to His own subsistence that He may subsist in it, as was said. Hence, it is not necessary that the human nature be identical with the person of the Word.

[7] From this also follows the exclusion of the sixth objection. For an hypostasis is less simple—whether in things or in the understanding—than the nature through which it is established in being: in the thing, indeed, when the hypostasis is not its nature; or in the understanding alone in the cases in which the hypostasis and the nature are identified. The hypostasis of the Word is not established simply by the human nature so as to have being through the human nature, but through it the Word has this alone: that He be man. It is, then, not necessary that the human nature be more simple

than the Word so far as He is the Word, but only so far as
the Word is this man.

[8] From this also the way is open to solving the seventh
objection. For it is not necessary that the hypostasis of
the Word of God be constituted simply by signate matter, but
only so far as He is this man. For only as this man is He
constituted by the human nature, as was said.

[9] Of course, that the soul and body in Christ are drawn
to the personality of the Word without constituting a person
other than the person of the Word does not point to a lessened power, as the eighth argument would have it, but to
a greater worthiness. For everything whatever has, when
united to what is worthier, a better being than it has when it
exists through itself; just so, the sensible soul has a nobler
being in man than it has in the other animals in which it is
the principal form, for all that it is not such in man.

[10] Hence, also, comes the solution to the ninth objection. In Christ there was, indeed, this soul and this body,
for all that there was not constituted from them another person than the person of God's Word, because they were assumed unto the personality of God's Word; just as a body, too,
when it is without the soul, does have its own species, but it
is from the soul, when united to it, that it receives its species.

[11] Thus, also, one answers what the tenth argument proposed. It is clear that this man who is Christ is a certain
substance which is not universal, but particular. And He is
an hypostasis; nevertheless, not another hypostasis than the
hypostasis of the Word, for human nature has been assumed
by the hypostasis of the Word that the Word may subsist in
human as well as in divine nature. But that which subsists in
human nature is this man. Hence, the Word itself is supposed when one says "this man."

[12] But, let one move the very same objection over to human nature and say it is a certain substance, not universal
but particular and consequently an hypostasis—he is obviously
deceived. For human nature even in Socrates or Plato is not
an hypostasis, but that which subsists in the nature is an
hypostasis.

[13] But to call a human nature a substance and particular is not to use the meaning in which one calls an hypostasis a particular substance. "Substance" we speak of with the Philosopher [*Categories*, 5, 2a11] in two ways: for the supposit, namely, in the genus of substance which is called hypostasis; and for the *what-it-is* which is "the nature of a thing." But the parts of a substance are not thus called particular substances—subsisting, so to say, in themselves; they subsist in the whole. Hence, neither can one call them hypostases, for none of them is a complete substance. Otherwise, it would follow that in one man there are as many hypostases as there are parts.

[14] Now, to the eleventh argument in opposition. The solution is that equivocation is introduced by a diversity of the form signified by a name, but not by diversity of supposition. For this name "man" is not taken as equivocal because sometimes it supposes Plato, sometimes Socrates. Therefore, this name "man" said of Christ and of other men always signifies the same form; namely, human nature. This is why it is predicated of them univocally; but it is only the supposition which is changed, and, to be sure, in this: when it is taken for Christ it supposes an uncreated hypostasis, but when it is taken for others it supposes a created hypostasis.

[15] Nor, again, is the hypostasis of the Word said to be the supposit of the human nature, as though subjected to the latter as to a more formal principle, as the twelfth argument proposed. This would, of course, be necessary if it were the human nature which establishes the hypostasis of the Word in being simply. This is obviously false: for the hypostasis of the Word is the subject of the human nature so far as He draws this latter unto His own subsistence, just as something drawn to a second and nobler thing to which it is united.

[16] For all that, it does not follow that the human nature accrues to the Word accidentally, because the Word pre-exists from eternity, as the final argument was trying to conclude. For the Word assumed human nature so as to be truly man. But to be man is to be in the genus of a substance. Therefore, since by union with human nature the hypostasis of the Word

has the being of man, this does not accrue to the Word accidentally. For accidents do not bestow substantial being.

Original Sin, Resurrection, Judgment

[Chapter 50] That Original Sin Is Transmitted from the First Parent to His Descendants

[1] It has been shown, then, in the points set down that what the Catholic faith preaches about the Incarnation of the Son of God is not impossible. And the next thing is to make plain the suitability of the Son of God's assumption of human nature.

[2] Now, the reason for this suitability the Apostle seems to situate in original sin, which is passed on to all men; he says: "As by the disobedience of one man many were made sinners: so also by the obedience of one many shall be made just" (Rom. 5:19). However, since the Pelagian heretics denied original sin, we must now show that men are born with original sin.

[3] First, indeed, one must take up what Genesis (2:15-17) says: "The Lord God took man and put him into the paradise of pleasure, saying: Of every tree of paradise thou shalt eat but of the tree of knowledge of good and evil thou shalt not eat. For in what day soever you shall eat of it, thou shalt die the death." But, since it was not on the very day that he ate that Adam actually died, one has to understand the words "thou shalt die the death" as "you will be handed over to the necessity of death." And this would be said pointlessly if man from the institution of his nature had the necessity of dying. One must, then, say that death and the necessity of dying is a penalty inflicted on man for sin. But a penalty is not justly inflicted except for a fault. Therefore, in every single one of those in whom one finds this penalty one must of necessity find a fault. But this penalty is found in all men,

Summa Against the Gentiles, IV, 50-52, 79, 96. Trans. Pegis, Anderson, Bourke, O'Neil, *On the Truth of the Catholic Faith, Book Four,* pp. 212-223, 297-300, 345-346.

even from the very moment of birth, for since that day man is born handed over to the necessity of death. Hence, too, some die immediately after birth, "carried from the womb to the grave" (Job 10:19). In them, therefore, there is some sin. But it is not actual sin, for children do not have the use of free will, and without this nothing is imputed to man as sin (which is clear from the things said in Book III). One must, therefore, say that sin is in them, passed on to them in their origin.

[4] This is also made clear and explicit by the Apostle's words: "As by one man sin entered into this world and by sin death, and so death passed upon all men, in whom all sinned" (Rom. 5:12).

[5] Of course, one cannot say that by one man sin entered the world by way of imitation. For, thus, sin would have reached only those who in sinning imitate the first man; and, since death entered the world by sin, death would reach only those who sin in the likeness of the first man sinning. It is to exclude this that the Apostle adds that "death reigned from Adam unto Moses even over them also who have not sinned after the similitude of the transgression of Adam" (Rom. 5:14). Therefore, the understanding of the Apostle is not that sin entered the world through one man by way of imitation, but by way of origin.

[6] There is more. If the Apostle were speaking of the entry of sin into the world by way of imitation, he should rather have said that sin entered the world by the devil than by one man; as is said also expressly in Wisdom (2:24-25): "By the envy of the devil death came into the world: they follow him that are of his side."

[7] David says furthermore, in a Psalm (50:7): "Behold I was conceived in iniquities and in sins did my mother conceive me." But this cannot be understood of actual sin, since David is said to be conceived and born of a legitimate marriage. Therefore, this must be referred to original sin.

[8] Moreover, Job says (14:4): "Who can make him clean that is conceived of unclean seed? Is it not Thou who only art?" One gathers clearly from this that from the uncleanness

of human seed there extends an uncleanness to the man conceived of the seed. One must understand this of the uncleanness of sin, the only one for which a man is brought into
judgment, for Job (14:3) had already said: "And dost Thou
think it meet to open Thy eyes upon such a one, and to bring
him into judgment with Thee." Thus, then, there is a sin
contracted by man in his very origin which is called "original."

[9] Once again; baptism and the other sacraments of the
Church are remedies of a sort against sin, as will be clarified
later. But baptism, according to the common custom of the
Church, is given to children recently born. It would be given
quite in vain unless there were sin in them. But there is no
actual sin in them, for they lack the exercise of free will, without which no act is imputed to a man as a fault. Therefore,
one must say that there is in them a sin passed on by their
origin, since in the works of God and the Church there is
nothing futile or in vain.

[10] But one may say: Baptism is given to infants not to
cleanse them from sin, but to admit them to the kingdom of
God, to which there is no admission without baptism, since
our Lord says: "Unless a man be born again of water and the
Holy Ghost he cannot enter into the kingdom of God" (John
3:5). This objection is in vain. For no one is excluded from
the kingdom of God except for some fault. The end of every
rational creature is to arrive at beatitude, and this cannot be
save in the kingdom of God. And this, in turn, is nothing
but the *ordered society of those who enjoy the divine vision*,
in which true beatitude consists, which is clear from the points
made in Book III. But nothing fails its end except through
a sin. Therefore, if children not yet baptized cannot reach the
kingdom of God, one must say there is some sin in them.

[11] Thus, then, according to the tradition of the Catholic
faith one must hold that men are born with original sin.

[Chapter 51] Objections Against Original Sin

[1] There are, of course, certain things which appear to be
adversaries of this truth.

[2] For the sin of one man is not imputed as fault to others. So Ezechiel (18:20) says: "the son shall not bear the iniquity of the father." And the reason for this is that we are neither praised nor blamed except for the things which are in ourselves. But these are the things to which we are committed by will. Therefore, the sin of the first man is not imputed to the entire human race.

[3] But let one answer that when one sinned, "all sinned in him," as the Apostle seems to say and so the sin of one is not imputed to another, but the sin is his own. Yet even this, it seems, cannot stand. For those born of Adam were, when Adam sinned, not yet in him actually, but only in his power, as in their first origin. But to sin, since it is to act, is proportionate only to one who actually exists. Therefore, we did not all sin in Adam.

[4] But let it be said that we sinned in Adam as though originally the sin comes from him to us along with the nature. Even this seems impossible. For an accident, since it does not pass from one subject to another, cannot be passed on unless the subject is passed on. But the subject of sin is the rational soul, which is not passed on to us from our first parent, but is created by God in each and one by one, as was shown in Book II. Therefore, it is not by origin that the sin of Adam flowed on to us.

[5] Further, if the sin of our first parent flows into others because they take their origin from him, then, since Christ took His origin from our first parent, He, also, it seems, was subject to original sin. And this is foreign to the faith.

[6] Moreover, what follows on a thing from its natural origin is natural to that thing. But what is natural to a thing is not a sin in it; thus, the lack of vision is not a sin in a mole. Therefore, sin could not flow into others by reason of their origin from the first man.

[7] But let it now be said that the sin flows from the first parent into his descendants by way of origin, not inasmuch as the origin is natural, but inasmuch as the origin is vitiated; this also, it seems, cannot stand. For a failure in nature's work takes place only through the failure of some natural principle;

due to some corruption in the seed, for example, monstrous births in animals are caused. But one cannot grant the corruption of a natural principle in human seed. It seems, then, that a sin does not flow from the first parent into his descendants by a vitiated origin.

[8] Once again; the sins of nature, appearing among its works by the corruption of a principle, take place neither always nor frequently except in a few cases. Therefore, if by a vitiated origin sin flows from the first parent into his descendants, it will not flow into all, but into some few.

[9] And if, furthermore, due to a vitiated origin, a failure appears in the offspring, that failure ought to be of the same genus as the vice which is in the origin, for effects are conformed to their causes. The origin, of course, of human generation, since it is a perfection of the generative power, which shares reason not at all, can have no vice in it which belongs to the genus of fault. For only in those acts can there be virtue or vice, which are subject to reason in some fashion. And so one does not call it a man's fault if, due to a vitiated origin, he is born a leper or blind. Therefore, there is no way for a blameworthy failure to come down from the first parent to his descendant by origin.

[10] Yet again; nature's good is not taken away by sin. Wherefore, even in the demons natural goods remain, as Dionysius says [*On the Divine Names*, c. 4]. But generation is an act of nature. Therefore, the sin of the first man could not vitiate the origin of human generation so that the sin of the first man should flow into his descendants.

[11] Man, moreover, generates one like himself in species. In things, then, which have no bearing on the generation of the species, the son need not be made like his parents. But sin cannot bear on the essentials of the species, for sin is not among the things of nature; rather, it is a corruption of the natural order. There is, then, no necessity that from a first man sinning other sinners be born.

[12] There is more. Sons are more likened to their proximate than to their remote parents. But at times it happens that the proximate parents are without sin and even in the

act of generation no sin takes place. It is not, therefore, by the sin of the first parent that all are born sinners.

[13] And again, if the sin of the first man flowed into others, and—on the other hand—the good is more powerful in acting than the evil (as was shown above), then by so much the more was the satisfaction of Adam, and his justice, transferred through him to others.

[14] If the sin of the first man, moreover, was by origin propagated to his descendants, by an equal reason the sins of other parents pass down to their descendants. And in this way the later would always be more burdened with sins than the earlier generations. Especially must this follow if, in fact, the sin passes on from the parent to the offspring, and the satisfaction cannot pass on.

[Chapter 52] Solution of the Objections Proposed

[1] Now, for the solution of these points one should first set down that certain signs of the original sin appear with probability in the human race. For, since God takes care of human acts so as to give reward for good works and set a penalty for bad works, as we previously shown, it is from the very penalty that we can assure ourselves of the fault. Now, the human race commonly suffers various penalties, both bodily and spiritual. Greatest among the bodily ones is death, and to this all the others are ordered: namely, hunger, thirst, and others of this sort. Greatest, of course, among the spiritual penalties is the frailty of reason: from this it happens that man with difficulty arrives at knowledge of the truth; that with ease he falls into error; and that he cannot entirely overcome his beastly appetites, but is over and over again beclouded by them.

[2] For all that, one could say that defects of this kind, both bodily and spiritual, are not penalties, but natural defects necessarily consequent upon matter. For, necessarily, the human body, composed of contraries, must be corruptible; and the sensible appetite must be moved to sense pleasures, and these are occasionally contrary to reason. And, since the

possible intellect is in potency to all intelligibles, possessing none of them actually, but by nature acquiring them from the senses, one must arrive at knowledge of the truth with difficulty, and due to the phantasms one with ease deviates from the truth. But, for all that, let one weigh matters rightly, and he will be able to judge with probability enough—granted a divine providence which for every perfection has contrived a proportionate perfectible—that God united a superior to an inferior nature for this purpose: that the superior rule the inferior, and that, if some obstacle to this dominion should happen from a failure of nature, it would be removed by His special and supernatural benefaction. And the result would be, since the rational soul is of a higher nature than the body, belief that the rational soul was united to the body under such a condition that in the body there can be nothing contrary to the soul by which the body lives; and in like fashion, if reason in man is united to the sensual appetite and other sensitive powers, that the reason be not impeded by the sensible powers, but be master over them.

[3] Thus, then, according to the teaching of the faith, we set it down that man from the beginning was thus established by God: As long as man's reason was subject to God, not only did the inferior powers serve reason without obstacle, but the body also could not be impeded in subjection to reason by any bodily obstacle—God and His grace supplying, because nature had too little for perfecting this establishment. But, when reason turned away from God, not only did the inferior powers rebel from reason, but the body also sustained passions contrary to that life which is from the soul.

[4] Of course, although defects of this kind may seem natural to man in an absolute consideration of human nature on its inferior side, nonetheless, taking into consideration divine providence and the dignity of human nature on its superior side, it can be proved with enough probability that defects of this kind are penalties. And one can gather thus that the human race was originally infected with sin.

[5] These things now seen, one must answer to the points made as contrary objections.

[6] Now, there is no awkwardness in saying that when one sins the sin is propagated to all in their origin, even though each is praised or blamed according to his own act; as the first argument attempted to proceed. For things go one way in matters of a single individual, and another way in matters of the entire nature of a species, since "by participation in the species many men are as one man," as Porphyry says [*Introduction to the Categories*, c. 3]. A sin, then, which refers to an individual man or his person is not imputed to another as fault unless he be the sinner, since personally one is divided off from another. But, if there is a sin which looks to the nature of the species itself, there is nothing awkward about its propagation from one to another, just as the nature of the species is communicated through one to others. But, since sin is a kind of evil of rational nature, and evil a privation of good, one judges on the basis of the missing good whether a sin is related to a nature commonly or to a person properly. Of course, actual sins which are committed by all men commonly deprive the person of the sinner of a good: grace, for instance, and the due order of the parts of the soul. This is why they are personal, and why, when one sins, the sin is not imputed to another. But the first sin of the first man not only deprived him of his proper and personal good—namely, grace, and the due order of the parts of the soul; he was deprived as well of a good related to the common nature. For—as we said above—human nature was established in its first beginning so that the inferior powers were perfectly subject to reason, the reason to God, the body to the soul, and God was by His grace supplying what nature lacked for this arrangement. Now, this kind of benefit which some call "original justice" was conferred on the first man in such wise that he was to propagate it to his descendants along with human nature. But in the sin of the first man reason withdrew itself from the divine subjection. And it has followed thereon that the lower powers are not perfectly subject to the reason nor is the body to the soul; and this is not only the case for the first sinner, but the same consequent defect follows into his posterity and to the posterity in whom the original justice

mentioned was going to follow. Thus, then, the sin of the first man from whom all other men are derived according to the teaching of faith was not only personal in that it deprived the first man of his own good, but natural, also, in that it deprived him and consequently his descendants of the benefit bestowed on the entire human nature. Thus, too, this kind of defect which is in others as a consequence from the first parent still has in others the essentials of fault so far as all men are counted as one man by participation in the common nature. For one discovers the voluntary character in a sin of this kind in the will of the first parent much as the action of the hand has the essentials of fault from the will of the first mover, which is the power of reason; as a result, in a sin of nature judgments are made about the diverse men as though parts of a common nature, much as they are made in a personal sin about diverse parts of one man.

[7] In this way, then, it is true to say that when one sinned, "all sinned in him," as the Apostle says, and on this basis the second argument made its proposal. Other men were present in Adam, however, not in act, but only in his power as in an original principle. Nor are they said to have sinned in him as exercising any act, but so far as they belong to Adam's nature which was corrupted by sin.

[8] Let the sin be propagated from the first parent to his descendants. Nevertheless, it does not follow, although the subject of sin is the rational soul, that the rational soul is propagated along with the seed; as the progress of the third argument had it. For the manner of propagating this sin of nature which is called original is like that of the very nature of the species, and this nature, although it is perfected by the rational soul, is for all that not propagated with the seed; such propagation is only of the body fitted by nature to receive such a soul. It was in Book II that we showed this.

[9] We grant that Christ was a descendant of the first parent in the flesh. For all that, He did not incur the contamination of original sin as the fourth argument concluded. For it was only the matter of His human body which He received from the first parent; the power to form His body

was not derived from the first parent, but was the power of the Holy Spirit, as was shown. Accordingly, He did not receive human nature from Adam as an agent, although He did receive it from Adam as from a material principle.

[10] One should consider this, also: The nature's origin passes along the defects mentioned because the nature has been stripped of that help of grace which had been bestowed on it in the first parent to pass on to his descendants along with the nature. Now, since this stripping came from a voluntary sin, the consequent defect has the character of fault. Hence, defects of this kind are faulty when referred to their first principle, which is the sin of Adam; and they are natural when referred to the nature already stripped. Accordingly, the Apostle says: "We were by nature children of wrath" (Eph. 2:3). In this way one answers the fifth objection.

[11] Clearly, then, from what has been said, the vice of origin in which the original sin is caused comes from the failure of a principle, namely, the gratuitous gift which human nature at its institution had had bestowed upon it. To be sure, this gift was in a sense natural: not natural as caused by the principles of the nature, but natural because it was given to man to be propagated along with his nature. But the sixth objection was dealing with the natural which is caused by the principles of the nature.

[12] The seventh objection proceeds in the same way, from a defect of a natural principle belonging to the nature of the species. Of course, what comes from a defect of a natural principle of this kind happens in but few cases. But the defect of original sin comes from the defect of a principle added over and above the principles of the species, as we said.

[13] Be it observed, also, that in the act of the generative powers there can be no vice in the genus of actual sin which depends on the will of a single person, because the act of the generative power is not obedient to reason or to will, as the eighth objection went. But nothing prevents our finding the vice of original sin—this refers to nature—in an act of the

generative power, since acts of the generative powers are called natural.

[14] The ninth objection, of course, can readily be answered from the points already made. For sin does not take away that good of nature which belongs to the nature's species. But that good of nature which grace added over and above nature could be removed by the sin of our first parent. This was said before.

[15] From the same points one easily answers the tenth objection. For, since privation and defect correspond to one another mutually, in that characteristic in original sin are the children made like to the parents in which the gift also, granted the nature in the beginning, would have been propagated to their descendants; for, although the gift did not belong to the essentials of the species, it was given by divine grace to the first man to flow from him into the entire species.

[16] This, too, must be considered: Let one by the sacraments of grace be cleansed from original sin so that it is not imputed a fault in him (and for him personally this is to be freed from original sin); for all that, the nature is not entirely healed; therefore, in an act of the nature the original sin is transmitted to his descendants. Thus, then, in a man who generates there is no original sin in so far as he is a given person; and it also happens that in the act of generation there is no actual sin, which the eleventh argument was proposing. But so far as the man who generates is the natural principle of generation, the infection of the original sin which bears on nature remains in him and in his act of generation.

[17] Be it observed, also, that the actual sin of the first man passed over into nature because the nature in him had been further perfected by the benefit bestowed on the nature. But, when by his sin the nature was stripped of the benefit, his act was simply personal. Hence, he could not satisfy for the entire nature, nor could he make the good of nature whole once more by his act. But the only satisfaction of which he was somewhat capable was that which had a bearing on his own person. Therein the answer to the twelfth argument appears.

[18] In like manner, of course, one answers the thirteenth, for the sins of later parents find a nature stripped of the benefit which was at the outset granted to the nature itself. Hence, from those sins no defect follows which is propagated to the descendants, but only a defect which infects the person of the one sinning.

[19] Thus, then, it is neither unsuitable nor irrational to affirm the presence of original sin in men, and thus the heresy of the Pelagians, which was a denial of original sin, is confounded. . . .

[Chapter 79] That Through Christ the Resurrection of Bodies Is to Come

[1] Now, we have shown above that we have been freed by Christ from what we incurred by the sin of the first man; and, when the first man sinned, not only was the sin itself passed on to us, but also death, which is the punishment of sin, in the Apostle's words: "By one man sin entered into this world and by sin death" (Rom. 5:12). Therefore, it necessarily is by Christ that we are freed from each of these; namely, from the fault and from death. Accordingly, the Apostle says in the same place: "If by one man's offence death reigned through one; much more they who receive abundance . . . of the gift and of justice shall reign in life through one, Jesus Christ" (Rom. 5:17).

[2] Therefore, in order to make each of these clear to us in Himself, He chose both to die and to rise. He chose to die, indeed, to cleanse us from sin; hence, the Apostle says: "As it is appointed unto men once to die, so also Christ was offered once to exhaust the sins of many" (Heb. 9:27-28). But He chose to rise to free us from death; hence, the Apostle says: "Christ is risen from the dead, the firstfruits of them that sleep. For by a man came death and by a man the resurrection of the dead" (I Cor. 15:20-21).

[3] It is, then, the effect of the death of Christ in regard to the remission of sin which we achieve in the sacraments,

for, it has already been said, the sacraments work in the power of the passion of Christ.

[4] But the effect of the resurrection of Christ in regard to our liberation from death we shall achieve at the end of the world, when we shall all rise by the power of Christ. Hence, the Apostle says: "If Christ be preached that He arose again from the dead, how do some among you say that there is no resurrection of the dead? If there be no resurrection of the dead, then Christ is not risen again. And if Christ be not risen again then is our preaching vain and our faith is vain" (I Cor. 15:12-14). It is, then, a necessary tenet of faith to believe that there will be a resurrection of the dead.

[5] There are, however, some who are perverse in their understanding of this and they do not believe in the future resurrection of bodies, but attempt to ascribe what we read about the resurrection in the Scriptures to a spiritual resurrection in which some arise from the death of sin by grace.

[6] But this error is rejected by the Apostle himself; he says: "But shun profane and vain babblings: for they grow much towards ungodliness. And their speech spreadeth like a canker: of whom are Hymenaeus and Philebus: who have erred from the truth of the faith, saying that the resurrection is past already" (II Tim. 2:16-18). And this was not understandable except of a spiritual resurrection. It is, therefore, contrary to the truth of the faith to accept a spiritual resurrection and deny a bodily one.

[7] There is more. It is clear from what the Apostle says to the Corinthians that the words cited are to be understood of a bodily resurrection. For, after a bit, he adds: "It is sown a natural body, it shall rise a spiritual body," wherein, manifestly, the body's resurrection is touched on; and a little later he adds: "This corruptible must put on incorruption; and this mortal must put on immortality" (I Cor. 15:44, 53). But the corruptible and the mortal mean the body. Therefore, it is the body that will rise.

[8] Moreover, our Lord promises both resurrections, for He says: "Amen, Amen, I say unto you that the hour cometh and now is when the dead shall hear the voice of the Son of

God and they that hear shall live." And this seems to pertain to the spiritual resurrection of souls, which even then was beginning to be completed, when some were cleaving to Christ in faith. But, later, it is the bodily resurrection He expresses, saying: "The hour cometh, wherein all that are in the graves shall hear the voice of the Son of God" (John 5:25, 28). For, clearly, souls are not in the graves, but bodies. Therefore, this predicts the bodily resurrection.

[9] The bodily resurrection was also expressly foretold by Job. For he says: "I know that my Redeemer liveth, and in the last day I shall rise out of the earth, and shall be clothed again with my skin, and in my flesh I shall see my God" (Job 19:25-26).

[10] Moreover, to establish that there will be a resurrection of the flesh there is an evident supporting argument which is based on the points made earlier. For we showed in Book II that the souls of men are immortal. They persist, then, after their bodies, released from their bodies. It is also clear from what was said in Book II that the soul is naturally united to the body, for in its essence it is the form of the body. It is, then, contrary to the nature of the soul to be without the body. But nothing which is contrary to nature can be perpetual. Perpetually, then, the soul will not be without the body. Since, then, it persists perpetually, it must once again be united to the body; and this is to rise again. Therefore, the immortality of souls seems to demand a future resurrection of bodies.

[11] Furthermore, there was shown in Book III the natural desire of man to tend to happiness. But ultimate happiness is the perfection of the happy one. Therefore, anyone to whom some perfection is wanting does not yet have perfect happiness, because his desire is not entirely at rest, for every imperfect thing naturally desires to achieve its perfection. But the soul separated from the body is in a way imperfect, as is every part existing outside of its whole, for the soul is naturally a part of human nature. Therefore, man cannot achieve his ultimate happiness unless the soul be once again united to the body, especially since it was shown that in this life man cannot arrive at his ultimate happiness.

[12] Moreover, as was shown in Book III, by divine providence sinners deserve punishment, and those who do well a reward. But in this life men, composed of soul and body, sin or act rightly. Therefore, in both the soul and the body men deserve reward or punishment. But that in this life they cannot achieve the reward of ultimate happiness is clear from the points made in Book III. And time after time sins are not punished in this life; rather, in fact, as we read in Job (21:7) here "the wicked live, are advanced, and are strengthened with riches." Necessarily, then, we must assert a repeated union of the soul with the body, so that man can be rewarded and punished in the body as well as in the soul. . . .

[Chapter 96] On the Last Judgment

[1] From the foregoing it is clear, then, that there is a twofold retribution for what a man does in life: one for the soul—and this he receives as soon as the soul has been separated from the body; but there will be another retribution when the bodies are assumed again—and some will receive bodies which are incapable of suffering and glorious; but others, bodies capable of suffering and ignoble. The first retribution is made to men singly and one by one, in that men die separately and one by one. But the second retribution will be made to all and at the same time in that all will rise at the same time. Every retribution, of course, wherein different decisions are rendered according to differing merits demands a judgment. Necessarily, therefore, the judgment is twofold: There is one, regarding the soul, in which separately and one by one punishment or reward is determined; there is another common one, however, regarding the soul and body—in it there will be determined for all at the same time what they have earned.

[2] And since by His humanity in which He suffered and rose again Christ earned for us both resurrection and eternal life, it is to Him that universal judgment belongs, in which those who rise are rewarded or punished. For this reason we

read of Him in John (5:27): "He hath given Him power to do judgment, because He is the Son of man."

[3] A judgment, of course, ought to be proportional to the matters judged. And because the last judgment will be about the reward or punishment of visible bodies, it is suitable that it be carried on visibly. Hence, also, Christ will carry out that judgment in the form of humanity which all may be able to see, both the good and the wicked. The sight of His divinity, however, makes men blessed, as was shown in Book III. Accordingly, this will be visible only to the good. The judgment of the soul, of course, since it is about invisible things, is carried on invisibly.

[4] Granted, of course, that Christ has the authoritative act of judging in that last judgment, nonetheless at the same time those who will judge with Him—sitting with the judge, as it were—who adhered to Him more than others. These are the Apostles, of whom it was said: "You, who have followed Me, shall sit on twelve seats judging the twelve tribes of Israel" (Matt. 19:28); and this promise is extended also to those who follow in the footprints of the Apostles.

Five Qualities of the Lord's Prayer

"Our Father who art in heaven." Among all other prayers, the Lord's Prayer holds the chief place. It has five excellent qualities which are required in all prayer. A prayer must be *confident, ordered, suitable, devout* and *humble*.

It must be *confident:* "Let us, therefore, go with confidence to the throne of grace." It must not be wanting in faith, as it is said: "But let him ask in faith, nothing wavering." That this is a most trustworthy prayer is reasonable, since it was formed by Him who is our Advocate and the most wise Petitioner for us: "In whom are hid all the treasures of wisdom and knowledge"; and of whom it is said: "For we

---

Exposition of the Lord's Prayer, Prologue. Trans. Collins, *The Catechetical Instructions of St. Thomas*, pp. 135-138.

have an advocate with the Father, Jesus Christ the just one."
Hence, St. Cyprian says: "Since we have Christ as our
Advocate with the Father for our sins, when we pray on
account of our faults, we use the very words of our Advocate."

Furthermore, this prayer is even more worthy of confidence
in that He who taught us how to pray, graciously hears our
prayer together with the Father, as it is said in the Psalm:
"He shall cry to Me, and I will hear him." Thus writes St.
Cyprian: "It is a friendly, familiar, and devout prayer to ask
of the Lord in His own words." And so no one goes away
from this prayer without fruit. St. Augustine says that through
it our venial sins are remitted.

Moreover, our prayer must be *suitable*, so that a person
asks of God in prayer what is good for him. St. John
Damascene says: "Prayer is the asking of what is right and
fitting from God." Many times our prayer is not heard because we seek that which is not good for us: "You ask and
you do not receive, because you ask amiss." To know, indeed,
what one ought to pray for is most difficult; for it is not
easy to know what one ought to desire. Those things which
we rightly seek in prayer are rightly desired; hence the
Apostle says: "For we know not what we should pray for
as we ought." Christ Himself is our Teacher; it is He who
teaches us what we ought to pray for, and it was to Him
that the disciples said: "Lord, teach us to pray." Those
things, therefore, which He has taught us to pray for, we
most properly ask for. "Whatsoever words we use in prayer,"
says St. Augustine, "we cannot but utter that which is contained in our Lord's Prayer, if we pray in a suitable and
worthy manner."

Our prayer ought also to be *ordered* as our desires should
be ordered, for prayer is but the expression of desire. Now,
it is the correct order that we prefer spiritual to bodily things,
and heavenly things to those merely earthly. This is according to what is written: "Seek ye first therefore the kingdom of
God and His justice, and all these things shall be added unto
you." Here Our Lord shows that heavenly things must be
sought first, and then things material.

Our prayer must be *devout,* because a rich measure of piety makes the sacrifice of prayer acceptable to God: "In Thy name I will lift up my hands. Let my soul be filled with marrow and fatness." Many times because of the length of our prayers our devotion grows cool; hence Our Lord taught us to avoid wordiness in our prayers: "When you are praying, speak not much." And St. Augustine says: "Let much talking be absent from prayer; but as long as fervor continues, let prayer likewise go on." For this reason the Lord made His Prayer short. Devotion in prayer rises from charity which is our love of God and neighbor, both of which are evident in this prayer. Our love for God is seen in that we call God "our Father," and our love for our neighbor when we say: "Our Father . . . forgive us our trespasses," and this leads us to love of neighbor.

Prayer ought to be *humble:* "He hath had regard for the prayer of the humble." This is seen in the parable of the Pharisee and the Publican (Luke 18:9-15), and also in the words of Judith: "The prayer of the humble and the meek hath always pleased Thee." This same humility is observed in this prayer, for true humility is had when a person does not presume upon his own powers, but from the divine strength expects all that he asks for.

It must be noted that prayer brings about three good effects. First, prayer is an efficacious and useful remedy against evils. Thus, it delivers us from the sins we have committed: "Thou hast forgiven the wickedness of my sin. For this shall every one that is holy pray to Thee in a seasonable time." The thief on the Cross prayed and received forgiveness: "This day thou shalt be with Me in paradise." Thus also prayed the Publican, and "went down to his home justified." Prayer, also, frees one from the fear of future sin, and from trials and sadness of soul: "Is any one of you sad? Let him pray." Again it delivers one from persecutors and enemies: "Instead of making me a return of love, they detracted me, but I gave myself to prayer."

In the second place, prayer is efficacious and useful to obtain all that one desires: "All things whatsoever you ask

when you pray, believe that you shall receive." When our
prayers are not heard, either we do not persevere in prayer,
whereas "we ought always to pray, and not to faint," or we
do not ask for that which is more conducive to our salvation.
"Our good Lord often does not give us what we wish," says
St. Augustine, "because it would really be what we do not
wish for." St. Paul gives us an example of this in that he
thrice prayed that the sting of his flesh be removed from
him, and his prayer was not heard. Thirdly, prayer is profitable because it makes us friends of God: "Let my prayer
be directed as incense in Thy sight."

The Seven Sacraments

We shall now consider the Sacraments of the Church. We
shall treat them under one heading, since they all pertain to
the effect of grace. First of all, that must be known which
St. Augustine wrote in the tenth book of *The City of God*:
"a Sacrament is a sacred thing" or "the sign of a sacred thing."
Even in the Old Law there were certain sacraments, that is,
signs of a sacred thing—for example, the paschal lamb and
other legal sacred signs or "sacraments" which, however, did
not *cause* grace but only signified or indicated the grace
of Christ. The Apostle calls these "sacraments" *weak and
needy elements*. They were *needy* because they did not contain grace, and they were *weak* because they could not confer
grace. In them, as St. Augustine says, the merits of Christ
brought about salvation in a more hidden manner under the
cover of visible things. The Sacraments of the New Law,
on the other hand, both contain grace and confer it. A
Sacrament of the New Law is a visible form of invisible
grace. Thus, the exterior washing which takes place when
the water is poured in Baptism represents that interior cleans-

On the Articles of the Faith and Sacraments of the Church, beginning of
sect. on Sacraments. Trans. Collins, The Catechetical Instructions of St.
Thomas, pp. 119-122.

ing which takes away sin by virtue of the Sacrament of Baptism.

There are seven Sacraments of the New Law: Baptism, Confirmation, the Eucharist, Penance, Extreme Unction, Orders, and Matrimony. The first five of these Sacraments are intended to bring about the perfection of the individual man in himself; whereas the other two, Orders and Matrimony, are so constituted that they perfect and multiply the entire Church.

The Spiritual and the Physical Life: An Analogy

The spiritual life conforms to the physical life. In the physical life man is perfected in three chief ways: first, by generation, in that he is born into this world; secondly, by growth, through which he is brought up into stature and perfect strength; thirdly, by food which sustains man's life and powers. This would suffice were it not that man is attacked by illnesses, and hence, fourthly, he needs something which will bring him back to health.

This also holds true in the spiritual life. First, man needs regeneration or re-birth which is brought through the Sacrament of Baptism: "Unless a man be born again of water and the Holy Ghost, he cannot enter into the kingdom of God." Secondly, it is necessary that man develop perfect strength, which is, as it were, a spiritual growth, and this indeed comes to him in the Sacrament of Confirmation. This is like the strengthening which the Apostles received when the Holy Ghost came upon them and confirmed them. The Lord had said to them: "But stay you in the city of Jerusalem till you be endued with power from on high." The third similarity is that man must be fed with spiritual food: "Unless you eat the flesh of the Son of Man, and drink His blood, you shall not have life in you." Fourthly, man must be healed spiritually through the Sacrament of Penance: "Heal, O Lord, my soul, for I have sinned against Thee." Lastly, one is healed both in soul and in body in the Sacrament of Extreme Unction: "Is any man sick among you? Let him bring in the priests of the church, and let them pray over him, anointing him with oil in the name of the Lord. And the prayer of faith shall save the sick man, and the Lord shall raise him up, and if he be in sins, they shall be forgiven him." Two of the Sacraments, Orders and Matrimony, are instituted for the common good of the Church. Through the Sacrament of Orders the Church is ruled and is spiritually multiplied; and through Matrimony it is increased physically in numbers.

The Seven Sacraments in General

The seven Sacraments have some things which they all hold in common, and some things which are proper to each one. That which is common to all the Sacraments is that they confer grace. It is also common to all the Sacraments that a Sacrament is made up of words and physical acts. And so also Christ, who is the Author of the Sacraments, is the Word made flesh. And just as the flesh of Christ was sanctified, and has the power of sanctifying because of the Word united to itself, so also the Sacraments are made holy and have the power of sanctifying through the words which accompany the action. Thus, St. Augustine says: "The word is joined to the element, and the Sacrament is made." Now, the words by which the Sacraments are sanctified are called the *form* of the Sacraments; and the things which are sanctified are called the *matter* of the Sacraments. Water, for example, is the *matter* of Baptism, and the holy chrism is the matter of Confirmation.

In each Sacrament there is required a *minister*, who confers the Sacrament with the intention of doing that which the Church intends. If any one of these three requirements is lacking, the Sacrament is not brought into being, viz., if there is lacking the due *form* of the words, or if the *matter* is not present, or if the *minister* does not intend to confer the Sacrament.

The effect of the Sacrament is likewise impeded through the fault of the recipient, for example, if one feigns to receive it and with a heart unprepared to receive worthily.

Such a one, although he actually receives the Sacrament, does not receive the effect of the Sacrament, that is, the grace of the Holy Spirit. "For the Holy Spirit of discipline will flee from the deceitful." On the other hand, however, there are some who never even receive sacramentally, yet who receive the effect of the Sacrament because of their devotion towards the Sacrament, which they may have in desire or in a vow.

There are some things which are characteristic of each individual Sacrament. Certain ones impress a *character* on the soul which is a certain spiritual sign distinct from the other Sacraments. Such are the Sacraments of Orders, Baptism and Confirmation. The Sacraments which give a character are never repeated in the same person who has once received it. Thus, he who is baptized need never again receive this Sacrament; neither can he who has been confirmed receive Confirmation again; and one who has been ordained need never repeat his ordination. The reason is that the character which each of these Sacraments impresses is indelible.

In the other Sacraments, however, a character is not impressed on the recipient, and hence they can be repeated as far as the person is concerned, not however as far as the matter is concerned. Thus, one can frequently receive Penance, frequently receive the Eucharist, and can be anointed more than once with Extreme Unction, and likewise he can be married more than once. Yet, regarding the matter, the same Host cannot be frequently consecrated, nor ought the oil of the sick be frequently blessed.

On the Future Life of Man

It is not fitting that men be corrupted in the same way that the other corporeal creatures are, for these creatures are totally corrupted and are consequently not restored as

Exposition of Job, Ch. 14, Lect. 5. Trans. V.J.B.

numerically the same. Man, of course, may be corrupted in his body but he remains incorruptible in his soul, which transcends the whole genus of corporeal things, so that the hope of restoration endures in this way.

Next he [Job] presents reasons for this view that are drawn from the qualities proper to man. In fact, man surpasses all lower creatures in two properties. One of these is his operative power, for he is the master of his action through free choice and this belongs to no other corporeal creature. Because of this, man is more powerful than any corporeal creature and as a result he may use others for his own sake. The other property in which he excels is intellectual knowledge. Though it is present within the mind, still some sign of it is evident in his body, especially in his face, which is quite different in man than in other animals. It is evident from these two properties that man is not corrupted as are the other animals, in the sense that he will not exist perpetually.

In regard to the first of these, he says: "Thou hast strengthened him a little while, that he may pass away for ever"; as if to say: It is not fitting that much strength be provided for man for a short time and that he will not afterward exist in perpetuity. In fact, it would seem stupid for a person to make a very strong instrument to be used for a short hour and then discard it completely. The power of each corporeal creature is restricted to limited effects but the power of free choice is directed to infinite activities. So, this gives evidence of the power of the soul, of the fact that it will endure without limit.

As to the property of intellect, he says: "Thou shalt change his face and shalt send him away"; saying, as it were: It is not fitting that Thou should change his face, that is, make it different from that of the other animals, and yet send him off from the state of life into a perpetuity from which he will not return, like the other animals. It is customary to take the face as a symbol of intellectual knowledge, because the face is peculiar to the rational creature. Now, intellectual knowledge can only be appropriate to an incorruptible substance, as is proved by the philosophers.

Of course, a person might say that though man does not return to life after death, he does not pass away forever, since in some way he lives on in his children. Indeed, Baldad's words give this impression, where he said above: "This is the joy of his way, that others may spring again out of the earth." But Job rejects this answer, adding: "Whether his children come to honor or dishonor, he shall not understand"; as if to say: Man grasps the eternal good through his intellect, and so he naturally desires it. Now, the good that is present in the succession of children cannot satisfy intellectual appetite, if man is wholly destroyed by death, so that he will not exist perpetually. Indeed, the intellectual appetite will find no rest, except in an intellectual good, and the good that lies in the succession of children is not understood by man, either while he is alive or after death, provided he wholly ceases to exist at death. Therefore, the intellectual appetite of man does not tend toward the eternity of this good but toward a good or evil that he possesses within himself; hence, he adds: "But yet his flesh, while he shall live, shall have pain and his soul shall mourn over him." In this he distinguishes two sorrows: one of the flesh within sensory apprehension, the other of the soul arising from intellectual or imaginative apprehension, and this latter is properly called sadness, being termed mourning in this text.

Charity and Sharing in Divine Life

The end for human life is felicity. Different kinds of felicity are distinguished according to different lives. Those who live apart from civic life cannot attain the civic felicity that marks the peak of this kind of life. Likewise, for a person to reach contemplative felicity, he must become a participant in that kind of life. Hence, the felicity that man can achieve, by his

On the Sentences, III, 27, 2, 2, Response. Trans. V.J.B.

natural capacities is in accord with human life. The philosophers have spoken about it; so, in the *Ethics* (I, 10, 1101a20) is the statement: "but happy, as men."

However, since we have been promised a sort of felicity in which *we shall be equal to the angels,* as is seen in Matt. 22:30, one which transcends not only man's powers but also those of the angels (who have to be led up to it by grace just as we, for it is natural to God alone)—it is, then, necessary for a man to become a participant in the divine life, in order that he may attain to this divine felicity.

Now, that which enables one to live together with another person is chiefly friendship. As the Philosopher says in the *Ethics* (IX, 12, 1172a5): "each person spending his time with his friend, doing the things they like best, wishing to live together as a friend with the one who has a high regard for his kind of life." Thus, some people go hunting together, others drink together, still others devote themselves to philosophy, and so on.

It was consequently necessary that some sort of friendship with God be made available, so that we might live together with Him; and this is charity, as we have said. Now, this sharing in divine life exceeds the capacity of nature, as does the felicity to which it is directed. So, nature must be perfected for this purpose by a superadded good; and this is the essential character of this virtue. Hence, we must say that charity is a theological virtue that is: *poured forth into our hearts by the Holy Spirit who has been given to us* (Rom. 5:5).

RECOMMENDED READINGS

CHENU, M. D. "Introduction to the 'Summa' of St. Thomas," *The Thomist Reader:* II. Washington: Thomist Press, 1958.

GARRIGOU-LAGRANGE, R. *Reality: a Synthesis of Thomistic Thought.* Translated by P. Cummins. St. Louis: Herder, 1950.